Four Years in Paradise

D1603373

0 11557 03130 0

SISTERS OF THE HUNT

Four Years in Paradise

OSA JOHNSON

FOREWORD BY MARY ZEISS STANGE

STACKPOLE
BOOKS

New foreword copyright © 2004 by Stackpole Books

Published by
STACKPOLE BOOKS
5067 Ritter Road
Mechanicsburg, PA 17055
www.stackpolebooks.com

Printed in the United States

First edition

10 9 8 7 6 5 4 3 2 1

Cover design by Tracy Patterson

Library of Congress Cataloging-in-Publication Data

Johnson, Osa, 1894–1953.
    Four years in paradise / Osa Johnson ; foreword by Mary Zeiss Stange.— 1st ed.
      p. cm. — (Sisters of the hunt)
    Reprint. Originally published: London : Hutchinson, 1941. With new foreword.
    Includes index.
    ISBN 0-8117-3130-8 (alk. paper)
    1. Johnson, Osa, 1894–1953. 2. Naturalists—United States—Biography. 3. Africa, East—Description and travel. I. Title. II. Series.
QH31.J72 A3 2004
916.762'043—dc22
                                              2003067218

FOREWORD

Osa Helen Leighty was born in 1894 in Chanute, Kansas, descended from pioneer stock. Her mother and grandmother taught her to cook, sew, and keep house. Her father, a brakeman for the Santa Fe Railroad, took her hunting in winter and fishing in summer, and from him she inherited a talent for gardening. By the time she was in her teens, Osa seemed solidly on a trajectory toward the life each middle-class girl of her time and place envisioned for herself, in which, as she later put it, "one married; one settled down; after that life flowed smoothly and with pleasant monotony to the grave."[1] Then at the age of sixteen, after a three-week courtship and more or less on a whim, Osa eloped with Martin Johnson, a fellow Kansan nine-and-a-half years her senior. From that point on, the script of her life changed in ways a genteel country belle could scarcely imagine.

To Martin Johnson (1884–1937), the idea of a settled life was anathema. He had early on exhibited talents both for photography (cameras were the only things he liked about working in his father's jewelry store), and for diverging from the social norm (as when he was expelled from high school for distributing trick photographs he had made of teachers in what appeared to be morally compromised positions). By the time he fell in love with Osa at the age of twenty-five, Martin had run away to live on his own in Chicago, vagabonded through Europe, worked as an itinerant portrait photographer in Kansas, sailed the high seas with Jack London on the *Snark*, and opened two theaters in his hometown of Independence, a few miles down the road from Chanute.

Part swashbuckler, part showman, Martin financed his dreams of distant adventure by giving illustrated lectures, complete with musical accompaniment, about his travels with London. He named his theaters Snark No. 1 and Snark No. 2 after London's fabled if ill-fated ship; Snark No. 2 had a ticket office in the shape of a ship's bow. It was there that he enlisted Osa—who harbored a secret desire to become an actress and film star—to substitute one Sunday evening for a singer who had come down with laryngitis. Her performance by her own account was less than stellar, but as Martin was tone-deaf that little mattered, and they married that same night.

Osa divided the next year or so between feathering their little love-nest in Independence and performing on stage in Martin's theaters. Then late in 1910 Martin, driven in roughly equal parts by wanderlust and financial necessity, confronted his teenaged bride with a truly life-altering decision, "a choice between a flat in Independence and a life spent in travel, between civilization and the wilderness."[2] For the next seven years the Johnsons toured the vaudeville circuit, Martin building up an ever more impressive travelogue and trading on the Jack London connection, with Osa performing ostensibly native musical numbers in "authentic" Hawaiian and Indian costumes she had stitched up herself. By the time they had amassed enough money for their first adventure together in 1917—retracing some of the *Snark*'s voyage, to the Solomon Islands—Martin and Osa were headliners on the prestigious Orpheum circuit, sharing billing with the likes of Will Rogers and Harry Lauder. Not unlike her older contemporary Annie Oakley, Osa Johnson's path to international notoriety ran through the world of show business.

It may strike a twenty-first century reader as odd that the Johnsons, who over the course of the next twenty years pioneered the art of live-action wildlife photography, were primarily entertainers. But the world of popular nature study was very different a hundred years ago: Prior to the advent of television and global air travel, the closest the vast majority of people got to exotic wild nature was through books like London's *The Call of the Wild*, zoos, circuses (and their frontier variations, the "wild west" shows), and illustrated lectures by world explorers, like Martin's travelogues. The replacement of the "magic lantern" slide show by motion pictures marked a sea change in this field, and Martin Johnson brilliantly exploited its implications.

Between 1917 and Martin's death in a plane crash in 1937, the Johnsons' extended trips to the South Seas, Borneo, and especially Africa resulted in ten feature-length films and over seventy silent short subjects. These films made superstars of Mr. and Mrs. Martin Johnson, as the couple was always billed: he as producer, narrator, and cinematographer, and she as his able assistant and leading lady. The movies to a large extent reflected the roles the couple played in real life. His job was to stalk with a camera. Hers was to hunt with a gun—in order both to procure meat for themselves and their large corps of native porters and to provide cover for Martin as he cranked his camera in frequently life-threatening situations.

Their marriage appears to have been both personally and professionally a true partnership, a theme that emerged as of particular importance in Osa's writings. "In the field," she wrote, "Martin relied on me and I relied on him. We were interdependent in every way, mentally and physically. I was his wife, his partner. The most important thing in my life was to know that I could be of help to him."[3] For his part, Martin remarked, "I have had the right sort of woman to take along with me into the desert and jungle. If ever a man needed a partner in his chosen profession, it has been I. And if ever a wife were a partner to a man, it is Osa Johnson."[4] Elsewhere, commending Osa's stamina in often stressful and uncomfortable circumstances, Martin declared, "For bravery and steadiness and endurance, Osa is the equal of any man I ever saw. She is a woman through and through. There is nothing 'mannish' about her. Yet as a comrade in the wilderness she is better than any man I ever saw."[5] Fellow filmmaker W. S. Van Dyke admiringly concurred, in a review of the Johnsons's 1928 film *Simba*:

> I never met Johnson but I would like to go on record as saying that I think his wife is a "peach" and game to the core. Not particularly because she faces the charge of big game, but because she drinks the water, eats the food, and smiles through the bites and annoyances of African bug life. There are few women who would stand for as much of it as she does.[6]

Of course, as such comments demonstrate, given the gender expectations of the day, partnership between husband and wife hardly meant equality. Osa's role model in many ways was Jack London's wife Charmian. Yet while the two adventurers' wives held each other in mutually high regard, the younger and less "liberated" Osa was far more willing to take a back seat to Martin than Charmian was to Jack. Both in her personal life and on screen, Osa defined her wifely role as clearly subordinate to Martin's leadership, which no doubt added to her popular appeal. As she explained in *Photoplay Magazine*:

> You might have an idea that I went along to play an ingénue role opposite man-eating lions and put a heart throb in the films. But even if it does look that way every wife knows better. I went along just because I am a wife.
> I went to Africa for just the same reason that lots of girls settled down on Main Street back home. . . .

She went on in the same article to remark that she always kept her cosmetics handy in the jungle, since "everybody knows what an American husband thinks of a shiny nose."[7] Elsewhere, in a series of pieces she wrote for *Good Housekeeping*, she reflected on being a "home body . . . not much different from the stay-at-home girl who started housekeeping . . . in a flat in Independence, Kansas. . . . The only difference between me and millions of other wives is that I make home 'on the go.'"[8] She subsequently wrote about preparing "jungle dinners," and offered recipes combining wild game with then-new convenience foods like condensed soups and canned ground coffee, bringing safari cooking back home to the American public.[9]

It seems that a part of Osa never left Kansas, and indeed never wanted to. Homesickness is a leitmotif in her bestselling *I Married Adventure*, and a constant theme in her surviving letters. Yet at the same time, Osa took to rugged wilderness adventure with unalloyed enthusiasm. And in this regard she shattered conventional expectations about a woman's proper place or behavior. The image of the petitely comely huntress venturing, rifle in hand, to within a few feet of trumpeting elephants and menacing rhinos became a staple in Martin's films. Audiences and critics alike appreciated the contrast between what the Johnsons' friend and benefactor George Eastman called Osa's "pink-silk-dress-little-girlness" and her toughness in the bush.[10] A comment in a review of their early film *Trailing African Wild Animals* is typical:

> Of course, one of the reasons for the film's attractiveness is the presence . . . of Mrs. Martin Johnson herself. She is seen in various positions unbecoming a timid lady, and she appears not to have the slightest objection to the tickle of a lion's whiskers across her cheek. . . . Her distinctly feminine personality forms a striking contrast with the barbaric and quite evidently dangerous surroundings. . . . The young lady not only takes a very active part in the proceedings, and proves herself possessed of courage and no little skill with the rifle.[11]

Osa Johnson was actually a spectacular shot. She was justly proud when, in 1930, she became the first woman to be issued a professional big game hunter's license in Africa.[12]

In the climax of the Johnsons's first big feature film *Simba*, after a reenactment of a native lion-hunt with spears, Osa herself guns down a charging lion, and her feat is celebrated by the African hunters. She then goes back to camp, and—in the closing scene of the movie—makes an apple pie. This depiction of her dual nature as hunter-housewife kept her comfortably enough within the bounds of conventional expectations to secure the affections of the movie-going public. And in many ways it reflected the "real" Osa.

Yet her letters suggest that she in fact felt rather confined by her role, however self-imposed it may have been. In a 1930 letter to her mother, from Nairobi when she and Martin were on their third of five protracted African trips, she bragged:

> I went out on the rifle range the other afternoon and I hit the bulls eye several times. The Gun smith who is a crack shot looked at me with his mouth open, and said I knew you would do it. I have heard a lot about you. . . . Mother before I leave this country I will take on some animal charging, and I will make the world set up and take notice, but I wont do anything foolish mother.[13]

Whether it was her idea or Martin's is unclear, but it eventuated that a rhino would be just the thing to provoke into charging. In 1931 she wrote her mother about "what a hard time we had trying to get a rhino to charge—we tried everything we could think of to get them to break up one of our cars for a picture, and I walked up to them even two at a time, but without luck."[14] Osa's account is corroborated by an eyewitness who fifty years later recalled: "Martin had a car padded on all sides with old tires and had Osa walk out in front to provoke the rhino to charge. It was a courageous thing for her to do, but all of their 83 attempts were unsuccessful."[15] *Congorilla* (1932), the first sound feature made entirely in Africa, which they were filming at the time, contains some exciting footage of Osa's repeated attempts to bait rhinos into charging her.

Osa finally got her wish in April of 1933, on their fifth and final trip to Africa. She wrote home:

> Also mother dear I took on a rhino charge—alone just Vern backing me—Martin and Hugh making the movies—I walked up to him and he came like a streak of lighting [sic]—and I brought him down just twenty feet in front of me—that will thrill the public when they see me bring the rhino down.[16]

This kill, which is thrilling indeed, appears in the 1935 feature *Baboona*. Yet Osa was equally proud of tracking and bringing down a huge lion wounded by a hunter who was staying with the Johnsons five years earlier, an event possessing personal satisfaction only, as Martin was not there to film it.[17]

In fact, actual shots of animals being killed are comparatively rare in the Johnsons's films. Such killing as does occur in their films is explicitly either for food or (as in Osa's case with the rhino) in self-defense. This was a matter of conscious design and marked a distinct departure from earlier depictions of life and adventure in Africa. Reflecting the biases of colonial expansion, down through the nineteenth and well into the twentieth centuries, the "Dark Continent" was in general seen as territory to be conquered. Animals, and native peoples as well, were cast in the role of inferior, if nonetheless lethal, adversaries—savage obstacles to be overcome. The same imperialist attitudes which supported trophy hunting were at work in the earliest exercises in "hunting with cameras;" that is, early still and moving pictures from Africa recapitulated the idea that Africa was literally there for the taking.[18] Such images simultaneously arose from and reinforced Europeans' and Americans' feelings of racial and cultural superiority.

Yet the early twentieth century also saw the dawn of the conservation movement on both sides of the Atlantic. The role unregulated hunting might play in mass extinction was only too clear from the fate of the North American bison, hunted to near-extermination by the close of the nineteenth century. Most ecologically concerned observers saw the eventual extinction of Africa's megafauna as a foregone conclusion. Among those so concerned was Carl Akeley, the naturalist, taxidermist, and sculptor responsible for designing and mounting the African galleries at New York's American Museum of Natural History. Martin Johnson was greatly influenced by Akeley's conviction that artists and scientists of their day owed it to the future to preserve what they could of unspoiled precolonial Africa. Largely through Akeley's agency, the Natural History Museum became a major underwriter of Martin's photo-safaris. And the films which had begun as adventure entertainment for the masses became tools for conservation education as well. As the opening of *Simba* proclaimed, the goal was to show "Africa as God made it, never disturbed by civilized man." In the opening sequence of *Congorilla*, the Congo is described as "a land where man and beast still live as in the Garden of Eden."[19] Hence, as was stressed numerous times in the films and in both Osa's and Martin's writings, while hunting was decidedly a part of life in the Garden, they placed a high premium on killing only when necessary.

To be sure, in trading the Dark Continent for Eden, Martin and Osa were exchanging one romance—the myth of heroic conquest—for another. *Simba,* the film that arose from their second African trip (their "Four Years in Paradise"), depicts one group of African natives in the light of the "age-old story of Man emerging from savagery," another group as an instance of "half-civilized" people who "have reached the pastoral stage, living off their sheep and cattle." Such armchair evolutionary theory is accompanied by images that are at times unabashedly racist. Yet here as elsewhere in the films, condescension toward African natives—both tribal peoples whom they encountered and the "boys" who worked for them—is coupled with affection and even admiration. The same tension is at work in the Johnsons's writing, particularly Osa's.

Johnson biographer Pascal James Imperato is probably right in arguing that there is a vaudevillian element to much of the racist humor in the Johnsons's films; and he is certainly correct that this element lessened over time.[20] The Johnsons were creatures of the period in which they lived, and if they were going to be able to "sell" their conservationist message, they had to appeal to popular beliefs about white, as well as male, superiority. Yet even as some progressive Americans criticized their attitudes toward Black Africans, many of their European, particularly English, contemporaries in Africa were sharply critical of the extent to which they treated African natives, particularly some members of their household staff, as equals. Both on screen and in her various writings, Osa particularly reflects the ambivalence her growing familiarity with African peoples had to have generated in a person who had grown up in a border state at a time when the memory of the Civil War was still relatively fresh. And she is remarkably guileless in her descriptions of the often complicated relationships in which she, as a white woman, found herself.

The Johnsons's last African feature film was *Baboona,* which recounted their 60,000 mile "flying safari" from South Africa to Egypt. As they had been the first to film wild animals undisturbed in their natural surroundings, foreshadowing contemporary nature photography à la *National Geographic,* they were also the first to film Africa from the air. It is therefore deeply ironic that their adventures together ended in a commercial plane crash in California, which killed Martin and left Osa badly injured. Yet while their marriage ended with Martin's untimely death at the age of 53,

Osa's career as Mrs. Martin Johnson was hardly over. She devoted the rest of her life to building upon the story of their partnership, as well as to raising public awareness about conservation issues.

Osa had commenced her writing career during their years in Africa, producing a series of articles for *Good Housekeeping* and the first two of her several children's books, *Jungle Babies* (1930) and *Jungle Pets* (1932). Faced with the need to carve out a living for herself, and under the guidance of her and Martin's publicist Clark Getts (who would become her second husband), Mrs. Martin Johnson set about creating her own, more independent, identity. For the first time, she lectured and published under her own name. She discovered that the adventure story that had created the films was, if anything, more powerful on the printed page. In 1940, Osa Johnson's *I Married Adventure* was the number one nonfiction bestseller of the year; it topped the *New York Times* bestseller list for several weeks and was the June selection of the Book-of-the-Month Club. The book, which is essentially autobiographical, was cast as a biography of Martin, since the publisher, Lippincott, did not feel a woman's life-story was sufficiently compelling. It narrated the Johnsons's travels from their prairie beginnings in Kansas through their last trip to Borneo and Martin's death, and sold a half million copies in its first year.[21] Building upon this book's success, Osa quickly produced its sequel, *Four Years in Paradise*, which was published in 1941, and is in many ways more Osa's story than Martin's.

Whereas *I Married Adventure* painted with a broad brush, comprehending Martin and Osa's beginnings and the twenty-seven years of their marriage, *Four Years in Paradise* focused in greater detail on the second of their five trips to Africa. This was the trip sponsored by the American Museum of Natural History, with additional funding from such benefactors as Kodak founder George Eastman, the purpose of which was to produce a series of African wildlife feature films. It was, in creative terms, probably the most productive period of Martin's career, during which he developed and perfected the techniques—like flash photographs and interweaving slow motion with real time shots—that not only would characterize his work from then on, but also would set the standard for subsequent wildlife photography.

For Osa, too, these years, from 1924 to 1927, were an especially significant period. After seven years of touring the vaudeville circuit, and seven more of exploring the South Seas and Borneo with occasional lecture tours worked in stateside to raise more capital, the Johnsons' complex at Lake Paradise was the first relatively permanent home the couple had had since that little flat they started out in back in Independence. Osa not only brought all her Kansas skills to bear on turning her Kenya house into a home, she also was largely responsible for managing the roughly two hundred "boys" needed to build the place and keep it running, as well as for organizing the several safaris the Johnsons undertook in the course of these years. When they were on safari (a term that, incidentally, the Johnsons introduced to the American lexicon), whenever she was not involved in filming—either providing rifle cover for Martin or performing her own star turn in front of the camera—Osa was hunting and fishing to provide meat for the entire entourage.

Four Years in Paradise possesses an intimacy and a degree of candor lacking in the more panoramically conceived *I Married Adventure*. As one reviewer remarked, "With an engaging honesty and frankness, with something akin to but deeper than naivete, Osa Johnson completely destroys the aura of mystery, bravery, and silent grandeur with which most heroes of the jungle surround themselves."[22] Osa's own distinct voice emerges in this book, and while the stress throughout remains on Martin's creative mission and leadership, she comes across as a rather more equal partner in the enterprise here than elsewhere in their writings.[23]

With *Four Years in Paradise,* and its accompanying 17,000-mile national lecture tour, Osa Johnson became a celebrity in her own right. She went on to write several more children's books, as well as two more narratives of her and Martin's life together: *Bride in the Solomons* (1944) and the posthumously published *Last Adventure: The Martin Johnsons in Borneo* (1966). She also designed and marketed, in conjunction with her children's books, a collection of realistic stuffed animals called Osa Johnson's Pets, each of which came with a pamphlet highlighting the animal's natural history. The popular stuffed toys earned the seal of approval from the National Wildlife Federation, which in 1950 named America's "First Lady of Exploration" honorary co-chair (along with Bing Crosby) of its annual Wildlife Week observance.[24]

Osa had a genuine flair for style. She brought out a line of designer casual wear for women and children, fashioned out of her trademarked "Osafari" cloth, in colors like Masai Bronze, Kenya Blue, and Uganda Flame. Her "Congo" line of pigskin and goatskin sports gloves in various colors sold well in high-end department stores. In 1939, she was named one of America's ten best-dressed women, along with trendsetters like the Dutchess of Windsor, Bette Davis, and Joan Crawford. Osa's particular contribution to the fashion world lay in her sense of nature-inspired colors and her use of natural materials: leather and furs, feathers, wood and bone. Queried whether she liked to shoot her own fashions, she

demurred that hunting was far more serious a matter than that. Still, she
allowed, "Whenever we kill a bustard (African wild turkey) we always save
the wings for a hat. And whenever we kill a guinea foul, we say 'The pom-
pon for a turban, the breast for a roast, the legs for soup and the other
feathers for a pillow.' Perhaps," she further ventured, "this is a survival of
my western pioneer ancestral thrift."[25]

Osa Johnson's later years were marked by turmoil. Her hoped-for
career as a film star never materialized. While she frequently spoke and
wrote about returning to Africa, she only made it back there once, as a
technical advisor on Daryl F. Zanuck's production of *Stanley and Liv-
ingston*. Her second marriage, to Getts, fell apart. Debt, and a tendency
toward depression and alcohol abuse, took their toll. She died of a heart
attack in her New York apartment at the age of 58.

It is probably the case that Osa never really recovered from Martin's
death. Shortly after the accident that took his life, she wrote movingly of
her desire to go home to the place she and he had shared:

> The jungle is co-operative. It gives that it may live. That
> is the secret of nature and of love. . . . Here, in civiliza-
> tion, I have found only a demand for action-at-any-price,
> even the price of sound thinking, noble feeling, and
> splendid health.
>
> . . . I grant that I have been so long away that I do not
> understand civilization—why it rears ugly things upon
> green places, why men and women so tenaciously and
> savagely cling to ideas that don't matter, how people can
> imagine that the possession of more things than another
> person owns can improve their lives and make for happi-
> ness. Perhaps the jungle has made me too simple.
>
> Yes, I am going home—to the little compound in East
> Africa which we built, my late husband and I, through
> the years. I could make a new home elsewhere, but I shall
> go there because I love the world as God made it, a world
> that every man loves, I think, in the secret places of his
> heart.[26]

Maybe because Osa Johnson never made it home to Lake Paradise in
actual fact, her journey there in *Four Years in Paradise* is that much more
compelling. For Osa, as for the readers of this extraordinary book, a wilderness home is truly where the heart is.

My special thanks to the Martin and Osa Johnson Safari Museum in Chanute, Kansas. Museum Director Conrad Froehlich and Curators Jacqueline Borgeson and Barbara Henshall were generous with both their time and their insights into the careers of Martin and Osa Johnson, and gave me free rein to sift through the Johnsons's personal letters and unpublished papers. For more information on the museum, call (620) 491-2730 or visit the website, www.safarimuseum.com.

Mary Zeiss Stange
Ekalala, Montana
July 2003

NOTES

1. Osa Johnson, "My Home in the African Blue," *Good Housekeeping* (January 1924), 49.
2. "My Home in the African Blue," 49.
3. See below, 235.
4. Martin Johnson, quoted in the epigraph to Osa Johnson's *Last Adventure*, edited by Pascal James Imperato, M.D. (New York: William Morrow and Company, 1966). A variation of this quotation appears as the headnote to Chapter 6 of this volume (66).
5. Martin Johnson, quoted on dust jacket of the first edition of Osa Johnson's *I Married Adventure* (New York: J. B. Lippincott, 1940).
6. W. S. Van Dyke, quoted in Pascal James Imperato and Eleanor M. Imperato, *They Married Adventure: The Wandering Lives of Martin and Osa Johnson* (New Brunswick, NJ: Rutgers University Press, 1992), 158.
7. Mrs. Martin Johnson, "A Wife in Africa," *Photoplay Magazine* (date unknown), 33.
8. Mrs. Martin Johnson, "My Home in the African Blue," *Good Housekeeping* (January 1924), 48, 167.
9. See Mrs. Martin Johnson, "Jungle Dinner," *Hearst's International-Cosmopolitan* (June 1937), 74–76, 79.
10. George Eastman, quoted in *I Married Adventure*, 299.
11. *New York World* review of *Trailing African Wild Animals*, quoted in Imperato, 112–113.
12. The license was issued to her by the Governor of Tanganyika (present-day Tanzania). Letter from Osa Johnson to her Mother Belle Leighty, January 28, 1930. Henshall Library, Martin and Osa Johnson

Safari Museum, Chanute, Kansas. All letters cited herein are from the Museum archives.

13. Letter from Osa Johnson to Belle Leighty, January 8, 1930. Spelling and punctuation as in the original. Both Osa's and Martin's correspondence reflect the fact that neither had finished high school.

14. Osa Johnson letter to Belle Leighty from Nairobi, February 21, 1931.

15. Dr. J. R. Gregory, the Johnsons' personal physician, quoted in Imperato, 164.

16. Osa Johnson letter to Belle Leighty, April 28, 1933. Vern is Vern Carstens, the Johnsons's pilot. Hugh is Hugh Davis, one of Martin's assistants.

17. Osa Johnson letter to Belle Leighty from Nairobi, sometime in 1930.

18. On the way hunting factored into and supported imperialism, see especially John M. MacKenzie, *The Empire of Nature: Hunting, Conservation and British Imperialism* (Manchester and New York: Manchester University Press, 1988). On the translation of colonial discourse into photographic images of conquest, see James R. Ryan, *Picturing Empire: Photography and the Visualization of the British Empire* (London: Reaktion Books Ltd., 1997).

19. As things turned out, *Simba* was the only film the Johnsons completed for the museum, since after Akeley's death in Africa in 1926 their relationship with the Natural History Museum became more tenuous. However, their subsequent films retain the conservationist sensibility first set forth in *Simba*.

20. See Imperato, 168–169.

21. Imperato, 209. He rightly points out that this sales figure is truly impressive, given the fact that the country was still pulling itself out of the Great Depression.

22. Rose Feld, reviewing the book for the *New York Herald Tribune*, quoted in Imperato, 215.

23. A Note about Authorship:

In their generally very helpful and insightful biography of the Johnsons, *They Married Adventure: The Wandering Lives of Martin and Osa Johnson*, Pascal James Imperato and Eleanor Imperato state, on several occasions, that both Martin and, more especially, Osa, relied heavily on ghost-writers. As the editor not only of this reprint series but also of an anthology of women's hunting writing which features an excerpt from *Four Years in Paradise*, I was troubled to read their assertion that Osa played virtually no active role in the production of either this book or *I Married Adventure*. When I questioned

Jacqueline Borgeson and Barbara Henshall, curators of the Martin and Osa Johnson Safari Museum, both replied that in their view what the Imperatos referred to as ghost-writing should more properly be regarded as the kind of editing many professional writers depend upon to get their work into publishable shape. Based upon a careful perusal of Osa Johnson's letters and manuscripts of several articles, including an early version of chapter 16 of this book, I can only agree. *Four Years in Paradise* reads like Osa, in its turns of phrase, its bubbly enthusiasm, its generous descriptions of other persons, and—alas—its tendency from time to time to lapse into breathless cliché. The draft of chapter 16, Osa's authorship of which was attested by her mother, demonstrates to my satisfaction that whatever editorial hands were at work, they had all the raw essentials and much of the best metaphorical language straight from Osa Johnson.

24. Press release dated February 25, 1950, in the Martin and Osa Johnson Safari Museum archives. The release explains that this honor for Osa is in recognition of "the important role of women in the cause of conservation."
25. Osa Johnson, "Osa Johnson Doesn't Stalk Hats and Coats in Jungles," *The Amarillo Globe* (Amarillo Texas, January 16, 1942), 20.
26. Osa Johnson, "Jungle," Guest Editorial in *The American Magazine* Vol.. CXXIV, No. 1 (July 1937), n.p.

To my dear mother,
who has stood by me all these
years and encouraged me to
carry on.

1

*". . . I have been home just four
months, and as soon as I can, I am
going back. I know exactly the spot
I will make for. It lies away out in
the blue, a good thousand mile trek
from Nairobi, in British East Africa.
It is Paradise, literally as well as
figuratively, and if it were charted it
would appear on the maps as Lake
Paradise. And I know of no place in
all the world that better deserves the
name. . . ."*
—MARTIN JOHNSON

WE STEAMED INTO Kilindini, the port of Mombasa. Great islands of waving cocoanut palms swept past the porthole and a familiar spicy-sweet odor filled the air.

"Martin, we're back in Africa."

"We're home, Osa," he said.

We hurried into our clothes, rushed up to the deck and watched the ship move slowly into the harbor. Sweeping rollers, with windblown crests, washed inward toward the rocky shore. Baboa trees, lifting their dwarfed branches from huge century-old trunks, made a colonnade along the bank, curving off toward the Palace of the Sultan of Zanzibar. Arab dhows with red and green sails scudded down-wind, and great barges began to head for us as we came to anchor.

The air was hot as an oven, even at this early hour. Although this was the winter season in America, it was the height of summer in British East Africa. We were on the other side of the world, and we would have to get used to sunstrokes and to flowers growing in January.

Behind us lay twenty-eight days on the *Mantola*, the little British steamer that had brought us out from London. Before that the trans-

13

atlantic voyage from New York. Of course, there had been weeks of preparation in London, long days of buying supplies, and of seeing officials and others concerned with the expedition. It had been the first day of December when we sailed from America and now almost two months had elapsed, but our long trek towards the wilds of Lake Paradise was actually only beginning.

Little native canoes drew alongside, piled high with finger bananas, mangoes, pineapples, papayas and custard apples, with sometimes a monkey or parrot perched right on top of the fruit.

Across the water we could see the great white fort, built by the Portuguese in the seventeenth century; and the new government buildings rose out of the bright tropical sunlight a mile to the west on the other side of the island.

Martin and I had seen it all on our first trip to Africa two years before, but sometimes returning can be more exciting than arriving for the first time. Now, the sight of Africa filled us with such excitement that for the moment our concern over the vastness of the undertaking to which we were devoting the next few years was temporarily forgotten.

It was a matter of only a few minutes to be examined by the government doctor who had boarded the ship. Then at last the yellow quarantine flag was lowered and soon we saw the giant cranes lifting our precious cargo from the waist of the ship. I watched our trunks and boxes overboard, all two hundred and twenty-five of them.

And to bring us even closer to Lake Paradise, there on a great flat-bottomed boat was M'pishi, our old cook, rigged out in a brand new suit of khaki in honor of our arrival, and Mohammed, our houseboy, wearing his "kanza" or native mother hubbard. When they saw us, their happy faces shone like black melons suddenly split open to reveal rows of glistening white seeds. I remembered that Martin had written to the Native Affairs Committee in Nairobi several months before, giving them the numbers and names of all our old boys, and asking to have them rounded up, and to send M'pishi and Mohammed to Mombasa to help us through the customs.

They took our small luggage, and we made for the wharf in a native boat. Then came the ordeal of going through customs. If we could clear our things in time, we could make the late afternoon train to Nairobi.

All our things were strewn about the dock. Everything from crates of Heinz's Fifty-Seven varieties to little boxes containing watermelon seeds from Kansas and hollyhock seeds from my father's garden in Chanute. Mountains and mountains of crates! There were shovels, wire, crow-bars, rakes and hoes for the garden, hammers and nails. Tents, chairs, cots and equipment which we had had made specially at the Benjamin Edgington plant in London. The precious lenses from Bausch & Lomb in Rochester and Dallmeyer in London. Boxes of cigars, a crazy-quilt which my grandmother had made, a butter churn from our back porch in Kansas. And all the cameras, acids, developers, and moving picture film that were to help us accomplish the work we had set out to do. There were enough drug supplies to open a corner drug store on the edge of the desert, for we were to be hundreds of miles from civilization, with no physician within call, and fifty to two hundred human beings to protect against accident and sickness.

Customs inspectors began opening crate after crate. It was incredible the things we had. What a list!

Cameras	Soap (mountains of it, a gift from
Guns	Sidney Colgate)
Sheets	Folding chairs
Pillow Cases	Folding tables
Blankets	Folding wash basins
Towels	Folding cots
Dish rags	Folding washtub
Aprons	Safari bags

Air-tight clothes boxes
Ammunition
Filing boxes
Chemicals
Cooking utensils by the score
Enamel dishes
Containers
Water filters
Galvanized tanks
Tanks for rain water
Pumps
Delco Electric system
Coleman stoves
Flashlights
Drying racks
Butter churns
Drying drums
Electric wire and fixtures
Electric fans
Enlarging equipment
Drug supplies
Printing equipment
Crates and crates of canned goods

Fish hooks
Bags of cement (for fixing our chimneys)
Nails
Axes
Shovels and spades
Crow-bars and picks
Rakes and hoes
Buckets and tubs
Typewriters and supplies
Wire
Scissors and shears
Chains (for towing)
Extra motor car parts
Flower seeds
Papers, pencils and ink
Magazines and books
Patchwork quilts
Bed clothes
Mats and rugs
Wearing apparel
—and an ape

It took nearly all afternoon to check off each piece, but the customs officials were courteous and helpful, and by five o'clock everything was passed.

The guns caused the most trouble. Each had to be unpacked and the number registered.

"Twenty per cent," Martin grumbled.

"That's right," the austere British official answered.

Twenty per cent duty on each gun. I looked at Martin. I knew that he was thinking of our first expedition to the South Seas, with one second-hand gun, an old hand-crank Universal camera, a few thousand feet of film, and all our worldly belongings in a trunk and two boxes. And no duty to pay.

"Come on. Let's get out of this crowd."

Hiring an old Ford, we drove from Kilindini to Mombasa through the maze of narrow, irregular streets.

Reaching the Metropole Hotel, we parked the car. The two boys carried the bags up the little wooden steps that led into the lobby.

"Mr. Johnson," the native clerk said, "I have several letters for you. They have been here for three weeks."

Martin's face lit up as he saw one familiar handwriting.

"It's from Blaney Percival, Osa. He's going to meet us in Nairobi."

"Blaney, bless his old heart! I knew he'd meet us," I said, for I felt as Martin did about him.

Blaney Percival occupied a corner all his own in our hearts. Twenty years as game warden in British East Africa had made him the greatest authority in Africa on the animals of the country. He knew all the various species, their habits and haunts, and was never sparing of his time and knowledge to help us. He had been with us on our first safari, and his advice and friendship had meant more to us than that of any other single person in Africa.

"He'll want to know all about how we made out with our finances. You know how we talked it over before we returned to the States," I said.

I thought of how the three of us had discussed our shoe-string budget and our dreams for preserving the wild life of Africa in our films. And what a dream it had all seemed then!

It had been a long road we had traveled through the years. But this time we were no longer traveling on a shoe-string. At last we were making an expedition as we had always wanted to make one. We were attempting what all but a few regarded as fantastic and impossible, to make an authentic film record of vanishing wild life as it existed in its last and greatest stronghold. And if in some over-civilized future, cities should crowd out the elephants and wars should bomb the giraffes from the plains and the baboons from the treetops, our films would stand—a record for posterity.

After dinner it was too hot to think of going to bed, so we sat on the veranda. Everything was still and warm and mellow in this tropical land. Martin said nothing for a long time. The smoke from his cigar rose in circles about his head.

"Exactly three hundred and thirty miles by that crazy wood-burning train and we'll be in Nairobi," he spoke finally out of the smoke.

I sat watching the soft tropical night.

"And then five hundred miles due north and we'll be at Lake Paradise. Here we are in Africa—half-way around the world from home; yet in point of time we're only half-way toward our objective."

2

". . . What a joy it was, after many gruelling months in civilization, to see again the real Africa we had come to love so very much. . . ."
—MARTIN JOHNSON

ALTHOUGH RAILWAY SCHEDULES in Africa are not too strictly observed, our train was scheduled to leave at five p.m. sharp, and we were there in plenty of time to check our many belongings and to see that our boys were safely aboard. Martin had even rented a special refrigerator car for the sake of his films, since the effect of excessive heat and moisture on the gelatin was just one more obstacle with which we had to contend.

"Do you know that they charge eighteen cents a mile for a first-class ticket?" Martin asked. "Multiply that by three hundred and thirty miles and see what you get."

"It must be enormous," I said, horrified.

"Fifty-nine dollars and forty cents apiece."

"That's outrageous!"

It cost us more to have our luggage and crates transported by the Uganda Railway from Mombasa to Nairobi than it had cost to bring them all the way from New York to London, and from London to Mombasa.

The following morning we woke to find ourselves in the highlands, passing through wide unsettled plains over which roamed great masses of game. Antelope and gazelle, grazing beside the

19

tracks, started up as we passed. Giraffe stared at us with surprised curiosity, and ostrich, zebra, wildebeest, baboons and monkeys were everywhere about.

The train huffed and puffed at decreasing speed to an altitude of over five thousand feet, and at noon I could see the outline of Nairobi rising abruptly out of the plains.

The city is a frontier town, not unlike our mining towns of the early West, but its buildings, though only two or three stories in height, are substantial and up to date.

We drew into a splendid modern railway station. Black porters in long-tailed khaki shirts were clamoring for our luggage, but M'pishi and Mohammed stood guard as if the Crown Jewels of England were in their care.

"Hello, Martin! Hello, Osa!"

We wheeled around at the familiar voice.

"Blaney, you old son-of-a-gun!" Martin squeezed his hand.

Blaney's blue eyes sparkled. He didn't look a day older than the first time Martin and I had met him in Nairobi. He had retired the year before and was living at his home on the outskirts of town, but retirement had in no way softened him. He was still the tough, weatherbeaten companion of our first trip to Africa in 1921, when he had advised and guided us. His sly, perpetual grin told us that he was still finding fun in the jungle and was ready to lead us to it.

There were those in British East Africa who referred respectfully to Blaney Percival as a scientist of no mean account. Undoubtedly he was the greatest authority on wild game on the entire continent. His own particular hobby was collecting birds and butterflies, and he had gathered several thousand varieties in his own private museum. Moreover, he had cultivated many of the most beautiful jungle flowers; in his garden bloomed rare orchids which attracted visitors from all over the world.

But to Martin and me, Blaney was no scholarly scientist. He

might have been one of our farming neighbors in Kansas, wearing his clothes with the same careless abandon and loving the land with the same devotion. He was a jolly, happy-go-lucky companion, and his wealth of good stories had filled our evenings around the campfire with rich and hearty entertainment. It was good to be back with him once again.

Watching him, I recalled that day on our first visit to Africa when he told Martin and me about Lake Paradise. He had shown us a thin, worn book written by a Scotch missionary in the early part of the nineteenth century. "He describes a crater lake which is on no map of this country," Blaney had remarked. "Nobody seems to know about it, and you may be certain I've kept my ears open."

A secret lake—an untouched game sanctuary! Magic words. From then on, it had become *our* Lake Paradise. Martin had shouted: "We mustn't waste any time. We must go right away."

At that time Blaney had looked at me warningly and said: "I wouldn't set my heart on going, Mrs. Johnson. It will be no trip for a woman."

Blaney knew me better now!

At any rate, we had found Lake Paradise, and that one brief visit had resolved us to return as quickly as we could to photograph its untroubled wild life and its unspoiled beauty.

"All right, boys! You can start now, but take it easy!"

Every one of the two hundred and twenty-five pieces of luggage had been carefully taken off the train and roped securely on trucks that would take the precious cargo to Blaney Percival's house until we were ready to leave Nairobi. The boys hung on to the sides and top of the trucks, shouting like youngsters as they pulled away.

"Well, that much is done." Martin wiped his brow.

"Looks to me as if you hadn't forgotten anything," Blaney said with a smile.

"No, for the first time in all our lives we have everything we need. We'll not be lacking any equipment on this trip." Martin spoke with great satisfaction.

"What are you going to do about all these boys?" Blaney indicated twelve grinning Kavarando porters hovering on the station platform.

Martin turned and saw the old porters who had been with us for almost two years on our last trip. We shook hands with each of them.

"You're all hired!" Martin shouted the words and their faces shone.

As the boys drove off, Martin looked around him. "I guess they have everything. And I hope they know how to drive. If they crack up with those cameras, we may as well take the next train back to Mombasa. Those are the most expensive cameras we've ever owned."

"They're good boys," Blaney said. "You can trust them, Martin."

As Blaney led the way to his car, he said: "Did I tell you that the Willys-Knights came? All crated. You'll have to assemble them."

"That will take some time, too," Martin reflected. "Mr. Willys had them shipped down here. Two trucks, and a touring car for Osa, and he's sending four more."

As we drove along, Martin told Blaney how we had gone to Rochester to see George Eastman.

"We told him that only someone who could see the idea and not the returns would have to back us," Martin explained. "He said he liked our frankness, and before we knew what was happening, he had promised to invest ten thousand dollars in the undertaking."

"The American Museum in New York is interested, too," I chimed in.

"You know, Blaney," Martin went on, "the thing I liked most was that Mr. Eastman said he believed in us both."

We spent the next day in the stores of Nairobi, and at Tarleton, Whetham and Burman, the safari outfitters. Among many other necessities, we bought a complete wardrobe of Solara clothing. This was an important item in our equipment since the cloth, made in London, was interlined with a red and purple weave to keep out the ultra-violet and red rays of the African sun. And we had to buy special tents made of selected canvas also interlined with red, and some of them made oversize, for stores. Tarpaulins, for their many uses, were added to our list of supplies.

As soon as we could get our cars assembled, and all the crates unpacked and loaded for safari, we would be off. It would require several weeks, Martin thought.

From daylight to nightfall we were busy unpacking all the crates and boxes and making them into loads that could be carried by the porters. The cameras were taken out of the camera trunks and rearranged and repacked for the drive to Lake Paradise.

There were hunting licenses to be obtained, for the British Government required us to supply our porters with a certain amount of game meat each week. And then we might occasionally find it necessary to shoot to protect ourselves.

Licenses are expensive in Africa. As a usual thing, one takes out a general license to shoot all the common game, the allowance being definite for each kind. A special license is issued for elephant, rhino, giraffe and ostrich, and other strictly protected animals.

We began choosing our native boys—porters, gunbearers, house servants, cooks and headman. Many of them had worked for us before and the news of our arrival at Nairobi had spread far and wide by the usual grapevine system. Our old boys were constantly drifting in, coming from all parts of East Africa, and we signed them on, usually because we had trained them carefully and were assured of their skill and loyalty, but sometimes out of sentiment and because we enjoyed their sense of humor.

We hired the best and most seasoned natives we could find. We selected Bukhari to be headman. Bukhari was a six-foot Nubian, black as ink, with the reputation of being a better shot than most white men, and possessing a powerful frame and features that told us he was not afraid of anything.

There was N'dundu, who was the head gunbearer; Suku, the first boy; Abdulla, who acted as chauffeur and mechanic as well as carpenter; Ouranga, camera assistant and laboratory boy; Thu, a young Kikuyu, who helped Martin with his picture work; Jagonga, a big strapping black, who acted as head porter for carrying cameras; and Nasero, who was the jack-of-all-trades, and acted as assistant headman, gun-bearer and porter.

"We've got twenty-four good men," Martin said at last. "We won't need any more until we get up country. But there are several cooks outside. You talk to them, Osa. You're the boss when it comes to cooking. And for Pete's sake find one that can bake bread."

While the veteran M'pishi had already been hired to be our cook, he would need an assistant, as well as several helpers, to take care of the large camp we planned.

"There's Mumbora," I noted, "and he makes the best coffee in Africa. But his wife didn't want him to go with us last time. She was troublesome about his salary, too."

I turned to M'pishi and asked him his choice.

"Mumbora is best man—my friend—good cook," he whispered.

It took quite a bit of persuasion to make Mumbora's wife see it our way, but finally things were arranged satisfactorily when we agreed to pay her one month's salary as a present, and to have a Nairobi bank pay her Mumbora's salary each month in advance. The only other condition she made was that he must have rice instead of posho at all times. His stomach would become ill, she swore; he couldn't sleep and he would die tomorrow if he had to eat posho. So we gladly made this concession to his sophisticated taste, and our personnel was complete. We were now sure of having the best coffee in Africa, and Martin was so pleased with the transaction that he promptly went out and bought Mumbora a pair of shoes and socks.

"Now, if we only had Boculy, we'd be all set," Martin remarked. "Where is that old half-brother of the elephants, Blaney, and why hasn't he shown up?"

Boculy was our old guide through the Northern Frontier on our first trip to Lake Paradise. We had come to trust him more than any of the other boys and it had been our secret hope all along that he would go to the Lake with us.

"Nobody has seen him for a couple of years," Blaney informed us. "I've heard a rumor that he was nabbed for poaching ivory."

We had to spend several days uncrating and assembling our motor cars. The native carpenters had to build bodies on the trucks, and compartments had to be built in, for carrying special equipment safely. Every inch was accounted for. There was space for copper stills for distilling drinking water. Beds were built in for sleeping-out on safari. Each truck had to be bound in heavy wire mesh to keep the luggage from falling out.

Martin's camera truck was specially designed. A trap door was cut through the roof so that the camera could be elevated. If, as we were driving along, Martin spied something to photograph, which would usually be gone before he could set up a camera, he could now be at the crank of the camera in a twinkling. The instrument was set upon a heavy iron unipod which elevated through the roof and could be turned in all directions.

In the front of the camera car we also built a developing laboratory the width of the body and just large enough for Martin to squeeze into. It had a complete sink, lined with black rubber, for washing film, and was fed with water from a tank on the roof. A little electric fan was run from the battery and there was an overhead red lamp as well as a movable lamp with a long cord. The solid window, covered with a fine copper screen to keep out insects, was padded with black felt and slid back to let in air from the front and to communicate with the driver's seat. Every inch of the unused space was equipped with racks or cabinets into which were fitted all the necessary chemical containers and utensils for developing and testing film and making prints.

For the first time we had a complete mobile safari, and for the first time we were carrying parts and supplies for the trucks. The Fisk Rubber Company had supplied us with about one hundred and fifty spare tires and tubes, and we had enough parts to take care of any repairs that might be needed—piston rings, fan belts, batteries, carburetors, spark plugs. We had almost enough parts on hand to build an entire new truck. Certainly, we were not lacking equipment in any department.

Whenever "Jack" Percival, Blaney's charming wife, went shopping, I took time off from the hundred and one preparations we were making to go with her. I have always enjoyed keeping house and shopping, and the markets in Nairobi were real entertainment.

The "white market" was maintained by English and Boer farmers, and there was also a native market, to which the natives and East Indian gardeners brought their truck produce. Here, for a few cents, I could get anything my heart desired, from great white-skinned potatoes to alligator pears, luscious red strawberries and green asparagus.

On the way to the open-air markets were neat, clean butcher shops in which were displayed wild game and all the meats of civilization, from pigs' feet in calves' jelly to spring lamb. Fascinated, I would walk along Government Road, shaded with eucalyptus trees, past the Indian bazaars and on along the bustling business thoroughfare.

Shopping in the "white market" of Nairobi was great fun, for it was not like shopping anywhere else in the world. Eggs and butter, flowers and fruits and vegetables, tinned goods and furniture were all sold at auction. I am sure the truck-farmers profited by the system. The strawberries about to fall into the hands of the lady with spectacles always seemed worth a few cents over their value to the fat lady with the mole on her cheek. The women of Nairobi went to market as most American women go to a bridge party, and because the supply was often limited they took a sporting interest in the price of a bunch of asparagus or a basket of alligator pears, and soon they were all shouting and yelling at the top of their voices.

Once, while "Jack" Percival was loading up her baskets with vegetables and fruits, two fluffy little Persian kittens came up for auction, and I couldn't resist buying them, much to her surprise and amusement.

Returning home, we came to the gate and saw an apprehensive gazelle that had strayed in from the plains and did not know how to find its way back again. It turned and fled. Even in the peace and comfort and civilized order of the little city, Africa meant animals. Animals roamed at will over the golf course and about the edge of the city, and one night lions chased two zebra down the main street and killed them near the Norfolk Hotel.

Every now and then, a leopard would make off with a pet dog, and one day Blaney and Martin scared one of the great cats from under Blaney's own veranda. Over and over again, the Nairobi paper repeated animal accident stories: HUNTER MAULED BY LION . . . SETTLER GORED BY RHINO . . . NATIVE KILLED BY LEOPARD.

On our first visit to Africa, Blaney Percival had taken me to the European cemetery in Nairobi. "If you're going to know Africa," he said, "this is a good place to begin." I could see what he meant. I counted nine tombstones with the briefly eloquent inscription: "Killed by a lion." There were other crumbling stones dedicated to men who had been killed by rhino, buffalo and leopards, or by accidental shooting.

One day Martin heard disquieting news. "Osa," he said, "we may be in the soup. There's a gold rush on the Amala River—down in Tanganyika." Martin spoke slowly and with deliberation. "That gold rush is going to hold us up. It's about two hundred miles to the south, and almost all the available wagons and oxen have gone down there. Just gobbled up." He was very worried.

So we appealed to Blaney, who, with his usual efficiency, secured sturdy mules for us. We investigated all possible sources of wagons, but Martin could secure only three old rattle traps. "They may last us until we get to Lake Paradise, but they certainly won't go any farther than that," he remarked as he inspected the rickety wheels.

"The rains are due in a few weeks." Blaney spoke with authority. "You must get to the Eauso Nyiro River before then."

The rains! When they really started the Eauso Nyiro River would be flooded in a few hours. And with our heavily loaded wagons and trucks we would probably be stalled for two or more months. The photographic materials would be ruined. The rains became our paramount concern.

"And you'll never be able to take everything on one big safari," Blaney went on. "You'll have to send one section ahead."

"I know. I'll have to wire to McDonough and Rattray in Isiolo. They can take care of the things until we get there if we send them in relays." Martin ran to the phone. "I'm going to send them a wire at once."

"Good idea," said Blaney. "Then you can follow in about a week."

Martin wired Captain McDonough, the government veterinary, and Rattray in Isiolo, and they replied that they would take good care of our equipment. They agreed to put up the transports and look after the boys until we arrived.

Our three mule wagons, heavily loaded, were sent on ahead, northward to Isiolo, two hundred and fifty miles on the way to Lake Paradise. Martin then wired Nyeri, halfway to Isiolo, where there was a lonely telegraph station, and ordered additional ox wagons with a hundred loads of posho and four hundred gallons of petrol to be sent along to the meeting juncture at Isiolo. Posho is a rough ground corn, not unlike American cornmeal, and is the staple food of the native boys.

At last we saw three mule wagons with black drivers leave for Isiolo. We were left with only our three motor cars.

Martin began taking stock. "I think everything is ship-shape."

I was going through the licenses. "Two hundred shillings each for game licenses—that includes hippo, buffalo, lions and leopards, and all the antelope, gazelle and zebra. There's one rhino license—that costs ten pounds, and one elephant license—fifty pounds. Do they check, Martin?"

We looked up as Blaney came into the room.

"There's something I want to ask you, Blaney," Martin said. "Can you come along with us on this safari?" There—at last, a question we had had on our minds for days was out.

"I knew that was what you were going to ask me, Martin, but I've retired, you know."

"But you know every inch of the country, and you're one of the crack shots of Africa," Martin pleaded.

Blaney had a twinkle in his eye.

"Of course, we can't pay you anything like what you're worth," Martin continued, "but you can see what this trip means to us and how we need you. You speak most of the languages and you would be invaluable to us. Besides, you enjoy going on safari. Why not come along?" Martin looked him full in the face.

"Please," I added.

"Well, Martin, I'll admit I'm a little restless. I'd like to get away into the 'Blue,' and have a few months of fun with you and Osa. I really would."

Martin and I stood as if before a judge pronouncing sentence.

"Of course, the answer is yes." Blaney threw back his head and laughed. "I always intended to."

"Blaney—you old son-of-a-gun. I thought for a moment you might—"

"And remember, Martin, I'm not going out with you for the money. But there's just one thing I don't understand." Blaney paused.

"What?"

"Why the deuce did it take you so long to ask me? I've had my things packed for three weeks!"

WILD ZEBRA IN TRAINING AT RATTRAY'S

After months of patient labor and discipline, the rancher
succeeded in breaking these spirited animals to harness.

CLIMBING UP FROM THE DESERT TOWARD LAKE PARADISE

The cars encounter the worst travel of the entire journey and in the blistering heat have to be rested and cooled, while porters make the trail ahead passable. Several days were spent covering these last few miles.

3

*". . . We are off into the blue.
Soon we shall find ourselves under
African skies, out in the open by day
and night. We shall not go to sleep
at night as quickly as the native
boys. We shall be hearing the night
sounds of Africa. During the long
weeks and months that lie ahead
they will come to be our lullaby."*
—MARTIN JOHNSON

"WE'VE GOT TO beat the rains! The rains are getting nearer and
nearer. We've got to beat them!"

Martin and I were getting our things in readiness for departure.
A young boy had arrived at daybreak with a box-body Ford
which we had rented. Martin loaded his own car with all the
film, plates and sensitive materials, and spread excelsior over the
top of the precious photographic equipment. Every nook and
cranny of the car was stuffed, and over all Martin spread a heavy
tarpaulin.

"You're not going to do that with my car, Martin Johnson,"
I protested.

I was very proud of my new touring car. It was the finest car
in Nairobi, and I didn't relish having it converted into a truck on
its very first trip.

"Sorry, honey," Martin laughed. "I'm afraid I'll *have* to put a
few things in your car."

A few things! My heart sank as I watched Martin and the boys
begin to pile the "few things" into my beautiful car. He loaded
film into the back seat, up to the sides. Then camp tables and
chairs were piled over the film, and two tents with poles over them.

On the running-board were strapped the black waterproof cases we had bought at Benjamin Edgington's in London. On the back trunk was the bedding, and on the fenders in the front were strapped big canvas bags of tarpaulins and ground sheets. But it didn't stop there. In every available inch of space boxes and small bags were stuffed. At the side of my steering wheel there was a holster for my .275 Bland and on either side of this were my 20 gauge Ithaca shotguns.

"Well, Martin," I said. "This is lovely! Is there any room for me to drive?" I was completely out of sorts.

"Sure, plenty of room," Martin announced cheerfully. "And you can carry Suku and Toto with you on the front seat. And the Persian kittens."

Well, that took care of that. My new car was accounted for. Or, at least, so I thought until Kalowat, the little ape, landed in the car and hooked her arms about my neck. I turned her over to Suku to hold on his lap.

Blaney Percival's parting gift was his pet cheetah, Marjo, which we also loaded on to one of the trucks. I was crazy about this big beautiful brown-eyed, golden beast. She had a black stripe running from the corner of each eye down across her cheek, which gave her a comical look, for all her proud feline haughtiness.

The other cars were loaded with cameras in padded cases, and tarpaulins and sacks were put into every possible nook and cranny. On the outside of the two cars, the men strapped tripods, extra tent poles, provisions, and the cook's outfit. The springs of the cars were resting on the axles when Martin finished his handiwork.

"Now, let's see. What about the chickens?" Martin picked up the crate of Rhode Island Reds which I had bought in the market for a shilling per chicken, and with one heave landed it on the back of my car, then tied it securely in place.

Blaney came out to watch us, walked around my car. "Lucky you're little, Osa, or Martin would have to leave you behind."

"I'll be all right, Blaney. But I wish you were leaving with us today." I tried to squeeze into the front seat beside Suku and Kalowat and Toto.

"Oh, I'll be catching up with you in about a week or so. I'll meet you at the Eauso Nyiro. And I'll bring somebody along to drive my car back."

"Now, let's see what's what here," Martin cried. "We've got four cars—three of ours and the boy's Ford. You and I will each drive one, Osa; Abdulla will drive the other, and Humadi will drive the last."

"What about the boys?" I asked.

Martin began to count noses. "Osa, you're taking Suku and Toto in your car. I'll take Semona in mine. M'pishi can go with Abdulla, and Thu with Humadi."

We all took our places as Martin said, "Our first stop is Thika. That's thirty-two miles from here. Everybody ready?"

The Percivals stood in the driveway, waving, as Martin led the procession of cars into Government Road. At last we were off. We coasted over the splendid modern boulevard kept in shape by native labor, through the plains, and made Thika, thirty-two miles distant, in an hour and a half.

We spent the night at the Blue Posts. The hotel boasted one big dining room and bar and office, all in one building, with about fifteen straw-thatched huts. Each hut was a numbered room. About four hundred yards away were the beautiful waterfalls of the Thika River.

I was surprised to find electric lights newly installed in the huts, until I discovered that the power was generated from the waterfalls. It was a remarkably modern hotel for this part of British East, and, above all, it was cool.

"I'm going to get up at dawn and fish," I told Martin as we tucked ourselves into bed for the night.

"Good!" he replied sleepily. "Catch me a nice trout for break-fast."

I could hear the musical rhythm of the nearby waterfalls. Martin spoke suddenly.

"You know, Osa, I believe this is going to be our most successful trip. We're not like so many people, constantly prodding around in the dark, not knowing which way to turn next, never knowing exactly what they want out of life. We know exactly what we want. I think we have a strong grasp on our kind of life."

I thought how true that was. Martin's life seemed always to have had a clear design. He knew what he wanted, and he went ahead and got it, regardless of the consequences to himself. It had always been as simple as that—as unconfused and uninvolved.

His great love of nature and his instinctive talent for photography were happily combined. But even more pronounced was his inherent love of adventure. Driving through an African wilderness, with all our resources and hopes pinned on outdistancing a challenge of Nature, I could always feel in him the determination which makes the strong succeed.

There had never been a time that Martin hadn't been in pursuit of something. All his life. When he was still a boy, he dreamed of adventure as he sat in the class room of a little white frame school-house in Independence, Kansas. The huge map of the world that hung on the wall of the class room ceased to be just a piece of dusty canvas, marked with splotches of green, blue, pink and yellow which said here was the Mediterranean, South America, North America, Canada, India, Africa. How silly it was to sit chewing a pencil and adding up a long string of figures! That might come in handy if one were going to be a clerk in the jewelry store. But multiplication, subtraction, addition—when there on the wall was a crinkled old map! There on the wall giant continents beckoned. An island reared its grassy back out of the blue expanses of the Pacific. Lofty mountains with snow-capped summits towered

to the skies. . . . Lands of color where queer people, in unfamiliar costumes, lived out equally unfamiliar lives . . . this wasn't
merely a map of the world: this was a map of the world that Martin Johnson was going to explore.

During his first twenty years, adventure had eluded him. But
always he knew that somewhere, sometime, it would come his
way, and when it did, he would close down on it and hold it fast.

When I was a little girl singing in the choir of the First Presby-
terian Church in Chanute, Kansas, Martin had run away from
home at Independence, a boy of sixteen, on his first brush with
adventure. He had a dream, and he held to that dream steadfastly
all the days that he lived. He crossed the Atlantic on a cattle-
boat. He worked on a carousel in an amusement park in Paris, and
at night he slept under the broad arches that spanned the Seine
in the shadow of Notre Dame. Then London, Liverpool, Budapest,
Brussels. But it was only the reflection of adventure that he had
found. It was second best, and second best just wouldn't do.

Martin returned from his globe-trotting, and sat long hours in
his father's jewelry store in Kansas, dreaming as he worked. There
was no end to his imagination, of his journeys in make-believe.
But all his dreams were presaging reality.

One fall evening, he happened to pick up a copy of *Cosmopolitan* Magazine. The date on the cover was November 10, 1906.
But it was what lay between the covers of the magazine that
counted. For there was adventure beckoning him in an article describing a proposed trip round the world on a little forty-five foot
boat, to be made by Jack London, and a party of five. And there
was the magic sentence, fairly leaping off the page, to the effect that
*one of the crew was to be someone in the United States, still un-
known, who had only to write a letter to Jack London sufficiently
convincing to win the place.*

The letter was written, the most important single document in the life of Martin Johnson. The trip was a reality. Martin sailed to the South Seas with Jack London. His life had begun.

The years that followed were full of excitement: days were crammed with danger, satisfaction, fun—and always adventure. The struggles, too, were there—the trials and tribulations which are the milestones in a life of ambitious dreams. After the voyage with the great American author, Martin returned to the States to show films of the trip and to try to raise funds for other trips.

My marriage to Martin occurred at this time. Then followed our first expedition together, to the New Hebrides to make a film record of the cannibals. Back we came to the States to raise more funds for more expeditions. Martin would lecture in any and all halls and theatres, and I danced and sang what passed for Hawaiian numbers to add variety to the entertainment! Next came a tour of the Keith-Albee vaudeville circuit from coast to coast. In modest rooming houses, packing trunks, drafty back-stages, cold dressing rooms, we lived the lives of vaudeville troupers, skimping, saving, planning, dreaming always, watching every penny! What a thrill it was to see the column of figures in the bank book rise with each succeeding week! More pictures. More experiences. There was the thrill of our first full-length picture being shown at the Roxy Theatre in New York. How delighted we were at the great response of the public!

And now we were faced with our greatest opportunity. We couldn't allow ourselves to fail with the official sponsorship of the Museum of Natural History in New York, and the financial assistance of George Eastman and so many of our friends.

I lay awake and my thoughts roamed back over the years. Everything seemed to have been leading logically and with design up to this moment.

Yet I began to worry. I thought of the urgency of reaching the Eauso Nyiro before it was in flood, and remembered how we had lost donkeys, supplies and equipment there on previous crossings, and that we must hurry or the season would be lost. I knew Martin was worried. It was not the danger that concerned him, though there would be plenty of danger. We could shoot and we knew how to take care of ourselves. But we had grave responsibilities, not only to those who were financing us, but to the many native boys whom we must protect and care for.

And I knew Martin worried about me. He kept saying that I might be lonely. I could never dispel the thought in the back of his mind that despite my love of adventure, of fishing, and the pleasures of our work, I longed for friends, for new clothes, theatres, dances, all those things that mean so much to most women. Well, of course, I did. But I had Martin, and I would never admit to him that these things mattered in the least.

"Osa, Osa! Where are you?" I heard Martin calling, and I ran into the hut.

"Right here, darling," I answered.

"You scared the daylights out of me. I wake up and find you gone." He was rubbing his eyes.

I held up a string of fat catfish I had caught by the waterfall. "Fish for breakfast." It was our first taste of "The Blue."

We started the day's run, Martin leading, I at the wheel of the second car, Abdulla at the third, and Humadi bringing up the rear. For the first twenty-five miles we passed hundreds of Kikuyu, some of them armed with spears, some driving goats, others squatting along the roadside gossiping. Every few miles we would come upon Indian dukas, little mud and grass stores that cater primarily to the natives, where they could buy a penny's worth of sugar and tea, cheap blankets, and "King Stork" cigarettes at twenty for a penny. Most of the duka shops also carried a few things that the passing white man might want, such as kerosene, sugar, flour and English-blended cigarettes.

We stopped briefly for lunch at Fort Hall, a government station

in the charge of a District Commissioner, known always in Africa
as a "D.C."

"If we make good time, we can reach Nyeri by late afternoon,"
said Martin as we finished a hurried lunch.

Leaving Fort Hall, we wound around mountains, down steep
roads where we could turn off our motors and coast like a sled
downhill. It was all I could do to drive around the hairpin bends.
I could feel the truck sway under the weight of its cargo as I
steered it past the dangerous turns. I gritted my teeth with nervousness as I saw a two thousand foot drop gaping up at me over the
rim of the narrow road.

We would pass groups of naked totos (babies) standing rigid
and saluting us as we drove by, as they had seen the askari or
native black soldiers do. Then they would run after us shouting
"jambo," which means "hello" in Swahili.

About three in the afternoon, our caravan pulled into Nyeri,
which is the center of a rich agricultural country. There wasn't very
much to recommend Nyeri. It had a general store, a few dukas,
and huts for the government officials and askaris. Its one hotel,
the White Rhino, was comfortable and attractive and furnished
in very good taste.

We remained in Nyeri about an hour, then set off for Nanyuki,
forty miles distant. That would make us one hundred and forty
miles from Nairobi. We were getting on!

As we motored on from Nyeri we came into the Mount Kenya
district, six thousand feet above sea level. From then on we were
in the part of Africa we loved best.

I could see beautiful snow-capped Mount Kenya, some seventy
miles away, its white peak and glaciers glistening in the sun and
rising to an altitude of 17,040 feet. It was hard to believe that it
stood exactly on the equator. Snow on the equator! It didn't seem
possible. I knew, too, that between Mount Kenya and Nyeri lay
an unbroken forest, full of wild elephant, buffalo and rhino.

We were now driving through mountain roads where the going was rough. The car I was driving constantly bounced over deep ruts. Suddenly I was conscious of a cackling and squawking some- where behind me. It sounded like a farmyard. I glanced back to find that the Rhode Island Reds were laying an egg every time I hit a heavy bump. I knew I had everything imaginable in my new touring car, but I hadn't expected it to carry eggs on top of the load. The two native boys who were riding with me went back and gathered this welcome produce.

"We can all have fresh eggs for breakfast if I can find enough bumps," I laughed. The boys smiled and held the eggs as if they were precious treasure.

As the first shadows of twilight fell, we reached Nanyuki, where we put up for the night at the Silverbeck Hotel. We had a good bath and cleaned up and after a good dinner with our old friends, Commander and Mrs. Hook, the owners, we spent a restful night in one of the bamboo and thatch bungalows which they had built for their guests.

We were up at dawn, and after a breakfast of fried eggs, we made ready to leave. The native manager of the hotel fitted us out with provisions, and a lunch was made up for noon-day. The tanks were filled to brimming with petrol.

"These roads won't be so bad for a while," Martin pointed out as we started up the cars. "We're soon going to get into hard, rocky, sandy soil."

"In other words, I won't be able to collect any eggs from the back seat today," I laughed.

"Don't count on it, honey. But they certainly tasted good at breakfast this morning."

In several places we had to ford small streams. The water splashed up in my face. It was cold as ice, since it came straight down from the Mount Kenya glacier that towered above us.

Up to this time we had seen little game, for plains animals do not come into the mountains. Of course, elephant and rhino and buffalo were numerous in the forest towards Kenya, though they could seldom be seen from the road. But here we did begin to see zebra. And gazelle bounded over the high plains in the distance.

We came upon flocks of ostrich, black-and-white-plumed males and pearl-gray females. The ostrich fed quietly until we came abreast of them, then they would start running parallel with our cars. We would step on the gas and race them for a while, but it was no use, the ostrich would always win. As soon as they were a hundred yards ahead of the leading car, they would put on an added spurt and cross the road in front of us, often falling and sprawling as their awkward feet hit the hard road-bed. This performance was repeated again and again during the morning. As lovely as ostrich are, they are the silliest and most comical of all birds, and I laughed at them until I could hardly steer the car. The native boys by my side watched with glowing interest, and nearly laughed their heads off.

After about fifteen miles of sheer descent, Martin signaled for us to stop. We were at the banks of the Ngara Ndara River.

"Let's have lunch here," he suggested, and we parked under a fig tree, so enormous that all four cars, side by side, were in the shade at the height of an African noon.

I arranged the lunch and we squatted on the ground and began to eat ravenously.

"There's a waterfall, Martin. I'm going to fish for a little while." I got my rod and line from the car.

"Well, don't be too long. We've got to pack up almost at once and push on," Martin warned.

But I had time to catch a fine mess of fish during the hour we spent there. I was coming back from the falls when I suddenly stopped short in my tracks. A ghastly sight lay before me on the ground.

There, under a tree, lay the body of a dead black boy. His

head was mashed in, his jaw bone broken, and blotches of dry blood smeared his face. There were ugly cuts on his arms and body.

"He died last night," Martin pronounced as he felt the body. "You know what this means, Osa."

I nodded. "Yes. I know. The Kikuyu tribe has left him here for the hyenas."

It is gruesome but true that when a member of the Kikuyu tribe dies, whether by violence or from natural causes, the others throw his body out in the jungle for the hyenas to devour. It is not only the dead that are thrown to the hyenas—the incurably sick and the dying meet the same fate. In spite of all that the British have done to try to stop it, this old tribal custom continues.

Martin wrote a note to the D.C. at Nanyuki, and sent it back with a passing native. There was nothing we could do, so we drove on.

How I wanted to visit Mount Kenya! On the shoulders of that vast mountain roamed all the big game, and I have never known a more beautiful garden of wild flowers: gladiolas, lupin, larkspur, pansies, violets, blooming shrubs. And nowhere are there better trout streams. But we could not stop; I never even suggested it to Martin, for I knew our caravan was waiting for us in Isiolo.

The late afternoon sun began to set, and we were passing through scrub country where there was no game. We began to pass Meru natives, driving herds of goats and sheep down from the Northern Frontier to trade. Once we passed a dozen camels carrying heavy loads of goat skins.

"We're coming on to the plains of Isiolo," Martin announced when we stopped to allow the motors to cool off.

When we had replenished the radiators with water and started up, we found that we were well off any beaten road. But the going was easy as we were on the descent and the ground was sandy. The game became plentiful again—zebra, oryx, gazelle, and several herd of giraffe. Martin stopped his car, and tried, without success, to get a picture of the giraffe. The animals would not budge as long as we kept moving, but the minute the cars stopped, they were off like a flash. Martin gave up, and we went on.

We crossed the Ngara Ndara River at several points as it wound across the plain. As we went we stirred up quail, partridge, spurfowl, grouse and bustard (wild turkey). And ugly vultures flew about us like shadows out of the night. With the dusk we reached a hill below which flickered the few lights of native campfires.

"Isiolo," Martin shouted back at me from his car, and we pushed on with renewed speed.

I could make out the huts of the quarantine station, and the mule wagons which we had sent ahead from Nairobi. Our men were sitting around the fires as we drove into the native settlement.

There were three camps at Isiolo. One was the veterinary station where our old friend, Captain McDonough, was in full charge. He lived alone, tending his duties, inspecting all domestic animals coming down from the Northern Frontier, checking them and inoculating them before they were allowed to pass on.

One of the other two camps belonged to another old friend, Rattray, and the third to the King's African Rifles. The latter served as a transport station maintaining thousands of oxen, mules and donkeys which were used to transport arms, ammunition and provisions to the faraway British outposts on the Northern Frontier.

Captain McDonough came out to greet us.

"It's certainly good to see you again." He shook our hands.

"Did everything get here all right?" Martin asked.

"Right as rain," the Captain replied. "I've never seen quite so much stuff. A complete safari."

The native boys who had come up with us began to mingle with the boys who had come ahead. The camp was loud with their jabbering.

"I'm worried about transportation," Martin said with concern.

"I don't see how we can continue without having more porters and wagons."

"There's nothing to do but scour the countryside. Maybe some of the Boer settlers back at Meru can let you have some," Mc-Donough suggested. "What's wrong down in Nairobi? No more wagons?"

"They've all been put in use for a gold rush down in Tanganyika," Martin explained.

We stayed only long enough to inspect the houses where our boxes and crates were stored. Fortunately, everything was intact, and we got into my car and drove four miles to Rattray's camp.

"Jove, I'm glad to see you again." Rattray took Martin's hand and shook it until I thought he would never let go.

"I guess we'll have to be here for about a week until we can get our transportation worked out," my husband told him.

"And, Osa! You're looking the same as ever." He held out his hand and I took it in mine. I noticed that it was twice its normal size.

"How is your arm?" I asked.

"All right. It will always be like this," he said quietly.

I could remember only too well how he had been mauled by a leopard while helping to bring in a zebra which I had shot just before we returned to the States on our last trip. The incident had sent him to the hospital in Nanyuki. And that was where we said good-bye to him when we left for home.

"I wasn't able to work for ten months, but I'm back on the job now," he went on.

And by his job he meant one of the most unusual occupations on earth, since Rattray's stock in trade was catching and training zebra to harness, and selling them to zoos.

"Of course, it's a little hard to work now," he pointed out. "I'm not quite as good as I used to be, but I manage."

"With all the mauling and bites that you had on that arm," said Martin, "it's a wonder that your muscles work at all."

"How about something to eat? I have some 'squeakers' for you, Osa." We could tell he didn't want to talk about his accident, so we said no more.

Rattray turned over one of his huts to us, and after a dinner of broiled young guinea fowl, we talked far into the night.

Martin sent native runners with letters to Nanyuki, and other letters to Boer farmers, appealing for wagons and oxen. We couldn't possibly spend more than a week in Isiolo if we wanted to beat the rains. We were wasting time. We would have to get our means of transportation somehow, so Martin sent to Meru for more porters. The posho and petrol had now arrived safely in Isiolo from Nyeri; all that we lacked were the ox-wagons.

Since there was no choice but to wait, we resigned ourselves to it and decided to make the most of our time taking pictures. We could see game everywhere about the settlement and knew from our previous visit to Rattray's that we might encounter anything in the high grass on the great plains which stretched off toward the mountains to the north.

I bagged some game birds the next day, and we had wild fowl three times a day until Martin got tired of it. Breast of partridge braised in butter, with little fresh vegetables from Rattray's garden, tasted good after a hot day in the field.

One day we found an ostrich nest containing thirty eggs, six of which we "borrowed," and that night we had a fluffy ostrich omelet, made from one egg, for five people. It was just as good as any French *omelette*.

Our Meru porters arrived, and with their arrival our troubles began. They immediately struck for twelve shillings a month instead of the regulation price of ten. Much against his better judgment, Martin had to give in to them, because he was worried about the rains. It had sprinkled a little the night before, and as we sat in our hut and watched the thin curtain of rain, he said:

"I'll bet you dollars to doughnuts that river will be rising to-morrow."

About noon, the native runners returned with the news that two mule wagons were on the way from Meru, and two ox-wagons from Nanyuki. Martin struck a bargain with the drivers of two of the Nairobi mule wagons to continue the journey with us to Bar-saloi where they would leave our supplies to be picked up by the other wagons for transfer to Paradise.

Rattray agreed to come along with his mule wagons, so that would give us four wagons to Barsaloi and four more in a few days to carry on the journey. We decided to leave the first thing in the morning.

"Now, if only Boculy would show up!" Martin said wistfully. "Then everything would be all right."

He went on with his checking.

"Come on, Osa. We've got to make out the kapandis for these new Meru porters. You read the names and take the numbers, and then I'll sign them on."

Every native in British East Africa must have his kapandi with his finger prints on it. It is a small paper which is enclosed in an equally small tin case, and hung either around the native's neck or about his waist. The kapandi must be signed by his employer whenever a native is hired, and on it is given the amount of his wages and the date on which he is hired. When the native leaves, he must have his kapandi signed off. This enables the white people to trace any deserters, since no man will hire a native who has not had his kapandi signed off properly.

"I'm going to have trouble here," said Martin, as we were mak-ing out the kapandi for two of the Meru porters. "They have both elected themselves headmen."

There stood two big husky Meru with red clay matted in their hair. They wore anklets of colobus monkey fur and carried fine spears with ostrich pom-poms on the tips. They called themselves "Neparas," and Nepara means "headman." Between themselves they had decided that they should be our headmen, and they stubbornly refused to recognize our own headman, Bukhari, and said they would not carry loads.

"There's nothing to do now, Martin, but give in to them."

"Yes, I know. We have to move on, so I'll have to let them have their way. But I'll fix them. I'll give them the heaviest loads when we get off in the desert."

4

". . . It is a big order we have undertaken. But we think we can fill it in four years of hard work. It will be hard work, we know that, but it will be work with joy in every minute of it. As I realize that I am at last off again for the wilderness, I feel like a man recovering from a long illness. Now, after nearly a year spent in civilization, I can begin to live once more."
—MARTIN JOHNSON

"BLANEY PERCIVAL WILL be meeting us at the Eauso Nyiro in a few days," Martin said, as we were getting ready to leave Isiolo.

It was four o'clock in the morning as we left. The wagons lumbered out first, and with them, the porters. Although the porters were loaded down, we ordered them to keep up with the wagons, for we knew that the drivers would need their help in getting across the bad places.

In order to save a few precious days, so important if we were to beat the rains, and on the advice of Captain McDonough, we decided to attempt a short-cut through the mountains over a route that was new to us, instead of taking the customary route that we had taken before, over lower ground through Archer's Post.

"Maybe we won't get away with this, but it's worth the try," said Martin.

It was twenty miles to the first water, and a steady ascent over a dangerous pass between two mountains.

"It will be bad going most of the way, and it is a dangerous road. So be careful, Osa."

"Don't forget to look out for lions when you pass the grassy donga," I shouted in return.

"The lions will take care of themselves; you just watch the road," he replied, as our cars picked up momentum.

Each of our motor cars carried three large petrol tins of water, each tin containing four gallons. We went along about ten miles and dropped the tins of water along the trail, with a boy to watch them. Martin wanted each porter to carry all he could and not be burdened down with water. But they would be extremely thirsty, for it was unmercifully hot.

After a hurried lunch under enormous fig trees on the bank of a beautiful stream, we drove along a trail through tropical African scenery. There were scrub thorn trees as far as we could see, and zebra raced alongside our cars and crossed the road ahead of us, as the ostriches had done on our way to Isiolo. Impala leaped in the air as they ran, some jumping as far as twenty feet. Giraffe craned their necks and great herds loped away as we passed them.

We could not drive as fast as we wished. The road was full of holes and gutters, some only a few feet apart. It was cluttered with volcanic rocks. I could feel the springs of my car bump on the axles, and I expected to break down at any moment. Fortunately, the springs took the strain.

In the late afternoon we came to the Kipsing River, a dry, sandy river-bed about one hundred yards wide.

"We'll have to push each car across," Martin ordered. "You drive and we'll push, and grip that wheel for all you're worth or you'll break the steering gear."

After several hours of sticking, pushing and pulling, we got the cars safely across.

All that afternoon we drove through semi-desert country, not a green growing thing to be seen except the thornbushes. We had to cross sand luggars, or dry sand beds, pulling and pushing our cars out of the soft spots until we were nearly exhausted.

As twilight fell, we came to the Eauso Nyiro crossing at Barsaloi. It was a beautiful spot, each side of the bank lined with palm and wild fig trees. The river ran swiftly, but it was only a foot deep and had a rocky bottom, so we had no difficulty in fording.

We had the native boys build rough huts at the edge of the stream. With their knives some cut down trees, others dug holes, and a third group gathered and bound sheaves of grass for thatching. The temporary shelters were soon completed.

"At least we're across the river, even if our wagons aren't," Martin commented as we put up for the night in our tent under the dom-palm trees.

The next morning I was up early and out fishing before Martin was awake. By the time he arose and walked down-stream to find me, I had already caught a dozen silvery fish, similar to our bass, each weighing over a pound.

I spent all that day fishing and when I weighed my catch at night I found that I had over one hundred and fifty pounds. Of course, I was simply delighted. The fact that we could eat only a few pounds didn't bother me in the least, for the porters would finish them off. If there were any left, the boys would smoke and dry them and carry them along in their pockets to eat like popcorn. This also saved them the bother of cooking meals.

While I was fishing, our little camp was deluged by droves of humpbacked cattle, camels, sheep and goats that were being driven down from the Northern Frontier by a band of Samburu men and women. With them came clouds of dust and millions of flies. The Samburu women screamed and chattered as they rushed to the edge of the stream to fill their gourds with water.

The Samburu men stood around us, over fifty of them, each with a long spear, and talked in low, unintelligible grunts. Suddenly, one of the burly black men noticed a mirror at the side of my car. At once they began to fight among themselves to see their reflections in the glass, and then the entire tribe, men and women, filed up to examine the marvel.

This might have gone on for hours had not our wagons and boys arrived shortly after noon. Rattray was in charge, and as the wagons creaked across the river bed, the Samburu began to disperse. We decided to buy five camels from them and paid twenty-five dollars apiece. These had been in government service in the North, and Martin knew they would make good pack animals.

With the arrival of Rattray and the boys, the Samburu had finished watering and cleared out. But they left their flies behind. Flies as big as wasps were buzzing all over the place.

Our wagons were across the river, but we decided to make camp here until Blaney Percival arrived. Rattray returned to Isiolo the next morning, and the boy who had driven our things up from Nairobi in the Ford left at the same time.

During the three days that followed, there were two light showers. My heart sank, for I knew what Martin must be thinking. But the sun soon shone again.

I spent this brief time in the field, or fishing. I knew it made Martin nervous to have me go off down the stream alone, and often without a gun-bearer, for at night we had already begun to hear the roar of lions and coughing of leopards. Game wardens had always told me to be careful of the streams. Many looked harmless enough, but were so swift that they might sweep one quickly into a deep pool among roots or brush, and drowning would be easy. And sudden rains or melting snows made freshets and tor-rents which swelled the streams without warning.

But my enthusiasm for fishing made me quite reckless. With or without waders, I would take long chances and often I came home dripping wet. It seemed to me that Martin scolded me more about coming home wet and late from fishing than for any other reason. The fishing "bug" had never bitten him.

His idea of fishing was to sit down beside a stream with the end of a rod under him or a line tied to his fingers, a fine cigar to smoke and an old *Saturday Evening Post* to read. He thought fly-casting a waste of precious energy. And he seldom complained that he caught nothing, if he could just be let alone. However, he never ceased to marvel at the quantities of fish I brought in, and seemed more proud of the catches than I was.

"If you see a nice pool, you invariably see a better one just beyond. Aren't you ever satisfied?" he would ask. But what true angler ever is satisfied? Frequently, I would start across a stream, balance on a smooth rock, slip and crash in over my head, taking a native boy, reel and tackle with me. But that was the sport, and who but a fisherman could understand?

One day, I had caught about thirty pounds of trout and my boy had strung them on a jungle vine which he carried over his shoulder. We started across a swift stream on logs and stones. He reached back to help me, and in doing so he slipped, as did I. We were promptly caught in a swirl of water up to our waists. Just below were large falls, and below them a deep pool. In trying to rescue me, the boy dropped the fish—and away they went over the falls. Safely on the other side, sick over the loss of my fish, I turned and gave him the dickens for losing the fish, then suddenly remembered that he had saved my life and told him that he was a good boy.

In the larger streams, such as the Eauso Nyiro, there are ample coarse fish to be caught: catfish, tiger fish, white fish, telapia, (resembling our bass), breem, bluegills, and pumpkinseeds.

All these, except catfish, will take a spoon or a fly. There are many varieties of catfish, many of them unfamiliar to us at home. The catfish will take grasshoppers, worms, beetles and similar live bait, but I have often tossed in on my hook merely a lump of meat and they did not seem to discriminate. The silverfish will take fresh bait, but will also leap to a spinner.

Resembling our carp is the whitefish, the meat of which is sweet and good, with bones about the size of the carp's. The whitefish is great fun to catch for, though not too clever, he's a fighter and offers plenty of sport. He will take a fly or small silver spoon. My cook would take out the large bones with a tweezer and then fry the flesh in a batter made of butter and flour, and the dish was something to remember.

The catfish is much more of a fighter than our variety of catfish. He inhabits the rapid waters and is full of life, striking hard. Many times the big ones have struck in a flash and have taken my leader in a single bite. There are brown, black, silver and even transparent fish. The last have the head of a catfish but a peculiarly-shaped body—long and thin, like that of a flounder, but not so broad.

The electric fish always scared the boys, who would shout, "M'baya sana" (very bad), cut my line and refuse to touch it. Out of the water, this fish blows up in size somewhat, and delivers a real electric shock to anyone who touches him. He is, of course, not edible.

Crocodiles raise havoc with fish. You get a nice strike and begin to play it, when suddenly the line goes light and you pull up a dangling fish-head, all that's left of your catch! The crocodiles usually drag their prey to the bottom to devour, but one day I hooked a huge catfish, which, incredible as it may seem, run to one hundred or more pounds, and had begun to reel it in when suddenly a croc struck it and rose out of the water with the fish in his huge mouth. He apparently could not take the fish to the bottom because of the swift current and tried to swallow it then and there. The fish was too large for his jaws and the tail stuck out of the croc's mouth, flopping about as the brute gulped and struggled to swallow. Finally, he bit the fish off and disappeared, and there went my fine catch.

God has surely provided the crocodiles with ample food. There are so many fish in Africa, running in great schools, that at times the water seems almost solid with fins and tails. It looks as though one could walk on them.

I have caught one hundred and ninety pounds of catfish and whitefish here in a single day, but they were all needed for camp. It took two boys, both grappling with him, to land one catfish I managed to hook.

The porters like fish and I often carried tackle for them, when our safari loads would permit this extra baggage, and they would take almost any quantity of fish I could catch. They fried them, grilled them, stewed them into their posho, and even ate them half-raw.

Eels are a nuisance, six to twenty feet long, and weighing up to twenty pounds. They get into one's line and make a mess of it. And line is precious on a safari hundreds of miles from a base. The boys liked eels for food, however, and begged for them.

The "gumbari" (protopterous), something like a catfish but with pink meat, like salmon, and with fins going the length of the body, was another one of the boys' favorites. It is popularly known as the lungfish, burrowing into the sand when the streams go dry. It was too "earthy" for me, however. It shows itself only in the rainy season. When the streams dry up and it "sees sun," it goes into the earth and hibernates. Lungfish have been brought back to civilization and "unearthed" months afterward and have revived on being placed in water.

The forests surrounding streams in Africa are sometimes so dense that it is not like fishing at home. Moving down a stream, one may have to fight brush and undergrowth, and even entangling vines, to reach the water. The water is also often filled with growth, but the fish are there, and what beauties! It was necessary to have my boy always at hand to help me cut loose from thorns and vines with his "panga," or knife. But the more hazards, the more fun!

In these surroundings, one could expect anything, from an elephant to a cobra, so caution became a sixth sense. Rhino thrashed out of thickets, buffalo charged from the tall grass, and hyenas were almost as frightening. Overhead, in the trees and scrub bush, were monkeys and river pigeons—and sometimes a leopard. Antelope and gazelle came down to drink, also eland, waterbuck, bushbuck and impala.

On one of these fishing jaunts, I told the boy to tie my old mule to a small clump of weeping willow trees near by. As the porter obeyed, I saw a big bull buffalo poking his huge head out from behind the bushes. The boy and the mule ran and I rushed for a tree, for nothing can charge with more speed and force than one of these big fellows. And he was enraged, for we had disturbed his nap. But the commotion frightened the buffalo as much as he frightened us, and off he loped to the safety and quiet of a thorn-tree grove.

Later that day, reaching the water, I found a towering rocky bank opposite me, and, protruding over a ledge, a tuft of feathery tail.

"Aba itu?" (what is that?) I asked my gun-bearer, Bukhari.

"A duck," said he, laughing. "Sitting on her eggs."

"I want her."

"M'baya sana!" (very bad) he exclaimed, and spoke of the puff adders and cobras and leopards that inhabit these spots.

But I wanted the duck and climbed above the projecting ledge, my fishing net in hand. Bukhari was petrified. He followed, saying: "I have guided Lady Northy, Lady Gregg, wife of the Governor, and Lady Byrne. And now is Lady Johnson. Since I was a 'toto,' " he continued pleadingly, "I have been a soldier. I am a Nubian and I have never had trouble. If anything happens to you, the Master will cut my head off!"

I took off my shoes for a better footing. Bukhari gave me up as hopeless, and pushed ahead to assist me and to test the path for danger.

"Much better that I die first," said he. But the climb was un-interrupted and soon I stealthily slipped my net over the duck. She was a teal, lustrously brown, and a beautiful specimen. I explained to Bukhari that I didn't want her for food, but just for a temporary pet, and to study her, and that it would be no disturbance for she didn't have an egg, after all.

Arriving in camp, late that evening, Martin exclaimed: "Thank God, you are back! What luck?" And he peered into my usually full creel to find only a few small fish.

"My best catch is a duck," said I. "I cast in, and here's what I pulled out!"

"Tell that to Sweeney," he said. And when I showed him the prize, he howled, "Just an old wag-tail; what next!"

I built a cage for her and kept and fed her for several days, and planned to release her soon on a fishing trip. But one day the boy went to feed her, lifted the cage—and out she flew. I hope that she went back to her mate.

Hornets were one of the worst pests at the Eauso. They were always buzzing about and when they stung they poisoned me terribly. Their nests hung everywhere in the trees and bushes, and I never leaned against a tree without first looking up to see if there were hornets there.

Many a time I came back from fishing with ugly stings, and one day my lower lip was so swollen that I could neither talk nor eat my dinner. A hornet stung me on the eye just as I got a beautiful strike one day, and while I played the fish my eye swelled completely shut, but I landed the fish.

The hornets didn't like Martin any better, and one day when he was fishing with me, they stung him so badly that his face, neck and back were all swollen. He developed a temperature and all night he suffered terrible pain. I got out our supply of household ammonia and bathed his body for hours, relieving the pain a little, and next morning he was able to be about.

5

*". . . This is one of the thrills of our
work. It is never possible to tell
whether the death with which we are
surrounded in many forms is going
to descend upon us or going to evap-
orate. Whichever happens it usually
happens quickly and without much
warning . . ."*
—MARTIN JOHNSON

"WELL, IT'S ABOUT time you got here," Martin shouted, as Blaney
Percival drove his ancient Ford across the river.

"I've just used my last drop of gasoline. If you'd camped any
farther on, I'd have had a fine time trying to find you."

Blaney had been a week in reaching us, but I wondered how he
ever got there at all, for his car was like a piece out of his own
museum. It was a high-backed Model T with a gasoline tank in
front where the windshield should have been, and the rest of it
was tied together with wire and strips of hide. One spring was
broken and blocked up, the seats were torn and shedding excelsior, and the contraption bucked, jumped and back-fired when he
drove. He had come all the way through that boiling hot sun with
no top on the car.

His boy was as primitive and picturesque as the car, a Wakamba
with filed teeth who looked like a raw savage, but Blaney assured us he was a good mechanic. He must have been, to keep such
a car running.

"That car," drawled Blaney, "was one of the first to come to
Africa. She has taken me everywhere, saved my life a number
of times, and I'm going to keep her till she falls apart."

I served Blaney tea and we at once began to discuss our plans for getting on, for the rains were now obviously very near.

We had discovered in our scouting trips that there were two possible routes through the mountains ahead. These we determined to explore, and the next day we sent Blaney in one direction while Martin explored the other.

At night they returned with the same story. Neither route was passable for our heavy vehicles, and it would take months to build a road through. The news was hard to take. We had wasted precious time and energy and supplies on a wild goose chase, and there was nothing to do but to turn back to Isiolo and take the familiar route through Archer's Post. We would waste another week, but we would probably get across the Eauso Nyiro River before the rains.

Worst of all, our wagons had gone back to Isiolo, so that we would have to transport our equipment by porter and donkey, which would mean several relays to move such a quantity of stores. Blaney suggested a short-cut for our foot-porters, and we left him to start the boys off while Martin and I dashed to Isiolo to head off the other wagons and take care of our supplies there. We then drove northeast to Archer's Post to receive the boys.

It took five days to transfer our equipment. On the short-cut some of the boys saw elephants, and one group was scattered by rhino. Lions were around them every night and they had to enclose themselves in thornbush corrals. N'dundu had to shoot into the air several times to frighten the cats off.

Archer's Post, once an important military station, was now nothing more than a group of half a dozen grass houses on the top of a barren hill, in charge of a few askaris and a commissioner who was an educated native. Beyond, to the north, lay the desert, like a gray sleeping sea; and about the place rose brooding mountains covered with scrub trees, thornbush, volcanic slag and boulders.

Here was the customary crossing of the Eauso Nyiro River, and, with our goods all safely on the other side, we felt that we had now at least accomplished our most important immediate objective, for we had beaten the rains to the spot where they would have caused us the most hardship.

But the rains could still bog us down in the mountains on our long climb to Lake Paradise, and we had more than a hundred miles of volcanic country and desert to cross before we would reach that area. So we determined to rush on, and we spent the night repacking our equipment and loading our cars and wagons. We would go ahead in the cars, leaving the wagons and porters to follow as rapidly as they could. By dawn we were ready to leave and were so sleepless that we decided to start at once and take advantage of the cool of the morning.

"At last we're off into 'The Blue,'" said Martin, giving me a squeeze. "From here on the world belongs to us, honey!"

At noon we made our first stop at Kissimini waterhole, generally known as "The Wells." Our cars were dry and we were glad we could fill them without cutting into our precious drinking supply.

A well about fifty feet deep was sunk here into the dry river bed. The Somalis were credited with digging it, and they relied upon it for watering their herds on the long treks from Abyssinia. Over the top of the well was a lid made of palm tree slabs, but I noticed that one of the slabs had been removed, which I thought queer.

I peered into the deep pit, and, as my eyes became accustomed to the darkness, I saw something floating on the surface of the water. It was the body of a young monkey. It had paid a heavy price for its thirst and its curiosity.

I told Martin what I had seen, and was thankful that we had had the foresight to hold back on our drinking water. But we did fill up the radiators of the cars. As I was returning for another petrol tin of water for my car, I saw several of the native boys bailing water out of the well.

"No . . . no . . . you can't drink that!" I shouted.

They seemed surprised, and I told them about the dead monkey. They only smiled, and said, "What's the difference?"

They drank the water, and apparently felt no ill effects from it. Sometimes I think an African native boy can stand anything.

Martin gave each boy a water-bottle, and a chargole, a canvas water-container holding a gallon.

We finally got under way again, and had miles of excellent road—excellent, that is, for Africa. The sky became overcast in the early afternoon, and it started to rain. Martin put up the tarpaulins across the cars, and we waited about three hours. The rain came down in torrents, but the sun broke through the clouds at last and we started on. The rain had been more help than hindrance since it had packed the sand down in the roads, leaving it hard and firm, and we made good time. We came to Karo at sundown, exhausted and glad to pitch camp.

Karo was a favorite spot on our first trip to Africa. Here, beside a lovely winding river, now a dry sand bed, a great park extended for about seven hundred yards in each direction, a park of gorgeous acacia trees, yellow-flowered and fragrant, and occasional palms. The place was a romantic oasis in every sense except that we had to dig for our water, but we found that plentiful.

To enable our boys to catch up with us, we decided to rest; and after the hardships of our trip thus far we would enjoy the cool shade and comfort of this little Eden. Martin also felt that we were likely to bag some good lion shots if nothing more, and he could limber up his cameras for what was sure to come later on.

Our hopes were stimulated by the signs of game on every hand. The bed of the stream was a mass of lion, leopard and plains game tracks and we soon saw the animals in numbers.

The air was clean, crisp and invigorating, although in the mid-

dle of the day the heat was terrific. I roamed about, exploring the
rock kopjes. Cactus, with long, striped, grass-blade leaves, was a
colorful relief from the oceans of sand and slag, and out of the
rock clefts grew gorgeous hibiscus, yellow flowers with brown centers. Dik-dik, about as big as a minute, leaped up and ran away on
stiff legs, bouncing like little rubber balls. Sometimes as I crept up
to them they would freeze and look at me with a baby's wonderment and then, with almost a baby's cry, dash off to the shelter of
a boulder or bush.

That night we set up our flashes and next day we worked from
quickly thrown-up thorn blinds, and, while the pictures that resulted were unimportant, we enjoyed the holiday like a couple of
kids.

Through our glasses, from the top of the boulder lookouts we
frequented, we saw distant lions, and we watched them track down
and scatter zebra and oryx, grants, tommies, impala and reed-
buck. On the third night we heard them close by and the next day
I spotted one sunning himself atop a broad rock, like one of the
familiar lions of Trafalgar Square. They were elusive, however,
and we managed to get only long shots, which we felt were not
going to be too successful, though some later proved to be excellent.

That night we took one of the best flashlight shots of leopard
that we ever obtained, and when we developed it in Martin's darkroom, rigged up in his tent, we were as happy as though we had
found gold.

But time was racing away, and after two days of this idyllic
rest, and the arrival of our boys and wagons, we packed and hurried on. All but Blaney, who had seen some rare birds he wanted
for his collection. So he stayed on, and planned to catch up with
us in a few days.

Almost immediately our troubles began. Pleasant groves gave
way to small scrub, and the earth was strewn with volcanic slag

and boulders. Our trail became so wretched that we often left it to pick our way over less bumpy ground among the rocks. We soon had to stop to repair two punctures.

Heavy sand luggars constantly cut across the trail. We were often caught in them without warning and spent tedious hours digging ourselves out or constructing tracks of brush and stones. The dry river beds were even more difficult to cross. We laid down roadways of palm fronds and thornbush and flat rocks, but the cars would slip off into the sand and bury themselves up to the axles. The first car to get across was a considerable help, for we could stretch a tow rope and help the tugging boys with the others.

On our second day out we encountered great washes from previous desert rains, and had to detour around over the rough ground. We spent hours of time moving boulders and small rocks, and literally made our road as we went.

Game birds began to appear in great flocks, especially the vulturine guinea fowl, and I saw one flock of these which must have numbered no less than five hundred. They often walked calmly across the trail and seemed astonishingly tame, but when we came within a few yards of them they scattered and completely disappeared into the bush. The guinea fowl gave us good fresh food and, tired as we were with the exhausting travel and work and heat, this was a welcome luxury.

We also saw numerous gazelle and antelope everywhere, as well as occasional lions and several leopards. One of the leopards was lying under a thorn-tree beside the road. He must have been asleep, for we were only a few yards from him when he started up and bounded away.

After several days of this pushing and pulling our way, with our cars boiling over and our water supply practically gone, we reached another welcome waterhole, which we also remembered from our first trip to Lake Paradise. This was Longaia, a winding dry river bed that ran for about a mile through a deep ravine, at a little distance off the trail. Elephants and other game liked this spot and there were tracks of elephant, rhino and lion everywhere about, and a considerable amount of fresh spoor.

The pools at Longaia were stagnant and we had to dig for clean water. The boys sunk several holes and while we waited for the water to seep in we decided not only to pitch our camp for the night but to set up flashlights and see what pictures we could obtain.

After concealing our cameras at the waterhole, we sent our boys back to camp, and with only light mattresses and blankets, we made our beds on a cliff above the dry river. This would be an ideal lookout, I thought, for a lion to use to stalk his game. Before we fell asleep I *heard* a lion, but Martin said:

"Oh, he won't come away over here—he's a long way off. Besides, they don't drink water; they drink only blood."

"That isn't so funny," I retorted. "I think we're a little crazy to sleep out here."

"It's all right," Martin assured me. "Try to get some sleep."

I wakened with a start, heard a crunching of stones on the cliff near us, and smelled the unmistakable odor of cat on the air. I screamed. There was a crash that seemed only a few feet away, and a heavy growl. I screamed again, at the top of my lungs, and off went the animal, which I knew to be a lion, pell-mell and with a great clatter of rocks. It seemed to me an hour before my heart stopped thumping, and we were awake the rest of the night.

"Well, what has happened to you?" Martin stared at me when daylight came. "Your eye, honey!"

I looked in the mirror in my compact. My eye was black, and swollen almost shut.

"What is it?" I asked.

"A mosquito. Maybe a spider. We'll get something out of the medicine kit and put on it."

OSA CROSSES THE EAUSO NYIRO RIVER

Her fine new car awash, she is towed across the ford enroute to Lake Paradise.

POPPIES ABLOOM ON THE DESERT

A field of gold and brown poppies, springing to life from the barren soil after the rains, on the way to Lake Paradise.

Suddenly Martin flicked out several spirrilum ticks from my blankets.

"There's what gave you your black eye," he said.

I knew that the spirrilum tick was one of the most deadly pests in Africa. It is quite unlike the American tick. About the size of a dime, it sucks blood until it swells up like a little balloon and falls off. I have seen ticks as large as a quarter on the sides of elephants.

Ticks are the pests that nearly drive elephants and rhino insane, and which the tick-birds and white heron pick off their backs. The ticks have a way of fastening themselves to an elephant behind his ear, or in some other inaccessible spot, and I have seen an elephant scratch and scratch against a tree to scrape the pests off. The ticks also frequent caves and old houses and huts, and carry infections from unhealthy and unwashed natives. The natives are more afraid of them than they are of the tsetse fly. There is no cure once spirillum fever develops. Generally in two weeks the victim is dead.

"Martin," I remarked as we returned to camp, "I didn't even feel that tick."

"You must have brushed it off in your sleep. And it probably wasn't fever-infected. There aren't any natives around here."

On our second day at Longaia we were more than ever determined to get those pictures. The game was so plentiful that we were sure of getting something unusual. I was miserable with the pain of the bad eye and my vision was impaired, but we resolved to build a rock blind for security and we dug in and slaved throughout the day with the porters. We built a well-camouflaged pile against the cliff, our cots inside, peepholes for the cameras, and we planted trees before the wall. We had other trees and bushes emerging from the top, as though they had always been there. The blind was finally completed, and we were sure that in addition to getting our flashes that night we could make some fine camera shots in the early morning when the animals came down to drink.

On these nights out Martin was always convinced that he would stay up to the wee hours and handle the cameras, but after our long hours of work throughout the day he was thoroughly tired and invariably fell asleep. I slept more lightly, so he relied upon me to be the watch-dog. As time went on, we divided the day, and after a good breakfast of bacon and eggs and a bit of morning sun, I would turn in for sleep, and this would enable me to keep a wakeful watch through the night while he rested.

At this waterhole I never saw anything but big game. The place was very isolated, and while the larger animals could take care of themselves against their enemies, the plains game probably feared to drink in that ravine where leopards and lions might pounce upon them. However, although we found a great wealth of game here, we got few pictures, and we decided that the wind sweeping through the ravine must have given the animals our scent and made them aware of us.

I reflected that we were taking great chances, whatever the protection, but I knew that we were out here to do a job and already there had been too much delay. Moreover, Martin was so eager to do what was expected of us by the Museum and the public, that I felt I must not let him see or feel any of my misgivings.

We climbed into our blind and he had no sooner struck his cot than he was asleep. I lay awake for a long time, listening to the silence and fascinated by the clarity of the sky and the crystalline stars. Far off a lion roared, and I wondered if he were our visitor of the night before and if a tick had got *him* in the eye. Elephants began to lumber in and I heard the swish of their skin and their low trumpetings. Rhino began snorting and fighting, and to the cadence of this grand chorus I fell asleep.

Suddenly I wakened with a sense of something wrong. I sat up. Something was scratching against the blind. I heard a snort, and

I knew it was a rhino. He rubbed and rubbed his back, evidently enjoying the sharp edges our stones provided. A rock broke loose and fell at the foot of my bed; some scattered stones fell beside my feet. More rocks caved in and one of thorn trees fell! I screamed, both in fear and in hope that it might frighten the rhino. He stopped, and I screamed again. He snorted and scuffled off. Martin leaped up and cut himself with the thorns and started to swear.

"This blind business is certainly not what it's cracked up to be. Here we are with all these animals around us and not a picture. Not a single doggone flash tonight!"

Presently he lit a long cigar, and I fell asleep.

6

". . . Thank heaven I have had the right sort of woman to take along with me into the desert and jungle. If ever a man needed a partner in his chosen vocation it has been I. And if ever a wife were a partner to a man, it is Osa Johnson. . . ."
—Martin Johnson

"Push! That's it. Push!" Martin shouted the orders.

The sand luggar was deceptive. It had looked easy when we drove into it, but my car was stalled. The wheels wouldn't budge an inch either way. It was the second time since we had left Longaia that the cars had been mired. Martin and the native boys helped to unload everything from my car, but it seemed that the wheels only went deeper into the sandy river bed. Abdulla unloaded his car. The same thing happened.

"We'll have to dig out or make camp right here in the middle," Martin said.

We got out the shovels and spades and worked until midnight. We dug the loose sand away and went ahead a few feet, then stuck again. The process was repeated every few feet until we got the cars across. It was well after midnight when the last car was safely out of the treacherous river bed.

We were so utterly exhausted that we turned in at once. My eye hurt, my back was stiff from pushing, and every muscle in my body was sore.

On top of this, we woke the next morning to find that we were being invaded by millions of locusts. They swarmed over the camp and got into everything, breakfast included. The ground was covered with insects and we trampled thousands of them.

At Longania waterhole, where we arrived at noon and decided to make camp, we found another miniature Eden. Up from a sandy river bed rose high banks, studded with scrub and topped by a park of thorn and great acacia trees. Game moved about everywhere and birds were making a great stir and chorus in the trees. It was a heavenly place to rest.

Martin and I had arrived in advance with only one boy, but the river bed looked passable and we determined to try moving our car across to the more agreeable opposite bank. We laid down a thornbush track across the seventy-five yards of sand and found it a bigger job than we had bargained for.

"It's too hot," Martin complained. "I'm going to take off this khaki shirt."

I started the car across the river bed, but a few yards out it slid into the sand and stuck. We unloaded it. Then Martin and the boy pushed while I drove. Three quarters of the way across the car stalled again and we became badly mired. But Martin seemed to be in greater distress than the car. He looked very pale and dizzy.

"My head is swimming," he said weakly.

I helped him over to the bank and he sat under the shade of a fig tree. That undershirt! Sunstroke, flashed across my mind. In this sun to expose one's head or spine for only a few minutes would be enough.

"Martin, after all this time in Africa, to do a foolish thing like that!" I bathed his head with a handkerchief saturated with eau de cologne and had hot tea made for him promptly. Then I soaked my bandanna in water, waved it to make it cool and wrapped it about his throat—a makeshift but effective relief—laid him in the shade and got him to go to sleep.

We decided to pack the supplies across, but to save precious time I helped the boy and carried sixty-pound loads to the bank.

They felt like thousand-pound loads in that soft, heavy sand. It was soon too dark to try to get the car out of the river bed that night, so we set up our cots under the trees and decided to sleep in the open and make the best of a bad situation. Martin had a temperature, and I watched him all through the night. But in the morning his temperature was normal; I gave him quinine and he seemed to be his usual self. He promised that he would never again part with his red-lined shirt and his hat as long as we were in Africa. And then he began to upbraid me for carrying the loads to shore.

The waterholes had filled with water, so we replenished our supply and as soon as our other cars came up we set out for Lasamis. This was the waterhole where Paul J. Rainey, pioneer in African game photography, took his first pictures. We sped along at a good rate of speed over well-packed volcanic slag and sand through desolate country with small scrub and thornbush, with nothing green to be seen. However, the zebra, giraffe, antelope and gazelle seemed sleek and fat, as though they fed on milk and honey or clover instead of this dry scrub. Their coats were shining as though they had just been curried.

In the early hours of the morning we came to the sand river of Merille, lined with dom-palm and mimosa trees.

We had no sooner arrived and replenished our water, than I saw a huge cloud of dust on the horizon, which would be natives, bringing their flocks to water. We waited, and sure enough, the camels began to arrive. Then came goats and sheep and hump-backed cattle, until the place was thick with dust. Dust filled our eyes and nostrils, and the smell of cattle and natives made a frightful stench.

Martin sent our boys to reassure the natives, who proved to be Rendille, and when they settled down to their watering Martin set up his cameras, but the dust made it difficult to take pictures.

Then what seemed like billions of flies swarmed about us. I had become accustomed to all sorts of flies, but these were the worst. They were as large and fat as ticks, and they fastened themselves to the body in much the same manner. They were the size of a big thumbnail—large, flat flies with many wiggling legs, reddish-brown in color. I had literally to pluck them from my skin. When I saw the natives close up, I noticed that they had bad skin diseases and their eyes had running sores. At the sight of the flies crawling over their bodies, I shuddered. And I was not a little worried about the diseases which the insects might carry. But we had a job to do, and we stuck to it. We had to make pictures, and here were unusual primitive types.

"Osa, I can't have those flies crawling all over the picture," Martin said as he finally began to crank the camera. "See what you can do about it."

The only thing to do about it was to shoo them off, so I borrowed a fly-swatter that had once been a giraffe's tail and swished away as Martin did his best with the camera. But the flies would crawl out on the noses of the natives and walk across their faces, and even swarm over the camera.

"That will look fine on an American movie screen," Martin said in disgust.

But the natives didn't seem to mind in the least, and seemed surprised that we should bother about it. So the only thing to do was to take the pictures, flies and all.

Then came large green blow-flies. These do not accompany the herds but feed upon kills left by lions, leopards and hyenas.

I could see these big blow-flies everywhere. Suddenly I noticed that they were getting into our supplies, and I knew that we would be in for maggots galore, so I had the boys hustle to close all the boxes. I tied netting about our fowl and game meat, and hoisted it into the tall dom-palm trees. The boys seemed to think this a lot of useless trouble, and they paid no attention at all to their own meat.

The Rendille natives continued to arrive with their herds until there were thousands of groaning camels. Except for carrying water, these camels are generally accumulated only for wealth and display. Such trade as the Rendille carry on is always in exchange for camels, and the trade is mostly for wives, which they also accumulate. A wife fetches as many camels as her beauty or her working ability seem to warrant, the rate varying from one to three camels per wife.

One of the chiefs in this conclave had fifteen wives, he said, but over a thousand camels left, along with as many goats, fattailed sheep and hump-backed cattle. We bought some of his camels for pack purposes and our headman had a grand day bargaining with his master's wealth, paying forty to sixty shillings apiece. On this basis Martin figured that the old chief would be worth in American dollars $12,000 in camels alone, and with his cattle and goats probably a total of $40,000, though he would not want the money and would not know what to do with it if he had it.

These natives subsist entirely on milk; fresh blood taken from their camels, goats and cows; and "ghee," a rancid butter. They never eat vegetables and they never kill their animals for meat although they occasionally eat a camel, cow or sheep that dies from natural causes.

By inserting a porcupine quill into the animal's jugular vein, they let the blood drop into a gourd. Then they mix it with milk. They stagger this process among their animals so that the occasional blood-taking does not weaken the stock. And certainly the native Rendille seem to thrive on the diet.

How these people could subsist entirely upon blood and milk always perplexed me. I have never been able to bring myself to taste camel's milk, but it is obviously rich and nourishing.

As the cattle finished drinking, the men herded them off, and the women came down to wash their children and to fill their gourds with drinking water, all from the same muddy pools.

"See if you can't get some of the women into camera range," Martin suggested.

I did my best. The Rendille women were extremely shy, but I finally coaxed them out in groups, and we got some good pictures. They wore their hair in fantastic coiffures of fan shape, or else hung in long, dirty braids. Done up as it was with red earth and castor oil, it provided a perfect lure for flies. One native woman had a queer hair-do exactly like a red floor-mop. Above a shaven neck and temples, the hair hung about six inches long, and it flopped about her head when she moved.

The men wore only loin cloths, except for the chiefs, each of whom wore a robe draped over one shoulder and made of cow-skin or hyrax, the little brown "rock rabbit" of Africa. The women wore becoming directoires of smooth skin draped from the waist. Some showed one bare thigh, others showed both knees and others the back of the legs, revealing shapely limbs. Above the waist the women were entirely nude. Some were buxom and a little stout, but for the most part they were beautifully athletic and shapely, and they stood very straight.

We spent the day photographing the Rendille natives, and toward evening they moved on. We had meantime bought some hump-backed cattle and sheep and decided to give our boys a feast and then leave for Lasamis at night, in order to avoid the heat. The moon was full and would give us good light.

I had M'pishi bring me the filet mignon and the saddle, giving the boys all other cuts, and we had a delicious dinner of roast Rendille beef. To the natives the cuts were all alike.

The boys' favorite was beef, and the camp was soon festooned with long strips of it, hanging on sticks and bars, and drying over the many smouldering fires. Dried meat was a great delicacy with the porters, who carried this "biltong" with them in strips and munched on it for days. Frequently they stewed lumps of it with their posho. Tripe, heart and lungs they also considered a great luxury, and our headman divided the supply among them equally.

The only trouble with these feasts was that the boys stuffed themselves and sat up most of the night telling tall stories. The next day they were not worth their salt. So we never had a feast when there was important work on hand for the following day.

After we had rested, Martin hustled the boys together and began packing. He went to the river bed to inspect the sand before we moved a car. We had no intention of spending the night stuck in a river bed and we knew the Merille to be treacherous, for the sand is fine and deep.

"We'll have to build a road across," Martin said.

With the work of building a road bed completed, first of scattered rocks, then of palm fronds and branches, we started the cars across. Notwithstanding all our care we stalled repeatedly, and had to harness all the porters to get the cars through. We had seen this river in flood, when it coursed over the landscape and roared down the main channel, carrying great logs and whole palm trees along with the current. Crossing was then impossible for days or weeks, so we were much relieved to have the Merille behind us.

We approached Lasamis just as dawn was tinting the horizon. On every side lay desert, sand, rocks and burnt hills, and in the early light the place looked more desolate than ever. Here, for centuries, caravans had come down from the Abyssinian mountains, and hundreds of graves scattered about under little mounds of volcanic rock gave the place the air of a vast cemetery.

We crossed cautiously through a wide sand luggar. I led the procession. About fifty feet from the opposite bank I felt the car sinking. I looked over the side. The car was imbedded up to the axles. I motioned to Martin to go around me, and not take the same track. He swerved several feet to the right, and sank. Abdulla, who was driving the third car, saw us and tried to take another path, but his fate was the same. This time we were bogged not in sand, but in mud. There was sand on the surface which had looked dry enough, but beneath was a foot or more of soft wet earth.

Martin jumped out of the car to investigate. He found that the mud patch was about a hundred feet in diameter. It seemed incredible that there should be mud here.

"Why in thunder must we get right into the middle of the only mud for hundreds of miles around?" he shouted.

"Well, there's nothing to do but dig," I replied.

We started to dig, but the more we dug, the more we sank. The mud touched the running boards. I was covered from head to foot with the sticky, grimy black, and I had to tug to get my legs loose and not become mired. We unloaded most of the stuff and carried it to the opposite shore.

We carried stones and threw them under the wheels, but it was no use. By late afternoon we were worn out. Martin stood on the shore and stared at the sinking cars.

"Martin, what are we going to do?"

He was silent. Suddenly his eyes lit up. I looked across the desert.

"Camels!" I shouted.

A caravan was on its way south from the government station at Marsabit. There were twenty drivers and askaris with them. They came up to us and everyone went to work. In a few minutes my car was out, and then we hitched a cable to it and with everyone lifting and pushing I stepped on the starter and we yanked the other two cars free. Martin gave the camel men a shilling apiece and they went happily on their way. As for us, we were definitely happier, if dirtier.

"At least my eye is nearly well," I said as we finally sat down to dinner. "I will always remember Lasamis for that."

For days I had been bathing the eye repeatedly, and had said many a silent prayer that I would be spared spirrilum fever. But I'd had no temperature and the swelling had now gone down.

Blaney later told me how near I had come to tragedy, and I was more than ever grateful for the good health with which I was blessed on these travels. Martin was often ill with malaria and other maladies, but either through a strange immunity or great good fortune, I have for the most part avoided them.

Grouse seemed to make Lasamis their capital, and literally thousands of these little birds came in formations in the morning at dawn, black streaks of them flying across the sky. It is a small game bird, about the size of our Kansas prairie chicken, and is delicious to eat.

At five-thirty came the first flight of the birds, so many that they covered the ground. They drank nervously and quickly and soon were gone, to rest on the desert in the boiling hot sun, in bunches of six or seven hundred, feeding on insects and berries with sand added to help digestion.

The next flight came at about six-thirty, the third flight at seven-thirty and the fourth about an hour later. This routine was repeated at sundown.

"Eh-a-a-a-a-ah," they chattered as they strutted about and spread their fan-tails. But two or three gulps of water to wet their little whistles seemed enough and they were off in a flash.

On one occasion, using my 20-gauge Ithaca shotgun, I managed to down fourteen with one shot, they were so crowded together. There were three different varieties among them.

"I'm going foraging for grouse," I told Martin the next day.

"Be careful of lions," he warned as I walked away. "If you ever see a black-maned lion, remember what Blaney once said— get him before he gets you."

"I've never shot a lion, Martin, and I hope I'll never have to."

"Well, a black-maned lion will make a trophy you'll be proud to have."

I left with a "toto" or personal boy, a youngster of about nine who helped around the camp. He was very alert and intelligent, and I liked to have him along on these walks more for the opportunity it gave me to converse with him and brush up on my Swahili than anything else, because he would have been quite useless in any danger. I carried my shotgun and a small 7 mm. rifle under my arm.

Suddenly we came upon a furrow through the sand, which told that here was the "drag" of a lion kill. Blood stained the sand, and told a story without words of struggle and death and feast. The furrow led to a rock kopje. These signs meant caution, so we silently inched along.

I crouched in the shelter of a boulder, and peered around it. There, in a small depression beyond, was a huge animal. Quickly I drew back.

"Bogu," I whispered to the boy in Swahili, meaning buffalo.

"Hapana—Simba" (no—lion), he whispered. He was very frightened.

Lion! My heart nearly stopped. I suddenly became aware of my tiny rifle. I felt helpless. I dared not move. Instinctively I looked for a tree. There was nothing in the immediate vicinity but a bit of scrub.

Then the beast came out into the open. A black-maned lion! Martin's words came back to me. "Get him before he gets you."

My knees shook, and as I leaned against the rock I felt sure that the lion must hear my heart pounding, for it sounded as loud in my ears as the beat of a kettle drum.

The little toto was almost white. "Hapana mpiga"—(don't shoot), he breathed.

The advice was hardly necessary. I tried to hide, but curiosity made me hold my breath and peer around the boulder for one more look. It was a black-maned lion right enough, and the largest and most incredibly handsome beast I have ever seen. He lay there in the sun, licking his chops after what must have been a heavy meal. Evidently he was drowsy and was about to take a nap in the sun. And, thank heavens, he was lying sideways from us. I thought quickly: if we got in here without his seeing us, perhaps we can get out.

I signaled to the native boy, and we dropped to our hands and knees and began to crawl away. Never had my boots seemed so large. My breeches scratched against every pebble and grain of sand. We made a safe distance, rose, and broke into a run for camp.

"What's the matter?" Martin cried. "You look as if you'd seen a ghost."

"I saw something all right, but it wasn't a ghost. Martin, I saw a black-maned lion." I whispered the words, as if the beast might hear me.

"A black-maned lion! Osa, are you sure?"

"Certainly I am. And he's still there."

"Well, what are we waiting for?" he shouted.

He caught up his camera, and with our gunbearers we quietly made our way back to the rock. The lion was there, panting and sunning himself.

Martin was as nervous as I had been, and as he set up his camera, somehow he made a noise. The lion heard it, and with one roar he bounded away. We followed him.

"He's the most beautiful lion I've ever seen," said Martin.

Half a mile away in a donga we found his kill. It was an oryx. And a mother lion and her three baby cubs were feasting on it. Fearing that she might charge, and that we might have to shoot, we contented ourselves with merely watching.

"Well, we're lucky just to have *seen* the king himself and his family at home," Martin said, turning to me. "Even if we didn't shoot any pictures, we didn't have to shoot any animals."

Leaving Lasamis, we bumped over the roughest ground we had

yet encountered—miles and miles of jagged volcanic rocks strewn over the earth. This we had to traverse, fearing punctures any minute, then climb up a steep escarpment between two great conical mountains with their sides blown out. This was our only route through the mountains, and, since great black boulders had fallen into the track, we had to ctop repeatedly to pry them loose and roll them off so that we could pass.

From the top of the rise we could see ahead the great Kaisoot Desert which we must now cross. The trail took us down through another valley strewn with burned rock and boulders. After several hours' traveling, this scorched and God-forsaken country suddenly ended, and we emerged on the clean golden sand of the desert which the rains had soaked and packed. This made a perfect race-track and we sped along for a short distance at a good clip.

Since we had a hundred miles to go before we could hope to reach water, we were glad of this chance to speed, and we made the most of it. Sometimes we would go miles without seeing a tree, although small brush was everywhere and constantly scratched the sides of our car; but occasionally there would be a little grove of thornscrub, and for the shade of these bushes the animals must have been grateful. In the heat of the day this would be their only protection against the scorching sun.

Thousands of every kind of game bird seemed to be about us— plover, doves, pigeons, sand grouse, lesser and greater bustard, common guinea fowl, vulturine guinea fowl and several varieties of partridge. Within a thirty-five-mile stretch we must have seen five thousand patridge. Often we stopped the car to let them pass. They had not been shot at and were quite tame, and they crossed the road, walking deliberately or flying low, in great flocks.

Whirlwinds and dust spouts rose to the sky, some so heavy that thornbushes were picked up and carried heavenward as if they were in the wake of a Kansas twister. The whirls came at you with a terrible growling. The natives called them "devils."

At one point a whirlwind turned my car completely around, leaving me headed in the opposite direction. When I faced about, I saw Martin ahead, pointing and motioning to me as he drove. Several ostrich along the road-side were caught by the whirling wind, their wings spread and lifted like a comical chorus in a fantastic ballet.

There were more ostrich here than I had ever seen before, sometimes seventy-five to one hundred in a single flock. Baby os· trich trailed along, so ugly with their long, thin necks and downy pinfeathers that they looked like the birds God forgot. Frisky cock ostrich, with their clean black and white plumage and pink legs, made the sombre gray hens seem a picture of solemnity.

The ostrich is a silly, vain bird. When the cock goes courting, his neck and legs become crimson, and he acts like a ridiculous little boy suffering from puppy love. He becomes very self-conscious, preens and struts about, and pecks and ruffs his handsome plumes. As a climax to his courting, the cock ostrich goes through a routine of awkward dances, calculated to make the hen admire him.

We also saw a number of fine gerenuk, the lean and sprightly gazelle with long graceful neck and slender legs which live off roots, shrubs and leaves, and are never seen to drink. Apparently they obtain from the greens all the moisture they require. Though they are very shy, we caught some splendid pictures of several of these animals, including one of a beautiful buck standing on his hind legs and nibbling like a giraffe from the branches of a small tree.

Suddenly I saw before me a vast blanket of white morning-glories with deep purple centers. They stretched as far as we could see, and I stopped the car. All around me, covering the ground, was an enchanted garden, brought up out of the apparently barren earth by the magic of the rain. I knew that water was probably twenty miles away, and I knew too that the flowers would remain

SAMBURU WOMEN AND HERDS AT LASAMIS

Having watered their sheep, goats and cattle, the native
women fill their water gourds from the same pools.

OSA AND MARTIN "AT HOME" ON SAFARI

After a day in the field, the Johnsons relax while Osa cleans a telescopic sight and checks her guns.

OSA BRINGS HOME CHRISTMAS DINNER
With Lazy Bones, her Abyssinian mule, and porters, she
returns with a thirty-five-pound African wild turkey.

OSA PLANTING HER GARDEN AT LAKE PARADISE
Laying out her first beds of American vegetables.

PAY DAY IN THE JUNGLE

Osa and Blaney Percival issue Kenya shillings to a group of porters at Lake Paradise.

for a short time only, then vanish, not to reappear until conditions were right for the seeds to blossom again, perhaps years later.

After fifteen miles of the dreamlike beauty of these flowers, we were again in the dusty desert. Further on we came to occasional clusters of white Easter lilies. They were nourished by the same quick rains, and continued to appear over a long stretch.

Mirages continually appeared—vast lakes and small lakes, oases with clusters of palms and acacia. But our headman repeatedly said: "Hapana margi" (not water), so that we wasted no time on these illusions. But I began wondering if the animals were as wise as he, and whether they were not often led to trek twenty miles or more by this sight of "water," just as men were, and how long it must take them to learn their way to the real waterholes. I wondered too by what signs they knew the trails and where they led and what a painful search they must have when familiar waterholes dried up and they had to look for others. One day in a blind was enough to show Martin and me how precious water could become. I looked at the distant mountains and was glad we had motor cars and did not have to trudge on foot that distance to drink.

Despite the scarcity of food and water, the thousands of plains animals about us seemed to thrive. They were sleek and fat and looked well nourished. Grevy zebra, thin-striped and large-eared, mingled with common zebra. There were reticulated giraffe, a plenitude of rhino, lions, leopards, oryx, and we began to see small herds of elephant in the distance. We felt that we were indeed approaching Paradise, for here, far from guns and other nuisances of man, the animals seemed to be friendly and unafraid.

We began to make altitude by slow rises, and the cars puffed and steamed and drew heavily upon our diminishing water supply. We settled down to making our next objective, Ret, a waterhole at the "end" of the desert. The mountains began to draw in upon us and converge.

Here were deep washes from recent rains, and animals in in-creasing numbers. As we made altitude, we came into sharp rises and had to pause to rest and cool our cars. We had, of course, left our ox wagons and donkey wagons and camels far behind, and had reduced our loads to the bare essentials of camera equipment and condensed food supplies and bedding. A good thing, too, for the boys now had to push and pull to help us over the bad spots. We often spent two hours covering one mile.

It was the worst part of the journey. I struck a rock and smashed my bumper. Martin broke the spring of his car. We blocked up the spring with wood and bound it with strips of eland hide. We had shot an eland the week before for meat, and we had kept the hide for just such an emergency.

While we were resting over this mishap, Blaney caught up with us. But he was in as bad condition as we; his water was low and he looked very fagged.

We pushed on to Ret, where we arrived, tired and dirty, water low in the radiators of our cars, and our stock of drinking water completely gone. The waterhole was dry and we had to rush on. I was so thirsty my tongue was hanging out. After hours without water in this terrific heat, I would have given anything I pos-sessed for a Coca-Cola or a cool pitcher of lemonade. I would even have enjoyed hot water at this point. But we pushed on toward Kampia Tembo, a waterhole in the hills, where we knew there was a spring. It was a favorite drinking place of the elephants. Here, also, on the edge of the forest, was a camp.

After weeks of the country we had just come through, this seemed the most heavenly place in the world. The forest was cool and fragrant and it was good to see things green again. Here, I knew, would be a hot bath, clean clothes, and a good dinner. And above all, I would drink cool spring water.

Lieutenant Harrison, the young English District Commissioner, greeted us, and a native sergeant and his askaris saluted us smartly and bustled about with our luggage.

Actually the place consisted of but a few mud and grass huts, one duka shop and the District Commissioner's headquarters, but there were trees everywhere, festooned with Spanish moss. Springs of cool water bubbled up beside the roadway, and before the D.C.'s humble boma was a garden filled with blooming canna, petunia and salvia.

While we were having lunch a native came up, saluted and addressed Martin and me. It was Boculy, our old elephant guide!

"We've been keeping him in jail for ivory-poaching," the young English lieutenant told Martin.

"I'll pay all his fines," Martin said, without even asking what they were.

Boculy was glad to see us. He grinned, and I could see the mark of deep devotion on his face. And needless to say, Martin and I were delighted to find him, for he knew every inch of this wilderness. As for elephants, he could track them and find them like no one else we had ever seen.

"Pretty lucky day for you," said Blaney. "You've got the best elephant guide that ever lived. But watch him: he's absolutely worthless for lions or anything else."

Boculy had guided us on our first trip to Lake Paradise. He was a queer little old man, but there was a definite nimbleness and youth in his gait and bearing, and, despite the deep lines in his face, he never seemed old. There was a quickness and intelligence about him which at once distinguished him from all the other African boys we knew, and his judgment about the forest was such that we would have trusted ourselves with him anywhere. The friendly warmth and humor of his smile immediately revealed his good disposition, and we had found him always to be good company on his many safaris with us.

"What do you suppose has happened to our porters?" asked Martin the next morning. "Bukhari, call the boys and fill every petrol tin with water. Abdulla, you start back in a car right away.

Take these tins. Go thirty miles and wait for those boys, if you don't meet them on the way."

As soon as Abdulla had left, Blaney Percival, Martin and I set off with Boculy as guide to look over the road toward Paradise.

We followed the road for about six miles and then turned into a scrub forest at a place where the grass was very high. Blaney walked ahead and guided us for about three hundred yards. Then we came into a well-developed trail that was so easy to follow we didn't need a trail breaker. Blaney got back into the car, and carefully we picked our way along for five hours. Then we could go no further in the car.

"We can follow this trail on foot," Blaney pointed out. "It will be an easy matter for the boys to cut through."

We returned to camp about dark. Martin and Blaney were happy: they were sure that we would be able to cut off many miles of the trail we had taken on our first trip to Paradise.

Abdulla had just returned, bringing with him five sick porters and their loads. He told us that the rest of the boys were about thirty miles away, and would make a short-cut to the Paradise trail. They had made remarkable time, but then they had had to hurry, as the waterholes were so far apart. The boys reported seeing a hundred elephants near Lasamis. There were probably only half this number, as native boys have the habit of doubling all their calculations. They thought our wagons would be about three days behind.

7

". . . Thick jungle closes it in. The Lake lies in the crater of a dead volcano. Thousands of birds twitter and call from the tree-tops around us. Down near the water are heron and egrets. The trees are laden with moss. Flowers grow profusely everywhere. . . . Lake Paradise, indeed."
—MARTIN JOHNSON

THE NEXT DAY we left Lieutenant Harrison and camped on the edge of the forest. This was the last leg of our journey. We had beaten the rains. Now we had only to wait for our porters, ox wagons and camels to catch up with us.

A few miles from Kampia Tembo we made our camp in an open grassy plain on the edge of a little donga. All about us was a dense forest, and the trees, centuries old, towered one hundred and more feet. They were hung with vines, creepers and Spanish moss. About our tents swarmed butterflies of every conceivable color—thousands of them.

"This is the greatest rhino country in the world, so don't be surprised if we have visitors," said Blaney as he bade us good night on our first evening in camp.

We found this to be no understatement, for every night we had rhino brushing against our tents or snorting about camp, and they gave us no peace. The porters were especially frightened of the big beasts. One night several boys came running to our tent and wakened us, saying:

"Rhino very bad. Please, master, come and shoot them."

"Oh, you're big brave boys; you're not afraid of a little rhino," Martin replied. "You're as big as a Masai, aren't you?"

The Masai were the bravest warriors in Africa, and every native envied them. This was the perfect end to such an argument, so the boys went back to their camp quietly, if not reassured.

From some inquisitive Boran native herdsmen who had heard of our presence in the vicinity and had come up to ask us for salt and sugar, we learned that there were not only great numbers of rhino but large herds of elephant near us. A large crater near by was full of them and this would be our chance to make some fine pictures while we were waiting for our porters to arrive.

We traded salt and sugar for milk, which the herdsmen carried in dirty calabashes. I never could stand this native milk, for the gourds were burned out on the inside with hot coals and everything carried in these containers had a burned taste, but Blaney drank the milk with relish. I don't think he liked it, but he made believe that he did to make his peace with the natives by offering them this gesture of friendship.

"Good stuff, Osa," he said, smacking his lips, and giving me a wink. But it tasted to me like poison.

Our porters arrived on the third morning. Martin and I were awakened early by the sound of excited voices and Bukhari came to our tent to call us. Outside, our personal servants were gathered around several porters who lay on the ground. Their lips were parched and cracked and they looked terribly done in.

"The safari ran out of water," Bukhari said. "The fools drank up all that Abdulla brought them on the first day, and have had no water since."

While Blaney and I took care of the boys, Martin and Bukhari went off at once with a supply of water to pick up the others, and the packs they had left behind. When the boys were revived, we set them to building rough shelters for themselves and determined to move on as soon as they were able to help with the work, without waiting for our wagons. Meantime, we would have at least a day of good pictures.

On the following morning, with Bukhari and several porters I set off for the nearby crater, leaving Martin and Boculy to come along with the cameras later. The crater was a vast hole in the earth, with a clean, clear grassy rim, and steep sides down which elephant and rhino trails led into thick forest. We could hear buffalo crashing about and the distant trumpeting of elephants. There were baboons everywhere in the trees.

I was too impatient to wait, so I stationed a porter to direct Martin and moved on down the principal trail. At the floor of the crater, the forest opened into grassy areas in the midst of which were miniature lakes, and beyond was a beautiful grove of acacia, so neatly arranged that it looked more like a park than a wilderness. It had taken us an hour and a half to reach the bottom of the crater, and after exploring it briefly, we selected a bit of high ground and here we concealed ourselves to watch.

As the afternoon drew on, several rhino came to drink and buffalo in considerable numbers came and went. Finally, elephants began to drift down to the water. We were well-covered and they did not get our scent, and I was fascinated, but very upset that I had no camera. Martin's delay began to worry me and I wondered what had become of him. Since it was growing late I determined to start back to the top.

Along the way we could hear the animals beginning to stir and feed in the forest on all sides. Rhino were crashing about and a leopard leaped from the crotch of a tree and ran off. About halfway up the trail, we came to a small clearing, and there, standing across our path, about seventy yards away, was a huge bull buffalo. He took one look at me and charged. It was evidently my life or his, so I fired and hit him. In quick succession I fired three more solid-nosed bullets, but on he came. I had only one bullet left in the magazine. I aimed carefully and the last shot struck him in the boss between his horns. I leaped backward, and as he fell he slid up to me and dropped dead only a few feet away.

Bukhari was standing beside me, shaking like a leaf, scared as much as I.

"God has been with you today," he said.

Our porters cut out the choice portions of the meat and we started back to camp. At the top of the crater, we found Martin and his boys. The porter had become confused and led them off on another trail, and he had been so worried looking for me that he had got no pictures.

"That was a crazy thing to do," said Blaney, "to go down alone in that crater. Two friends of mine were killed down there just two years ago. Thank God you're back."

That night, our Meru boys, who were always too tired to work but were always hungry, became very concerned about wasting that food down in the crater. They took lanterns and torches, which they made by winding grass around sticks, and went off to salvage the rest of the buffalo. If there were enough boys, enough noise and enough lights, they always felt safe, no matter how much big game was around. The combination always seemed to work.

Next morning, we began moving our camp on toward Lake Paradise. We turned every able-bodied boy out with shovels, pangas, picks and crowbars. One crew went ahead cutting big trees that had fallen or been pulled down by elephants. Another gang threw out loose stones; another cut the shrubs and grass; the end gang broke big stones too heavy to move and filled in the small depressions.

Soon the boys made a passable trail for the trucks. They worked so well and so fast that we could see the road grow before our eyes. After a mile, however, they were held up for the remainder of that day by a steep rise of one hundred feet over immense boulders that had to be broken, pulled up, and smoothed.

The next day we got over the bad place, and for a mile the boys scarcely touched the trail. Then another very bad stretch held them up for several days.

This went on for an entire week. Martin sent a couple of boys back along the trail to wait for the wagons. On the sixth day they arrived, and we set the ten additional boys they carried to work with the road gang.

The following morning we pushed on. The forest became more dense and the trail more difficult as we climbed higher; but we didn't want to camp in this rough country another night, so we urged the boys to make all speed. Boculy and I scouted the route ahead while Blaney and Martin worked with the road gang. With luck, we would reach Lake Paradise that day, Boculy predicted.

At about four o'clock we broke through the forest into a clearing at the top of the mountain. We knew we were now but a few miles from Lake Paradise, and we determined to reach it before dark if we could.

After a brief rest, we followed Boculy across the clearing and into the forest in the direction of the vast crater which held the Lake. We were now moving along a well-defined elephant trail. Smaller trails led in from both sides and the main trail became clearer and broader until it resembled a road. For centuries elephants, coming from all parts of these mountains, had walked over this route to the Lake for water.

The trees became larger and taller and the undergrowth less dense, and about us there was a cathedral-like silence. The sun was now lost in the towering branches above us, but it was still light and the air so clear that I felt buoyed up and wanted to sing. Here at last, was our Paradise! Boculy and Bukhari shared my excitement and we hurried on to another clearing beyond which we could see the vast opening of the crater.

We stopped suddenly. There was a low booming from within the crater, like cannon. As we moved on the booming grew louder and nearer and echoed through the forest.

"Elephants!" said Boculy. "Elephants down below. Breaking trees. They are going crazy!"

Blaney and Martin came up, and we all crept nearer and stood in the wide trail which formed the entrance to Lake Paradise. The elephants were either feeding in very large numbers or else were on a rampage. Added to this, we could hear the bellowing of buffalo, the snorting of rhino and the shrill barks and screeches of baboons, all mingling in exaggerated echoes.

"What a dramatic entrance to Paradise," said Blaney. "You're not going to have a dull moment here!"

Martin was beaming with satisfaction—he looked ten years younger.

Boculy was standing on one foot, rubbing the top of his head and trying to look calm.

I felt nervous little shivers of excitement running up my spine and into my hair, and goose-bumps stood out all over me.

I looked about me, slowly, breathlessly. I saw a spot of unsurpassable beauty—a cool, turquoise lake surrounded by clean, virginal forest where fantastically beautiful birds colored the trees. I listened, and knew that if I could hear all the ageless echoes which had resounded against these cliffs, it would be no familiar human sound, no heartening melody of companionship.

This, I realized, was the end of our journey. This was to be our home for the next several years. The thought struck me with sudden force, and in some strange way I seemed to withdraw from the spell of excitement which held the three men.

It was as though we had been dropped into the Garden of Eden, which had never before known Man.

Then, curiously, I saw another picture within my mind, the picture of a tidy little lot in Independence, Kansas, where I once thought Martin and I might build a house. It was on a quiet street where children played and housewives visited over the fences. The spot had been laid out by plan, long before I had come there, and

I knew exactly where our little house would be placed. I knew where we would buy the lumber and the paint and the furnishings. I knew every detail of making that home for Martin, because all the other women on this street had done the same thing before me.

But that house had never materialized. The home which I must build for Martin was to be here, in this far-off corner of Africa, where there were no neatly laid-out streets, no fenced-off lots.

Our home must be created out of the jungle itself; out of the trees which would be cut down to make our cabins; out of the mud and clay and rocks about us. Our furniture would be whatever our own hands could make. There was no way of buying end tables and floor lamps and kitchen cabinets.

I was suddenly appalled by the immensity of the task, and not a little afraid to tackle it.

And then, across the waters of Lake Paradise, my mind did catch an echo, though it was the echo of no voice ever heard in Africa. It was the voice of my grandmother out home in Kansas, and her tone was crisp and challenging:

"What do you think our covered wagons found in Kansas?" it seemed to demand. "Sears Roebuck catalogs?"

And then I laughed, and reached out to Martin, and my fear was gone. What lay ahead was to be the greatest adventure in all the world. My home here in the wilderness would be the loveliest place on earth. I knew it!

I heard Martin saying, "If it weren't so late, I'd get the greatest elephant picture ever made."

"Never mind, dear," I soothed him. "You're going to have plenty of time for that. But I think we'd better pitch camp before dark, don't you?"

So we retreated to meet our boys and set up camp in the clearing.

We were almost too excited to eat, but after a good dinner we decided to go and see the "circus," as Martin put it. Boculy estimated that there were twenty-five thousand elephants in the forest around Lake Paradise, and from what we had just heard I was sure most of them had come to greet us.

We asked Boculy and Bukhari to come along and bring the cooks and personal boys, if they would enjoy it.

"Boculy and I are ready," said Bukhari, "but the boys are very tired." From his sheepish grin, however, I knew that he meant they thought we were just a little crazy.

Taking our largest rifles and our flashlights, Blaney, Martin and I set off with the two boys. Our confidence in Boculy was such that we would have felt safe with him anywhere in this country, at any hour.

By a round-about trail we picked our way to the edge of a cliff overlooking the Lake. The racket had subsided, but elephants were still there in large numbers, and as we listened we heard the buffalo and rhino, a leopard coughing near by, baboons everywhere, and up from the water the night cries of geese, ducks, egrets, coots and heron.

Below the cliff ran the main thoroughfare of the elephants, down from the crater's rim through the forest that banked the sides, to the great lake below. As we sat there, groups of the great animals lumbered up from the water in a continuing parade under the spotlight of the moon. And we watched, fascinated and undetected, far into the night.

In spite of our resolution to rise early the next morning, it was eight before we stirred. I had wakened for a few moments at dawn to hear the sounds of the forest—a crescendo of animal and bird calls. And then I fell asleep again.

Our cook had breakfast waiting. We sat down at the little table, and looked out over a grassy plain that broke into a donga immediately in front of the tent. Beyond, the donga rose gradually into a long hill. As I was devouring American bacon and wild guinea-fowl eggs, I suddenly spied something over the rim of my coffee-cup. I nudged Martin. There, outlined against the sky, were three elephants.

They strolled toward us, moving slowly, as if they were too lazy to lift their feet in the early morning heat. They were not feeding. They were just enjoying the sun and air. Every once in a while they would stop and throw a trunkful of dust over their gigantic backs.

Martin called for a boy to bring his camera, and we set it up on the other side of the valley. The wind was in our favor, and the elephants drew nearer and nearer.

"Osa, get into the picture!" Martin said.

I walked slowly toward them. They looked sleepy and good natured. In spite of their huge size there was nothing terrifying about them. So I grew more bold and went just a little closer, a little closer than Martin had intended me to do.

Suddenly they saw me. They stopped short. Their trunks went up and out in alarm. They extended their huge ears until the tips stretched a dozen feet apart.

"They're going to charge, Osa! Come back here."

Instead of doing that, I screamed, at the top of my lungs and on the highest note I could reach.

The elephants ducked their heads as though someone had hit them. They looked bewildered and stood staring at me for a moment. Then they spun around and hurried off at a good gait.

I ran after them screaming. Every time I screamed they turned and shot a glance at me, as though I were something pretty fearful, and ran faster, their tails straight out behind them.

"Did you get a good picture, Martin?" I came back to the camera puffing and laughing.

"You little son-of-a-gun!" said Martin, very cross. "What will you do next? They might have made mincemeat out of all of us."

"Martin is right," chimed in Blaney, frowning at me and meaning it. "You ought to be spanked and put to bed."

Then Boculy came rushing in with the news that he had spotted elephants at a near-by pool, and we were all off at once to see them. Presently Boculy left the trail, and plunged into the forest, motioning us to follow. Suiting our pace to his, we crept along cautiously, climbing quietly over great rocks. Then we looked at a never-to-be-forgotten picture.

Below us stood a big bull elephant, knee deep in a pool. He was the very picture of drowsy contentment. Save for the slow swinging of his trunk and the languid fanning of his huge ears, he was almost motionless. His bath was built of great rocks, covered over with beautiful lichen and mosses, green and gray and rusty-red. Floating on the water were large blue and white water lilies. The pool was shaded by magnificent trees festooned with silvery moss. Thousands of butterflies—blue, yellow and white—fluttered around the animal.

The sky had been overcast, but at this moment the sun broke through. Herons and egret, ducks and coots, storks and cranes strutted and flew about the water. Trees swept in crowded ranks to the rim of the donga. Beyond, magnificent in its vastness, eerie in its reddish-gray bareness, lay the great Kaisoot Desert, stretching clear to the Abyssinian border. The sun sank behind a dark cloud.

I glanced at Blaney Percival, then at Martin, who pressed my hand tightly in his.

Boculy rubbed his stomach, smiled, and looked very, very proud.

We stood watching the pool. The big bull elephant decided finally that his bath was complete, and that he had had enough to drink, so he turned to pick his way up the rocky slope into the forest. Wound firmly around his switching little rope-like tail, as if it had been tied on, was one of the blue water lilies.

I laughed as he trundled out of sight. We sat on a rock watching the flashing birds and the many-colored butterflies. Nothing had ever seemed so beautiful on God's earth. Then the sun dimmed and the sky grew overcast with heavy clouds.

Before we reached camp, the "big rains," which we had dreaded for weeks, began to fall.

8

". . . There was nothing about Lake Paradise that suggested civilization. We seemed to be in another world, a Garden of Eden, in which it was easy to be good and happy, and in which men and animals lived at peace with one another."
—MARTIN JOHNSON

"ISN'T IT EVER going to stop raining?"

I felt depressed. I was sure it had never rained so hard before. Certainly it had never rained in Pago-Pago the way it did the day after we arrived at Lake Paradise.

It rained all the first night, and in the morning it was still pouring. In the afternoon the downpour slackened into a drizzle, and Martin had the boys gather grass and poles and construct more shelters. He gave them the extra blankets that were wrapped around the cameras, and we pegged out tarpaulins around the cars, making tents for the boys who, with those we had added en route, now numbered over one hundred and fifty. At night we had roaring fires in front of the tents, and it would have been almost comfortable if everything hadn't been so damp. We spent every dry moment drying our blankets in front of huge fires.

It was wonderful what those boys could stand in the way of exposure. The rain was cold, and each boy had to sleep on the wet ground, wrapped in a wet blanket, yet they seemed content. Apparently they took the hardships as part of the game, for at home they would have been no better sheltered. I tried to keep up their spirits by giving them extra rations of tea and brown sugar. Let them have their stomachs full and they will start a ngoma (dance) no matter how hard it rains.

The day following it was still drizzling. We went out with Blaney and several boys to select a site for our permanent camp. There seemed only one logical place for it, a half-cleared plateau on the rim of the crater where we had pitched our tents on our first visit.

"Bogu," (buffalo) said Boculy, as we approached the spot.

Sure enough, there were buffalo, a great herd of them, grazing contentedly in the open space and milling about among the trees. There were easily five hundred of them, and a number of calves, which meant that the mothers would be jittery. Nothing can be more deadly than a buffalo charge, and we quickly made for high ground where we could watch them and be out of their way.

We shouted, waved, and made a great hullabaloo to frighten them. They all raised their heads and stood stock-still; then slowly they drew together into a circle, the big bulls forward in their customary formation for a charge.

"I guess they mean to keep the place," said Blaney. "They were here first, and their lease hasn't expired."

The bulls snorted and pawed the ground, trying to make up their minds how to get to us. Then they began to bellow and pandemonium broke loose.

They swept off to the left as though to get away from us, but that trail led to the Lake. They whirled and got into formation again and stampeded our way, making a terrifying noise. Then the sea of glistening jet-black bodies swept past us and up the trail, breaking bushes and small trees, hooves making a great clatter on the rocks.

"Whew," said Martin, "I thought we were going to go through the sausage-grinder."

It showered without respite the first week at Paradise. But it

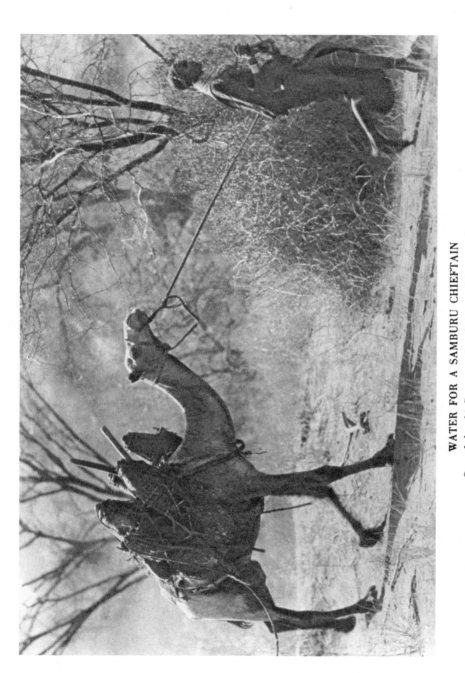

WATER FOR A SAMBURU CHIEFTAIN

One of the chief's many wives brings to his camp, from the Eauso Nyiro River, the evening's supply of water.

TRIBAL CHIEF AND HIS FAVORITE WIFE

He provided the Johnsons with porters at Meru. The stone in his ear weighs five pounds; her brass jewelry twice as much.

would have taken more than rain to stop us from getting down to work. Time was precious, and we knew it would take us months —and perhaps a year—to get fully settled here.

Since we were at an altitude of over 6,000 feet, with temperatures ranging from 57 degrees at five a.m., when we usually got up, to 69 or 70 at noon, and then down again, it was a problem to keep warm. We dressed in heavy underwear and sweaters and the boys wore overcoats and even blankets.

On the second day after our arrival, I got out my big bundle of seeds, and went hunting for a good garden spot. I donned my overalls and rubber hip-boots, and took along several of the boys, who carried picks and shovels. Soon we had set out beds of beans, peas, sweet corn, carrots, potatoes, tomatoes, artichokes, celery, cucumbers, turnips, squash and beets.

In about a week all our wagons arrived, with the remainder of the boys and donkeys. Six oxen were lost, two of them killed by lions. One donkey and one mule had been bitten by tsetse flies and had died of sleeping sickness. The tsetse fly of British East Africa is fatal only to domestic animals; it never seems to bother wild animals.

Blaney and Martin immediately went into the forest with saws and axes, and began felling logs for our houses. There were more than a hundred boys occupied with this work of heaving and tugging at the logs, bringing them up and down ravines, through the forest and into camp.

When we showed our Meru boys the saws with which to cut down trees, they stared and exclaimed:

"O ti, (Oh, my), it has teeth just like the crocodile."

They were very fearful about taking this strange and dangerous-looking instrument in their hands, but when Blaney showed them how to use it, they went to work with a will and were soon chanting as the saws sliced through the tree trunks:

O ti,
O ti,
Uh-ugh,
Uh-ugh,
Hi-yah!

keeping up the chant until the tree crashed.

Everyone was at work. Blaney supervised most of the building operations, and Martin did every sort of job imaginable, laying out plans, carpentering, cleaning, unpacking, oiling cameras. Every afternoon I would make the rounds of the various gangs, into which the boys had been segregated for special jobs, to see that they were working. I would find a lazy Meru who had slipped off and gone to sleep, but a few cracks of the rhino kiboko in mid-air would soon stir him from his slumber.

"So, you think we brought you all the way up here to sleep while the rest of us work?" I would say, trying to shame him. And he would think up some lame excuse as the other boys poked fun at him.

At lunch time I would blow the horn of my car and they would all congregate in a body for their noon-time meal. Then back to work, and I would make another inspection tour late in the after-noon. Meantime, I was busy selecting sites for the houses and lay-ing out the vegetable and flower gardens.

At five-thirty everyone quit work for the day, and each boy would bring in a log for the campfires. Some of the good-for-nothing Meru boys complained about the work, whatever it was, and complained even if they weren't working, but a word or two from Martin would set them straight again. They might not have grumbled so much if they hadn't worn big heavy woolen caps like Arctic explorers, sometimes with the ear and chin flaps down, in the heat of the day. But this was the fashion among the natives.

Kalowat, our pet gibbon, whom we had brought up from Nairobi along with my two Persian kittens and the cheetah, would go out to the fire with the boys and dip her hand into the posho pot, just as they did, and eat with relish and smack her lips. She preferred this to eating with us, though Kalowat and all the animal pets were usually on hand when our dinner was served. She would sit down at the table with us and apparently enjoy our attentions and then skip out to the fires and join the boys, who loved her and gave her the most affectionate care.

Kalowat had her own blanket, about the size of a baby's. The boys always shook this out for her and made up her bed as though they were attending an important personage. They were very kind to her, and shared with her the fruit they gathered. When the beautiful yellow poppies on the desert turned to burrs, and she got these in her feet and her fur, she was pathetic until the boys picked the burrs out. She would hold up her foot, pucker her mouth and begin hoo-hooing, and she even managed to squeeze out tears for them. They called her the "toto of the Big Missus."

She was never still a minute. She would stand on her head, turn somersaults, romp over the tents and trees, and steal the boys' caps. She found they always enjoyed these antics and she loved to show off and get their applause.

Martin built a fourteen-foot-square building to house our electric plant and machine shop, pushing it to completion in a little over twenty-four hours.

Blaney helped him to install the plant. When the work was completed, Martin said:

"Wish me luck, Osa," as he seized the wheel and gave it a twirl.

I shut my eyes and crossed my fingers. I may have uttered a few words under my breath, I can't be sure, because when I opened one eye to peek, the lights were on.

"You've done it, old man!" Blaney congratulated Martin.

Martin smiled and sighed. Boculy stood on one leg like a stork and seemed very proud. The natives let up a chorus of Ah-h-h-h-hs. I remember noticing how their wet, black bodies shone in the sudden light of electricity.

We rushed ahead on the work of constructing our permanent

buildings. Since we would be here for a long time and in all kinds of weather, and might even have elephants trying to push us over at night, we wanted these buildings to be made of sterner stuff and to have more durability than the usual mud and straw shacks found in British East.

First of all, we selected good stout logs, sinking them into the ground and standing them upright in African native fashion. These we tied together with vines, stuffing the spaces between the logs with Spanish moss, and plastering both the outside and inside with a mixture of clay and elephant dung which ultimately dried to the firmness of concrete.

In these first weeks we were as busy as a camp of loggers. Despite the frequent rain we built our village as Noah built his ark. Everyone was up at the crack of dawn. Sometimes because we were six thousand feet high, the fog was so thick we couldn't see each other at a few feet. There were days when the fog didn't clear until 11 a.m. This went on for some time, but we never slackened our work.

I loved to go out and watch the boys making the "cement" for our huts.

They dug a large shallow pit and in it made a big mud puddle. When the pit was full of wet clay, dung, water, and a certain amount of chopped dry grass, they would tramp it and mix it with their feet. As our "cement" squished through their toes, they chanted their rhythmic work-song:

> Yo Ee Yo
> Yo Ee Yo
> Yo Ee Yo

Then a little fellow would chime in with his falsetto version:

> yo ee yo
> YOO EE YOO
> yo ee yo

After the mud was mixed, the boys would make big cakes and sling them with all their strength at the log framework of the house.

"Rusha!" (splash)

"Aya!" Another boy slugged his shot like a Mack Sennett pie.

"Rusha!"

"Aya!"

They "let her fly," until the wall was plastered and packed with mud.

Then the native carpenter would come with his trowel and call a halt to this mud-slinging and smooth the surface into a flat-finished wall. Then, because the rainy season was still on, it would take a couple of weeks for the wall to dry.

After it was all over, the boys would come to me and beg for soap. They would be covered to the knees with muck.

"Look, we are so dirty," they would say in Swahili. "Please, Missus, give us some soap."

Then I would shave a cake of soap into forty pieces and give them each a sliver. We weren't tightwads, but we couldn't carry tons of soap; we had to carry cameras.

In the forest, I discovered a white lime rock and a rose pink rock which we crushed together, making a dusty pink plaster wash for the inside walls of our bedroom. I left the outside walls the same dark chocolate-brown color of the dried mud. I painted my bathroom white with many coats of real paint until it gave out a soft milky glow when the sunlight filtered in through the great shade trees outside.

Accidents of necessity can sometimes turn out as well as the art of a decorator. The furniture I now made was in this category, for I used up the odds and ends of materials left by the carpenters. The stripped poles made legs and supports. Animal rawhide cut into strips made seats and backs for the chairs. My tables I made from packing boxes nailed onto legs.

What I had learned in the manual training class at school in Kansas certainly stood by me now. It had been the one class I really loved.

I made shelves for Martin's laboratory and other uses. I fitted and planed a four-shelf bookcase that would hang on the wall of our living room, and then painted it black from some of the paint left over from Martin's dark room. I even made a little serving table, out of clean white wood, with four straight planed legs. The long-earlobed carpenter was some help, but I did most of the leveling, for he never knew when a level was level. His earlobes hung to his shoulder, except on dressed-up occasions when he wound the lobes about his ear stumps to look like cauliflowers.

When I'd ask him to do anything, he was quick to say, "Mi mi náskia" (I understand).

"What did I say?" I would ask, to check up on him.

"I don't know," was the prompt reply.

But he was always willing, whether he understood or not, and generally I managed to penetrate his dull brain.

From tree branches I made towel racks, and from curved roots I made stands for wash basins, and clothes pegs of antelope horns.

Of course, the furnishings took a great deal of time and energy. But after all, we might be here for years and we always felt that whatever we did to provide ourselves with comfort and convenience was worthwhile, for upon our health and relaxation depended our success.

I felt I must soften our place as much as possible. It was a natural urge, and I also knew how much it meant to Martin to have things cheerful and attractive—especially how welcome the little comforts were after a hard day in the sun or locked up in his suffocating dark room.

Whenever we were on safari and I saw nice flowers, I stopped to dig them up for my garden. Martin would shout, "Hey, come on!

You're holding up the whole safari for a weed!" But he loved to see them grow and bloom just the same.

Blaney was a great help, for he knew every flower that grew and he brought me in plants or slips or rare orchids almost daily. There were wild morning glories; yellow hibiscus; mauve salvia; violets; forget-me-nots; heather; large pansies; delicate white "Mayflowers"; black-eyed susans; red pom-poms; leopard orchids (a spray of white and mauve petals); a golden orchid with brown polkadots; a large and lovely purple ground orchid; another ground orchid in pineblock but with a vile odor; and endless other variations of floral beauty.

We always had cut flowers for the dining and bedroom tables. Outside my bedroom windows, I made flower-boxes which I kept filled with a variety of ferns and wild flowers from the forest. It was pleasant to lie there and look out through the lacyness of the ferns at the Lake and the glorious unspoiled forest beyond.

I filled old stumps with nasturtiums and brought in forest creepers, colored foliage and wild begonia for boxes for the other buildings and for the edges of my walks and garden. I also brought up stones from the Lake and laid them out as edges for my flowerbeds, and made an attractive rock garden, decorated with tiny ferns, shrubs and flowers.

My windows I hung with home-made curtains of flowered chintz which made the room very gay indeed! The bedroom floor I had made of the ends of boxes which had contained our American tinned foods, a patchwork of American advertising slogans— Bartlett Pears, Heinz Tomato Catsup, Mammoth White Asparagus, Dutch Cleanser, Bon Ami, California Prunes, Unguentine. I stepped out on "Chili Sauce" every morning until I could stand it no longer, and got down on my knees and worked for a whole day with the carpenter to plane it all down to a bare, smooth surface.

"But why?" asked the carpenter. "It is so pretty."

The living room was now as comfortable as that of any country home. It was fourteen by seventeen feet, with a big screened veranda across the front. There were guns and horns on the wall which gave the atmosphere of a hunting lodge, zebra skins on the floor, and in the evening a fire in the open fireplace. It was a fire, too, without soot or much smoke, because the only wood in the forest was hard and gave out a most comforting warmth and color—a yellow flame which was like burning driftwood. Seated around the fire in the evenings, it seemed almost as if civilization, which we had tried to escape, had caught up with us.

Religiously, morning and night, I had our boys bring clear, sparkling water and fill our bath tubs. Martin was just as particular, and enjoyed his bath as much as I did.

I have always tried to make a home wherever we have gone. After all, our work was pretty well cut out for us. Martin's task was to photograph: mine was to keep the home running so smoothly that my husband's work could go on without interruption or annoyance. And I enjoyed my job just as much as Martin enjoyed his picture-taking.

I was delighted when Martin installed our laundry. He had a special building erected where all our washing was done in huge tubs. Clean boiling water was used, and I was thankful for the real irons and sturdy ironing boards we had toted along. Of course, all the suds in the tubs fascinated the natives. Only our personal boys possessed clothes of their own to wash. All but our well-trained personal boys thought we were very foolish to worry about washing and ironing. "Clothes only get dirty again," said one of the porters.

In order to rush the laboratory and other urgently-needed buildings, we had still not completed our kitchen.

"Martin," I complained at last, "it's time I had a decent stove."

I was thoroughly tired of trying to cook on open campfires the kind of meals I knew he ought to have.

"All right, honey. You send right down to the hardware store."

But with Blaney's and Boculy's help I made a stove just as good as any range.

First, Blaney made our own fire bricks. Then, cutting away part of one side of our kitchen, and building a heavy foundation of stone from the ground up, we laid our bricks, making a low fireplace and chimney. The fireplace we built out into the center of the room like a large stone oven. One end of this served as a regular oven. The other end had an open top and this I used as a stove, covered with a piece of sheet iron that had come up from Nairobi with our supplies. Into the sheet iron we cut holes. I admit that the holes weren't very round and some were nearly square and others zig-zagged, but they held my pots and pans and did the job.

"Gosh, what smells so good?"

Martin loved to eat, and whenever he came home and found me cooking, he would burst into the kitchen and sample whatever I had on the stove.

He would turn to M'pishi and say, "The Missus is number-one cook here, but you are number two." M'pishi would swell up and smile as though a great compliment had been bestowed upon him. "And Mumbora is number three," added Martin, whereupon Mumbora would also beam. They were true cooks and they liked to be appreciated.

I have always loved to cook, and, I think, next to fishing it is the one thing I enjoy doing the most. This passion for cooking gave me one of my narrowest escapes from injury.

I was cooking in the open one day, at a fire around which Omara had heaped rocks to hold my pots and pans. I had just stepped away from the fire when there was a loud explosion, and a fragment of hot rock flew past me and struck one of the porters on the cheek, giving him a deep cut and burn. Had I not moved away from the fire, I might easily have been killed.

I later learned the cause. Most of the rocks in this area were of volcanic origin and had sealed up in them gases which exploded upon being heated.

As time went on, I often heard rocks exploding at the boys' fires and saw the boys scattering. Every once in a while I would have to treat one of them for these injuries.

But even over the open fires during these early weeks at Paradise, we managed to have good meals, with breakfasts of bloaters and kippered herring and ham and eggs. And I made Martin some of his favorite desserts. I even made him floating island pudding.

As soon as our meal was over, Mumbora would clear the table, but instead of eating our food, he would go out and squat down with the other boys and, with his fingers, eat his ground posho, sometimes mixed with a few bits of meat or vegetable. Although Mumbora's wife had made a bargain with us to give him no posho, he would eat little else.

"That's his corned beef and cabbage," said Martin. "He's having a real good time."

To make our supplies last longer, and because we liked fresh foods, we got things that grew wild in the forests and on the plains whenever we could find them. The boys would show me new foods constantly, and if I looked skeptical, they would eat them first to reassure me. When I learned from experience which foods were edible and which agreed with us, I gathered armfuls of wild asparagus and quantities of other vegetables and fruits.

I found a delectable wild spinach, similar to the American variety. Mushrooms were to be found all over the place. There were wild plums, sweet and tart, growing in the woods, and these were welcome refreshment on a hot day. There were raspberries and blackberries such as we have at home, and there was a nameless small berry, very like a blackberry but sweeter. Best of all, the forest was full of wild Abyssinian coffee, great beans that make an excellent brew. I roasted this coffee in a pan, with a bit of butter to brown it. Then I ground it, just as we used to grind our coffee at home in the old days in Kansas, and I always had a fresh supply.

The arrival of our big galvanized iron water tanks by ox-wagon from Nairobi a few months after we reached the Lake enabled us to complete the most important building in the village—the laboratory.

Even though it was only mud and thatch it was the best laboratory Martin had ever had, and it lacked nothing we could obtain to increase its efficiency.

"Hollywood wouldn't think this much to look at, but it has everything," he said as he saw the tanks lifted up to their supports. They would give him plenty of water, day and night.

He had started laying out that laboratory on the day of our arrival. And he had put into it more affectionate care than into all the rest of the buildings combined. I marveled at the clever gadgets and arrangements he had devised and at the comfort and order and efficiency he created there.

It was the skyscraper of the village, with its ridgepole nearly thirty feet from the ground. The room was eighteen feet by twelve, and it housed the big drying drums, storage cases, tables and racks, and a large dark room. It was equipped with running water, developing vats, storage tanks and everything necessary to the making of professional pictures. It was so wired and lighted that Martin could work at night.

Fresh water was all-important in the laboratory work, and eight hundred gallons a day were brought up from the Lake on the backs of mules and camels. The water was filtered through charcoal and sand, and finally through cotton. In the rainy season Martin hit upon the idea of having a roof gutter and a rain barrel.

Most important of all was to keep the sensitive film and chemicals in perfect condition. Martin managed this by using special drying compounds and having continuous shipments of fresh stock sent from the Eastman Kodak plant in Rochester, and brought up from Nairobi by runners.

When the film was exposed, it was my job each night to wrap the two-hundred foot rolls of negative in black paper, place these in tins and seal the tins with melted paraffin wax.

For refrigeration, I had a spring-house sunk into the ground like a cellar. Blaney's home-made bricks lined the walls, and the flooring was made of boards from Martin's crates. It had two thatched roofs, one about a foot above the other, so that the warm air would not penetrate the cool, dark interior. No cave could have been more cool—or more dark. Martin strung a wire from his laboratory so that I could have some light, and I made shelves to hold my home-made preserves. Our milk stood in pails on a table and kept delightfully cool: a watermelon placed in the spring-house at noon would be just right for dinner.

So that we would have an ample supply of fresh milk, I made a trip to Kampia Tembo and bought from Boran herdsmen eleven fine, hump-backed cows and seven calves. For them we had to build a special corral and shelters, and we employed a young Boran to take care of them. There were large meadows within the crater and plentiful grass around the crater's rim, so that he never had to take them far away for grazing.

Every bit of the milking I supervised myself while we were at Lake Paradise, and I saw to it that the boy sterilized his hands and took every precaution to keep our milk as clean as in the dairy at home. All the milk was strained through cheesecloths which I also kept sterilized. We skimmed the cream and I did all the churning myself. For some reason, I could never teach the boys to churn properly, not even my cook, and I was always concerned about their cleanliness. Martin was very fond of buttermilk, and now he could have all he wanted. I had some little butter moulds with a pattern of roses, and when I took the moulded butter into the laboratory to show it to Martin, he always seemed very surprised and pleased.

We continued building at full speed, and at the end of fifteen months we had a miniature village on the shores of Lake Paradise. In due time other buildings would go up. There were to be guest houses. And we must have a better garage, tool house and carpenter shop. And of course the garden would be enlarged. On the far side of the garden, like a row of soldiers' barracks, stood the grass huts of the native boys. Our buildings, several acres of vegetable gardens, our regiment of black boys, our chickens, donkeys, cows and camels, our cars, ox-wagons and carts, all were enclosed in a stockade of thornbush six feet high. It looked like a stockade built in our great-grandfathers' days in America to keep the settlers safe from the Indians. It was an impressive little village.

We even made a small stockade for Marjo, the cheetah Blaney gave me, so that no animal could get at her when we were off on safari. We were all very fond of her and I never tired of watching her capers. A cheetah has the head of a cat and the body of a dog, and is the fastest animal on four legs, faster than a greyhound or a race horse. Marjo had been brought up with Blaney's children and had even slept on their bed, so that she made a very gentle and ideal pet. She had the run of the house and she was there at meal times with the Persian kittens and Kalowat, waiting for the tidbits we always threw to them.

Marjo got fatter and fatter, until I began to suspect something other than the tidbits. She had had the run of the place and had often gone off into the forest, staying away for hours at a time, and now I wondered if she might not have found a mate. Sure enough, one morning the boys came up to the house laughing and carrying four little cheetahs which had been born the night before in the corner of one of their grass huts.

They were perfectly darling, the cutest things I have ever seen, and Marjo was as proud of them as I was. They looked like a litter of little fluffy clowns and they chirped like birds. I named them the "polky dots" and Martin and I had many a good laugh over them from then on. They were great company for me.

At first the Persian kittens wouldn't have anything to do with the baby cheetahs: they turned up their tails and flattened their ears and spat. But the kittens relaxed and soon all six of the little animals were playing hide and seek in and out of my petunia beds.

Another great favorite of ours was Lazy Bones, who, incidentally, was appropriately named. No Missouri mule ever was more leisurely than he. No matter what happened, no matter how much I protested, he took his own good time. But I was fond of him nonetheless. He had a personality all his own.

On our way up to Lake Paradise, Martin had bought Lazy Bones for me from an Abyssinian trader for forty shillings. The mule and I had liked each other at sight. He was a sturdy animal, sure-footed for mountain travel, and his grayish-white coloring gave him quite an aristocratic air. He walked like a little prince of mules.

As he ambled about Lake Paradise, I would chatter to him in Swahili, and he would wiggle his long ears and screw up his comical, sad little mule face just as though he understood every word I said.

His most extraordinary habit was that he would "point" at game. But only at big game—buffalo, rhino or elephants. It may have been his one fear—I don't know. But the moment he sensed the presence of big game, Lazy Bones would stop dead in his tracks, his long ears would go forward and he would "freeze." Not a muscle would move. Invariably, when we followed the direction, we found big game. Boculy dubbed the mule "God's animal," and insisted that Lazy Bones saw and heard things that we did not. I'm not sure that Boculy wasn't right.

We were moving along on safari one day when we were charged by a rhino, and Lazy Bones, who was being led by a boy, broke away. After the charge, we searched for him and found his saddle and all his equipment strewn through the forest as if it had been stripped off him in his headlong flight. I was sure he would be eaten by lions and counted him lost. But back at Paradise we found him browsing about. He had found his way home.

The first time he saw elephants at Lake Paradise, he quickly retreated behind a hut. Martin and I watched him, very amused. He was quiet for a few moments, then he stole slyly to the corner of the hut and peeped around, got another good look at the elephants, then turned and trotted in quick-step over to his corral where we had a little hut for him. He slunk into it, like a dog retreating from danger. But he used his head. There he stayed until the elephants left.

One day I found a genet cat baby curled up on the limb of a tree, apparently abandoned, or, more likely, its mother had been killed. He was a cute little ball of golden fur, with black spots, and a long tail with black rings. I at once named him "Spots" and adopted him.

He was as tame as any house kitten and grew to the size of a large squirrel. Martin loved him and the pet was always about, especially at dinner time, when he would stand up and beg and Martin would feed him. He followed me around like a hungry kitten and would get so excited he would go around in circles at the smell of food.

He liked to walk along the rafters overhead and had great fun jumping down on the bed or on the mosquito netting, like a circus acrobat. He made great leaps: if a door were closed he would leap in at the window. He loved to play hide and seek with me in the garden, and romped with the kittens as though he were one of them.

One day during the late afternoon, I lay in bed resting. The genet came to the bedside cautiously and I expected him to spring up as was his custom. He crept up close and I reached down to pet him—and he bit me! I yowled and he scooted out the open door. Then I saw that "Spots" was above me on the rafter, watching the show. He had brought in a wild "friend" to show off his comfortable home. The friend never returned.

Even in Africa we had mice, and we hadn't been installed two weeks before the mice arrived with all their succession of litters. Our little Persian kittens were kept busy. But even so, as I started to put on my boots one day—I always turned them upside down as Blaney had taught me, to shake out any insects and to make sure there were no night adders or scorpions in them—out fell a mother mouse and seven little new pink babies. Meanwhile, the kittens were asleep in Martin's chair in the living room.

Blaney had also taught me to put Flit in my boots, and cautioned me against an almost-invisible insect called a jigger, a little flea no bigger than a pin point, that crawls in your boots and lays about one hundred eggs under your toe-nails. A jigger not only itches terribly, but in a few days may cause a dangerous infection.

One day I found a nine-inch centipede in my dressing gown and killed a large one in a food box.

We sat down to dinner one evening and lighted the Coleman lamps which hung from the rafters. I had made a brand-new peanut soup which I had concocted out of peanut butter, and as I dipped into my plate, a moth miller and two small insects fell into it. I yelled.

"Oh, you'll get used to those little pets, Osa," said Blaney calmly. "Just skim them back and go on eating."

At first I was worried about insects and was very cautious. Whenever I was bitten, I used ammonia on my skin, but soon grew so tired with much work and with the millions of pests that I just "took" them. I felt that if the boys could endure them I could

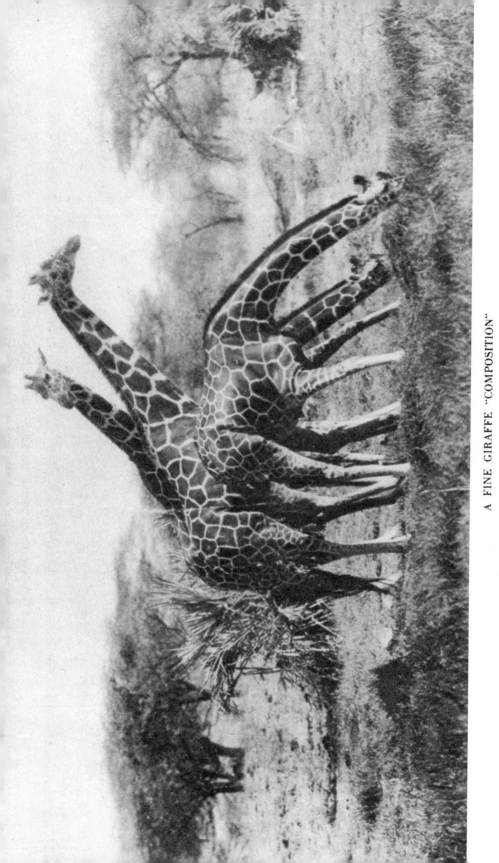

A FINE GIRAFFE "COMPOSITION"

At Chobe waterhole, four beautiful giraffe make this unique photograph for Martin Johnson's camera.

A CHOICE PRIDE OF LIONS POSES FOR THE JOHNSONS

Two lionesses and six young males look up from their feast while Martin takes their photograph with a 3-inch lens and Osa covers the party with her gun. The Johnsons provided the zebra.

MORNING GLORIES IN PARADISE

Following the rains, Osa finds a vast field of native flowers that have sprung up on the plains.

TWO ELEPHANTS BEGIN TO FEED

Waking in the late afternoon, these fine tuskers are just beginning to browse. They feed in the evening and through the night, sleeping in the heat of the day.

and I determined to pray for protection and not worry. The boys soon made me familiar with good and bad pests and snakes, which relieved me of at least half of the burden. The rest was a matter of luck.

Among the insects that made me shudder were the huge flying ants, larger than wasps. But the boys ate them as a delicacy! Only twice a year in Africa do the flying ants come along. They are said to live for only two days before their wings fall off and the birds and the boys eat them. M'pishi, who had just finished serving us a fish chowder, sat outside the tent and grabbed them out of the air and crammed them into his mouth. He told us we didn't know what a good thing we were missing. We took care to see that we never learned!

As the rains dragged on, many of the boys fell ill. Although in the first week there was no illness, and in the second only three cases, by the fifth week eighteen reported at the laboratory for treatment. We set aside a certain time each evening after dinner for doctor's office hours.

Martin and I both served as doctors in this jungle clinic, but as time went on and Martin became involved with his film work, I took over the office and the boys called me "Doctari Johnson," or sometimes "Little Missus Big Doctor."

To the very few that seemed really sick we gave a reasonable dose of quinine or whatever the patient seemed to need. And we soon found that we needed all the supplies we had bought in London, for quinine and such vital medicinal items dwindled rapidly.

Plenty of malingerers also showed up at the clinic. It seems to be a universal thing to feign illness to get out of work, but I soon learned to spot the make-believes, for they were always a little sicker than the others. With their moaning and groaning, you could always hear them coming. To this ever-increasing group of sufferers, we would give a whopping big dose of powdered quinine, epsom salts and castor oil. We made quite sure that they swallowed each dose. It was a good prescription, too! The patients quickly decreased in number.

On the Meru boys who complained of being ill constantly, I experimented with aspirin. It worked wonders.

But aspirin was too precious to ladle out by the dozen, so I had M'pishi roll some tiny pills of boiled flour and sugar. These I gave the patients one morning in place of aspirin and the boys said they were "much better" and my pills became very popular.

When I ran out of pellets, I would tell the Meru to come tomor-row, that this was a very special medicine and I had to have time to prepare it.

"Ndiyo," they would say and faithfully wait for their dose until the next day. Finally I tumbled to the fact that it was the sweetness of these pellets which appealed to them and that it was I who was being fooled.

In all kinds of weather, good or bad, we kept busily at work. The job had to go on, for we were there for a purpose and at such expense that every day was precious to us.

I organized one crew to work in the garden with me, and since Martin was constantly delayed from doing his work by the frequent downpours, he lent me his helpers, knowing that we needed fresh foods as soon as possible and that these would mean health for the boys as well as for us.

I wandered about in the garden in my hip boots, weeding, picking bugs, and noting with pride that little green shoots were beginning to break through the mud.

9

". . . How strange to be a man in this alien animal world! How strange that civilized man's need to work should have brought me into this world that knows no work! How strange to go to sleep, looking forward to a day of routine photography, from a stuffy blind looking out on an African waterhole! A day of routine in a land where even routine can be called adventure. . . ."

—MARTIN JOHNSON

As a means of getting my thousand and one domestic duties accomplished with as little confusion as possible, I worked out a regular routine. My headquarters were in the storehouse where I kept and issued all supplies, ranging from posho for the porters to drugs and medicines, blankets and bedding, and tools of every kind.

One day each week we had a thorough inspection of camp. We went through each and every building, from our living quarters to the boys' huts and corrals. We swept and scoured their quarters one day a week, just as a housewife at home cleans every Spring, for they needed it. In one week cobwebs would collect everywhere, and we cleaned them out, along with spiders, scorpions, centipedes, lizards and scores of insects of every size and color.

The chameleons I never touched, unless to take them outside and put them back in the bushes. I liked to watch them change color, from the blue of my scarf to the color of the flowers in the garden. Everyone in Africa respects them, and Blaney and Martin were as fond of them as I. We used to place them on a bouquet of flowers on our dinner table and watch them catch mosquitoes on their flashing tongues. They were better than Flit any day. Even the horned chameleon was a nice pet, though he did remind me of a miniature rhino.

"Here, Osa, he won't bite," said Blaney, as he caught a small chameleon and put it on my arm. I felt pretty squeamish as the little creature crawled up to my shoulder, running his long slender tongue over my skin. Goose bumps came out all over me, and I wasn't sure whether I was afraid or just ticklish. At least I wouldn't admit to Blaney that I was afraid.

The day after house cleaning, I checked our stores, not only to keep our supplies in balance, but to make sure they were not spoiling. The boys' posho would mildew quickly in the damp weather, and since their health depended upon this staple food, it had to be good and fresh.

White ants were a nuisance. They were large and vicious and ate their way wherever they went, through gunny sacks, duffle bags, blankets, sheets or any cloth materials. I developed a great respect for them when I saw them kill a centipede. They swarmed over him, stung him and clung to him until he grew tired of the fight and wilted, probably unconscious from his enemies' bites. In the same way I saw them dispatch two scorpions, and that was good riddance.

Safari ants, which we often encountered on the plains, did not come into Lake Paradise, for which I was grateful. When they attacked in a great black column, like flowing oil, I always let them alone for they were soon gone, having removed what they wanted. If I tried to stop or scatter them, they got into my boots and clothes and hair and left me covered with deep, irritating bites, worse than mosquito bites.

Another weekly chore was to scrub down the laboratory and check our equipment. This we regarded as our most important task. The quarters had to be kept spotless for perfect negatives and prints, and our cameras, lenses, binoculars, carrying cases and everything we used in the field had to be in top condition.

Another day was devoted to my kitchen. As soon as we finished our churning in the little dairy house adjoining, and had made the butter into moulds, we scrubbed things down. Churns, moulds, pots and pans and cheesecloth strainers were scalded and sterilized, and everything in the place was checked and put in order.

I missed no utensils until one day I found a roast pan gone.

"Where is that nice pan I brought from America?" I demanded of M'pishi.

"Maybe the Boran have taken it. I don't know," he said with suspicious innocence.

"I will have Boculy ask them," I stormed, "and if we find it I will ask them how much they paid you for it!"

"But I think a hyena took it, memsahib," said M'pishi weakly. "I left fat in it last night and they like fat."

"I suppose he will wear it for a hat," I said, wondering how many months it would take me to get another roast pan from Nairobi.

To be sure that the boys were strong and fit, we set apart one day each week to give them a rigid health inspection, with Bukhari acting as chief and Boculy and Ouranga as lieutenants. Some of the boys were so primitive that they had no sense of sanitation, and we had to teach them as best we could to keep their clothes and bedding clean and to take care of themselves. If anyone were off his diet or looked suspiciously dull, I promptly took his temperature and pulse, for we could not risk an epidemic of any kind.

"Sick of work, that's all," Blaney was constantly saying. "They love attention but you're spoiling them. Why, they have more money now than they've had in years. Their poor wives at home are the ones you should pity. Bring those boys up here to work and I'll cure them quick."

Our corrals also came in for their day of cleaning and inspection. Cows, camels, chickens and mules had to be watched
constantly for disease. And our cars and wagons had to be gone
over for the damage the drivers did to them; they had to be repaired and kept ready for use.

Martin liked to come home and find me looking my best. So
once a week I washed my hair in rain water that I stole from his
developing tanks, set it and waved it, put on my most attractive
dressing gown or tailored satin lounging pajamas. Martin was
always appreciative of any little feminine touches; and it made
me happy to dress for him. He noticed everything—little gay
colored handkerchiefs and scarfs, a new blouse, or a flower from
the garden tucked in my hair.

"Doggone it, honey," he would say, "all you are going to see
around here besides your husband is an elephant or rhino!"
But from the way his eyes twinkled, I knew he was pleased.

Besides our weekly tasks and our special jobs, there was always the garden. I was constantly at work in it, for with all the
pests we had, in addition to the animals and birds, the only
way to get plants to grow was by daily vigilance. White ants attacked my turnips, radishes and everything that grew underground. Caterpillars were equally devastating, and there were
plenty of bugs and grubs to keep me and the garden boys always
on the jump.

My chief pride, of course, was the garden. Out in Kansas, my
father had loved his garden and had given me his enthusiasm for
growing things. He would come home each night from a long
run as engineer on the Santa Fe and, tired as he was, would go
out with a hoe to attack the weeds on the little plot where he grew
everything from string beans to roses. He taught me how to tree
tomato plants. He taught me the blights and pests which were
the enemies of good vegetables, and how deep to plant the seeds.

And he used to say, "Osa, when you have a home and grow water-melons, don't forget to plant them in sandy loam."

I broke four acres of virgin soil and spent months clearing and burning the trees and roots. The rotted leaves and underlying humus, undisturbed for centuries, made an extraordinary rich-ness, and the sun and rain were both so abundant that I had a veritable hot-house going wherever the boys cleared enough room for my planting.

Imitating my father's orderliness, I laid out long and square raised beds, with paths between, like a conventional home garden, with provision for proper protection and drainage. I followed the seasons with appropriate foods and also "staggered" certain plantings of the same foods so that we had a continuance and variety of the things we most wanted.

We had, of course, brought a quantity of American seeds. And a friend of ours in Nairobi had sent me by courier some of her best strawberry slips, carefully wrapped in burlap and con-stantly sprinkled to keep them moist.

Coming from Kansas, we liked watermelon and corn, and took plenty of these seeds from home, as well as those of old-fashioned musk-melon and several varieties of cantaloupe. Some of our watermelons grew to weigh eighty to ninety pounds each!

We also had lettuce, curly endive and tomatoes, greens, onions and cucumbers. The tomatoes and cucumbers which we couldn't eat, I canned and pickled.

We were very fond of celery, so I gave it special care and planted it near my bedroom where I could watch it at all times. I made little cardboard huts to keep out the sun and bleach it properly. It grew only to about the size of our Belgian endive, but was very white and crisp with a really choice flavor. I had to make a special donkey and camel caravan to Ret to get proper sand for this celery bed. Celery is a most difficult plant to grow, and I was proud of succeeding with it in the jungle.

Kansas sunflower seeds had been sent us by friends, and we soon had a hedge of them growing. The birds loved them and flocked about the place. Some of my father's hollyhock seeds produced beautiful giant plants in the fertile African soil. Black-eyed susans grew richly; and there were nasturtiums, cosmos, sweet peas, zinnias, marigolds (large and miniature), salvia, baby's breath, cannas, carnations and roses. Cannas grew so profusely that I constantly had to thin them out and plant them farther and farther apart. Elephants often trod them down. I even planted the canna bulbs out in the forest and there they throve, and I suppose are still thriving.

In order to have more carnations, Martin's favorite flower, I decided to transplant some of the original patch, and made outlying beds and set out the plants. The next morning I went down for a look and found all the slips carefully picked out of the soil. Bewildered, I looked about and saw a huge elephant track. He had evidently sampled my carnations and found them not too tasty, whereupon he "played" with them and left them strewn about the ground. But I wasn't going to let an elephant stump me, so I patiently replanted the carnations and to my relief he never touched them again.

With my own native flowers, I planted gorgeous orchids, colorful shrubs and decorative plants I found in the forest. These added a luxurious note to a simple American garden. It was truly a glorious spot, and I never saw too much of it. It was always in bloom, one brilliant patch of color following another.

When I was most tired, particularly after a hot safari on the dry, dusty plains, I always found relaxation and refreshment in my garden. It was my shop window of loveliness, and Nature changed it regularly that I might feast my hungry eyes upon it. Lone female that I was, this was my special world of beauty: these were my changing styles and my fashion parades. Often when we were away from home, surrounded by strange natives plastered in castor oil and red clay, I longed for the fragrance of my garden with an almost physical ache.

At night, as I walked down the narrow paths between the different beds, I seemed closer to home than at any other time. I could almost hear my father, back home in Kansas, saying approvingly:

"Good girl, Osa. You've planted your patch of beauty. Seems to me the best a body can do, besides his regular job, is to plant a little beauty in the world."

I suppose that the winds and the birds have now carried the seeds of my garden throughout the forest, and I hope the crater is abloom with the flowers on which I spent so much care, and with which we left a part of our hearts.

While we did see occasional snakes in the forest and in the garden, contrary to general opinion there are not many snakes in Africa. I have seen more in one afternoon on a Connecticut estate just outside of New York City than in an entire year in Africa. But what snakes I did see were deadly poisonous.

At night I always feared them, especially the adders. A puff adder killed my two sweet little kittens which I had brought from Nairobi and carefully reared; I found them one morning, puffed and swollen. An adder's bite means sudden death. They grow six to seven feet long and are night prowlers, and consequently I dreaded them most of all.

One of our porters, Alagi, was bitten by a puff adder. I hurriedly lanced the wound, a porter sucked it after the native fashion, and I doused it with pure permanganate of potash. The porter lived but shrank to skin and bones, and for nearly a year we had to nurse him and feed him specially, for he could keep very little food on his stomach. So I always carried a knobbed stick and was careful to watch where I trod. I never picked flowers or disturbed clusters of dense leaves without poking into them first.

My seventeen Rhode Island Reds had multiplied and had grown out of the boxes I had built for them into a full-sized chicken house. I tended them, fed them and gathered the eggs every day.

But one day I noticed that my best rooster was acting queerly. He jumped around nervously, his comb was inflamed and his feathers were falling out. I saw that some of the hens also were affected.

"Ticks," said Bukhari. "Small ticks like seeds."

So we had to burn the boxes and all the straw. The boys didn't want to do this for fear of getting ticks themselves. Then we had to dip each chicken in a delousing bath of kerosene and scrape the ticks off with a knife, and then "Flit" the hens daily for weeks.

Suddenly I began to miss my best hens, one by one, and suspected the boys of taking them. I called Bukhari, Boculy and M'pishi and asked for an explanation.

"Maybe medicine doctor has been here and put the Voodoo on your chickens," said M'pishi, rubbing his beard. "It's not me!"

Boculy rubbed his hands and looked very solemn. "Maybe God is mad with us."

But Bukhari with his more practical mind said, "Just wait for a day. I'll watch out and find the thief."

Whereupon he made a systematic and thorough search of all the boys' huts and belongings. I heard him saying to the boys, borrowing Martin's favorite threat but with no authority to execute it, "If I find any of you stealing or touching one of the little Missus' chickens, I'll fine you twenty shillings!"

But on the following day he came to me with the report that he had been out all night to watch and sure enough a leopard had got into the corral and made off with a chicken. So that was the thief! But worse was to follow.

One day I found my choicest setting hens killed and lying scattered about the stockade. On examining them, I found the fine marks of a genet cat's teeth where he had held each fowl's neck and sucked the blood.

We promptly rigged up traps, catching over a score of leopards and genets. At first I took them miles off in the forest and released them. But as the raids continued and I found that the cats were killing in numbers far more than they could eat, and apparently just for the joy of killing, I was at the end of my patience.

"Shoot the vermin," growled Blaney. "This is what I've gone through for twenty-five years on my farm!" Thereafter, I followed his advice.

The boys grew so accustomed to my chickens that they treated the birds as pets and would let them come right into their huts to roost. They would let the hens lay eggs right under their beds and when they had a turban full they would bring the eggs to me as a surprise.

"I am so happy today," a boy would come up to me and say. Then he would produce a bag of eggs and offer them to me.

"That's just fine," I would say approvingly.

"They sleep with me at night in my house," the boy would add proudly. "Don't you think it is wonderful that I let your chickens sleep in my house?"

"I am so happy," I would reply, in my best Swahili.

"Then don't you think I should have more tea and sugar?"

I would give in, with a smile. The boys were all the same. They loved their presents.

"Why do the chickens in your house lay more than those in mine?" I would ask.

"I give them wild red chili pepper," he'd answer, "and keep the hurricane lamp burning all night."

This last was a rather serious waste of precious oil for the sake of a few eggs, so I would have to send Martin and Bukhari down to investigate.

In the forest I had found an entire family of baby wild guinea fowl chicks, just hatched. I put them in the pockets of my coat and took them home to join our already generous menagerie of forest pets. I kept them from harm until they were well grown and then put them out with the chickens, and the hens took care of them as tenderly and proudly as they did their own chicks.

One day the guinea fowl disappeared and I supposed that they had returned to the wild. I had not clipped their wings, for I wanted to see what they would do when grown. I soon found out.

Next day, a great flock of guinea fowl descended upon the garden and went for the lettuce. I dared not shoot, for it suddenly flashed upon me that my pets were probably there amongst them. No doubt they had brought in their jungle friends, saying, "Come on over to our house and see what a fine place we have—corn and everything!" But after that one visit they never returned. Often I wondered, as I saw guinea fowl in the forest, if they were my pets.

Our principal bird friends were the starlings and they were a constant entertainment. They came and danced before our houses as we rose for breakfast, and we grew to love them. Their blue and purple plumage glistened in the sun as they hopped about or flew around us. They ate the insects and took scraps I threw them. Their feathers were as bright as though brilliantined. Kalowat and I used to talk to them and they would chirp merrily back and never seemed to fear us.

The "honey guide" was a little larger than our sparrow, but, with a very shrill and challenging voice, he acted like the Major General of the bird world. Very confident and commanding, he was reputed to live on honey and to be an unfailing guide to honey trees. The natives believed in him implicitly and Boculy was sure he was a true guide. I was very skeptical of all this legend and was sure the boys were jollying me, as they often did.

Chasing after one of these birds one day, Boculy and my gun-bearer and I trailed it for miles. The bird would fly on, chirping merrily, and perch on a limb until we caught up with him; then he'd go on again, like a will-o-the-wisp, and I was ready to give the whole thing up as a wild goose chase, when the boys yelled that he was "in the honey." Sure enough, he had led us directly to a tree occupied by a swarm of bees which we promptly smoked out. We found nearly nine pounds of delicious wild honey.

Now thoroughly sold on the bird's special gifts, I followed the next one I encountered, and after walking about five miles I found—a buffalo, who promptly charged me! Boculy said, "One day good, one day bad," and I felt that I was right after all.

But I questioned the boys as we plodded back to camp and Boculy came out with the bright, face-saving explanation that the bird was really just being cunning, that he was the true honey-guide, but that he was too smart to lead others to the caches that he himself loved and needed for food; that he had led us true just once to show us that he could do it, but that he was now misleading us so we would not take his precious treasure.

Finally, the settlement was finished. It had taken me a long time to see my dreams of a home come true. But here under African skies, I at last had the place I could call home. And I loved my jungle home as I have never loved any other. There were other buildings to go up, much lay ahead; but the main work of construction was done. The village was now quite picturesque, with its collection of golden thatches, green garden areas, acres of flowers and climbing vines, and spears of tall corn that gave us a touch of our Kansas landscape. Set within the stockade of palings and thornbush, our little army of black boys; the string of motor cars, lorries, carts and trucks; flocks of Rhode Island Reds; herds of donkeys, hump-backed cows and camels, made me feel very proud of what we had so far accomplished.

With the advent of fair weather we could now set about the business of making the pictures we had traveled so far to obtain.

As a celebration, we had a great barbecue of oxen which Martin had bought from the neighboring Boran natives. Late into the night the celebration lasted, the great open fires blazed to the skies, and the chant of a hundred-odd natives in camp resounded through the forest, mingling with the distant trumpeting of the elephants and the other sounds of the African night.

"Many elephants tonight," said Boculy excitedly, as he rushed up to our veranda.

The racket had begun just before we had finished dinner. From all four quarters of the compass, elephants seemed to trumpet to each other. Their notes ranged from the deep hollow tone of the old tuskers to the shrill squeaky trumpeting of the babies, answering their mothers.

They seemed to be tearing down the forest. The creaking and snapping of trees was terrifying. Sometimes the noise seemed to come directly from behind our very houses, and tonight the boys did not have to be told to keep the fires piled high with brush to warn off the elephants that seemed to be edging in about us. Only Boculy was calm.

True, the elephants were not rioting, but simply feeding in an orderly elephant fashion, making an orderly elephant noise. They liked the slender shoots at the top of young trees, and in order to bring them within reach they had to bend and break the trees. Often, in broad daylight, I have watched the animals bracing their feet carefully, testing the ground to see if it would bear their weight, and then reaching up with their trunks to grasp high branches, and slowly dragging down the succulent shoots within reach. A creak, a crack, and a snap, and the elephant had his meal.

We went out to the cliff to watch, and wished that our cameras could pierce the dark and catch this action.

"Good," said Boculy. "Tomorrow we will follow them."

10

". . . I have no scientific training in anything but photography. But my cameras have an exactitude that no human being could attain. They can record the animal story accurately. They can repeat it over and over without forgetting and varying. And I believe, too, that they can make better pictures of animals and natives who do not know that they are being watched and photographed. . . ."

—MARTIN JOHNSON

"Oh, it's good to get up in the morning,
When the sun begins to shine. . . .
At four or five or six o'clock
In the good old summer time. . . ."

MARTIN YAWNED AND stretched and rubbed his eyes, but the song came through sleepily.

Our day at Lake Paradise followed a rigid pattern. The alarm clock went off at five in the morning and we were up in a jiffy and had breakfast. Then we carried out our plans made the night before.

Every trail at Paradise led somewhere. The forest was laid out by generations of big game tramping back and forth to food and water, with main thoroughfares leading to the Lake and waterholes and out into the plains, and with side streets and avenues that came in at right angles from the deep shady places where the animals loved to doze in the heat of the day.

But the trails were so many and the forest so dense that we could easily have been lost except for Boculy's keenness and sense of direction. He was like a human compass. And when we found a trail worth following, he would mark it for us, not by blazing the

126

CHRISTMAS PRESENTS TO THE STAFF

The Johnsons' personal boys and special porters receive sugar, tea, soap and extra shillings on Christmas Day.

KANSAS WATERMELONS AT LAKE PARADISE

Two of Osa's gardeners enjoy melons grown from seeds out of her father's Kansas garden.

trees but with sticks and crotched twigs that made signposts in a system all his own.

With uncanny accuracy, he seemed to know not only which springs and waterholes the elephants frequented, but actually where elephants would be that very day and hour. When the light was right and we wanted pictures, he always took us straight to elephants.

"How did you know they would be here today? Why not at the Wistonia or Old Lady waterhole?" I would ask.

"Oh," he would reply solemnly, looking very proud and brushing imaginary dust from his blue jersey, "I talked to them yesterday."

Martin and I had learned to distinguish some of the elephants individually. A frequent visitor at one of our favorite waterholes was a big bull with one fine long tusk and one broken one. He may have lost his tusk fighting, or in using it as a lever for moving logs, or simply in poking about, digging for roots in the crannies of the rocks about the Lake. He would come down to the pool early in the morning, testing each foothold on the trail before he trusted his weight to it, and he would stay in the water most of the day.

Once we watched him for hours. He blew about and ran his trunk over the rocks as if he were searching for something. Then he sprayed water over himself and settled down for an hour's nap, during which he moved scarcely more than a statue. Then he roused himself and reached up for a branch. After munching on it, he went to sleep again, and so he alternated, sleeping and eating, until the sun sank in the west. When the rays came level through the trees, slowly, ponderously, he left the pool. Overhanging the trail was a limb bright with green leaves. It was just out of reach of his trunk, but, nothing daunted, he raised himself slowly from the ground and, standing on his hind legs, gathered it into his mouth.

Another one of my favorites was an old lady. African elephants live to be about a hundred years old. Some have been thought to live even longer, and Blaney estimated that, based on tusks he had seen, some lived to be two hundred years old.

This old lady was thin to the point of emaciation. Her skin hung in great wrinkles on her mammoth frame. She seemed almost to totter, but she still had a fighting spirit.

One day Martin stepped out on the trail leading to the waterhole to photograph her as she came out. She got a whiff of him, and made for him, trunk and ears and tail straight out. When she was within fifty yards, she stopped, puzzled. At that distance, she could see nothing, and as the breeze was on the ebb she could smell nothing. Disgusted, she turned off on a branch trail, and we saw her go as though greatly relieved.

We were as relieved as she, for we didn't want to shoot, but Martin said: "Doggone, what a picture we missed, and I had my best lens all ready for her!"

We often saw a female elephant with crossed tusks and we dubbed her our "good luck elephant." Whenever we saw Boculy standing with crossed fingers, or with one leg crossed over the other, we knew she was coming.

For several months we missed her, and then one day she appeared at her old waterhole, with a tiny baby. Boculy speculated on whether the baby would have crossed tusks and be a "good luck toto."

Another old bull had four notches in one ear which gave him a very moth-eaten appearance. Boculy said that Abyssinian poachers had undoubtedly attacked him out on the plains, but, being poor shots, had only left their trademarks on his ear.

One of our elephant visitors at the Lake had a bobbed tail, and Boculy, always quick with a story for every occasion, swore that as a baby this elephant had been caught by natives and had had his tail cut off to make an elephant hair necklace or bracelet.

Boculy went scouting with a Meru boy one day and found a

splendid herd of elephants. He told the Meru to climb a tall tree and keep the elephants in view, while he came back to get us.

We returned to the spot, a walk of four hours, and found the Meru still in the tree, but sound asleep. The elephants were gone, he had no idea where.

"You shenzi!" yelled Boculy, as he cuffed him. "You lazy savage!" The one unforgivable sin with Boculy was stupidity.

"He's surely earned that punishment," said Martin. "Eight hours of mountain climbing for nothing."

After this we had Boculy take with him one of our best porters for such expeditions.

Boculy did have his temperament and his whims and we always indulged his moods with amusement. We were trekking home one day when Martin asked him:

"How far do you think it is to camp?"

"Three hours, Master."

Some time passed and Martin again asked how far we were from home.

"Eight hours, Master," he replied solemnly.

"Now, Boculy, how can it be eight hours when it was just three hours, unless we are going away from home?"

"That is the way it is," said the rascal laconically.

"I know," Martin said to me in an aside. "He's just sore because we wouldn't go after that herd of elephants, even if it is going to rain."

Usually, the elephants at Paradise were easy subjects for Martin's camera, because they were apparently not afraid of us. Although they must have been hunted by Abyssinian poachers on the plains, here in this sanctuary they were unmolested and unafraid. Yet there was always danger and we had to be alert at all times, for when they were suddenly excited or when accompanied by young, we never knew what to expect and as often as not there would be a charge. Furthermore, as we became bolder we went nearer and nearer to the elephants, for we wanted sharp, clear pictures and in our eagerness to get them we were apt to minimize the risks.

Beginning with long-focus lenses which would bring distant objects very near, we were dissatisfied with the results because the pictures were unsteady and gave us fuzzy foregrounds. So we worked within shorter and shorter ranges until we were using six- and three-inch lenses, which necessitated our getting within a few yards of the elephants to obtain detail.

The narrowest escape Martin and I had in Africa was all over before we had time to be afraid. It occurred only a few days after we had returned to Paradise. Boculy suddenly appeared, very excited, with the news that there were seven elephants in a clearing less than a mile from our Paradise village and in a good position for photographing. That was all we needed to hear.

Martin and I took one camera and followed where Boculy led. There, sure enough, were the seven elephants, browsing. Among them was a bull with the finest tusks we had yet seen.

After making several fine shots, Martin turned to me and said, "I'll go out and get a little action, Osa; you take the camera."

He took his double-barreled .470 express rifle, and crept up until he was within seventy feet of the leading elephant. The elephant saw him and charged furiously. Martin took careful aim, as he had been instructed to do by hunters, at the vital spot just below the center of the head, and let him have a hard-nosed bullet.

The elephant halted for a second, but instead of toppling over, as we expected, made straight for Martin. After their leader came not only the six who had been feeding with him but a number of others who had been concealed in the forest. Martin stopped just long enough to fire another bullet into the leader and then turned and ran toward me and the camera.

An elephant gun is a double-barreled high-powered rifle: it is not one of today's modern repeaters. Both barrels were now empty. But as Martin ran, he managed to get another brace of cartridges out of his pocket and into the chambers of the gun. I never knew how he managed it, but he did. When again he turned to fire, the elephants were almost upon him. He fired both barrels into the leader's head. The elephant never faltered. As he bore down on Martin, towering above him, Martin reached for more cartridges, but gave it up as futile.

Through all this I stuck to the camera, and kept turning the crank. Martin and I had made a solemn pact that no matter what happened, whichever one of us was at the camera would stick to it until the last moment.

This, however, was the last moment. I let go the crank, snatched my gun and fired at the leader of the herd. He turned, barely missing Martin, went off to one side, nearly kicking over the camera as he passed, and toppled over dead. The herd that came in his wake, seeing their leader down, divided and went off, some to one side, some to the other, and disappeared into the forest.

When it was all over, my knees gave way, and I sat down shakily on a log.

Martin sat beside me. Neither of us spoke. Finally Martin wiped his brow and said:

"Osa, in that moment I wondered how it was going to feel to die. I thought my picture days were over, sure enough."

"Let's go home to Kansas, Martin. I think I've had enough elephants," I replied weakly.

But our boys had no such sentiments. They raised me to their shoulders and carried me back to the village, singing over and over: "Memsahib has killed an elephant. Memsahib has killed an elephant. Little memsahib is a big one. Little memsahib is a big one."

That night Martin sat up late. He was writing a letter. I glanced over his shoulder and read, as he typed on the ancient Remington machine. It was addressed to Mr. Pomeroy of the American Museum of Natural History in New York.

Dear Mr. Pomeroy:

Our laboratory is finished and we have moved in. We are now busy unpacking and setting up equipment. I have already set up the big movie developing tanks and they are soaking with fresh water. In a few days I will start testing cameras and developers, although I have made a few pictures. I will send you something and in a few days I will be able to be making good prints. But this letter can't wait as I must send it off to catch the monthly mail. Next month I will send you some good stuff.

I have never had a finer laboratory. The walls are high and the entire inside is covered with white canvas. The canvas in the darkroom has been painted black and I have four ruby lights at convenient places.

Now that the rains are over we are finding a wealth of good things to eat. We have found a substitute for spinach—in fact, it may be a wild spinach, and it is equally as good as that which is raised in America.

Blaney Percival is going back to Nairobi shortly. We shall miss him, for he has been an invaluable help to us.

I will write more the next time. It's no easy task we have set for ourselves. We know that. But I have been preparing myself for it for nearly twenty years. As you know, for nearly twenty years I have been going to school in the tropics, learning tropical photography, which is far different from any other kind of photography, learning how to live in the wilderness, learning how to deal with wild people and wild animals.

We shall not fail you. Mrs. Johnson is well, and joins me in sending you our very best wishes.

Sincerely,
MARTIN JOHNSON.

It was true enough; photography is an exacting science. Films of remote countries and primitive people, and wild animals, are usually little more than moving-picture books. They show a series of scenes, for the most part unrelated and assembled with an eye to pleasing some commercial producer. The titles are usually sensational, inaccurate or both. The pictures themselves are often "staged" for the camera and are no more representative of the actual lives of savage men or wild animals than they would be if they were taken on a Hollywood lot, as they often are.

But Martin wanted to make pictures of Africa that would be different and authentic. It would be the whole story of the country —its peoples and its animals, slowly unrolling against a background of magnificent scenery; wide, grassy plains dotted with sparse mimosa groves, peaceful wooded hills, rugged, barren mountain ranges, rich forests, desolate lava fields, swift rivers, broad reaches of sandy desert. It would show the natives of Africa at war, at peace, at work, at play, unconscious of the camera. And it would show the animals, not hunted and afraid, but natural and unaware, untroubled by man.

It was not an easy task. But we had never had easy tasks and were used to adversity. Ever since we were children in Kansas we had learned that our dreams all came true if we only had the courage to stick to them.

After dinner, Martin and Blaney and I would go out to the crest of the crater and seat ourselves on a ledge above the spot where the elephant trail entered the crater and led down to the water. Here the elephants had probably lumbered down to the Lake, undisturbed by man, for centuries. Martin would light his big cigar and we would sit there silently under the moon and the stars, completely enveloped by the vast and primeval solitude and enchanted by the sounds of life about us.

A leopard would cough, revealing his stealthy presence, and immediately baboons would panic in the trees and mothers, fathers, grandfathers and babies would raise a tremendous racket with their barking and terrified screaming. Hyenas uttered their mournful wails, rhinos lumbered in, snorting about and starting their nocturnal battles; buffalo bellowed as they came to the scene. There was the timid bark of the little Abyssinian bushbuck, ducks, cranes and coots cried up from the water, millions of crickets screeched and jackals called—until the chorus and its echoes throbbed through us.

Ultimately, an elephant trumpeted shrilly and others answered. We strained for sight of the approaching herd on their padded feet. Then came a sound like the swish of taffeta skirts—swish-swish, swish-swish, and the huge forms emerged below us and lumbered past, their stomachs rumbling like thunder.

Some nights there might be thirty-five, forty or fifty, and again only a half-dozen or a single pair. When there were babies along, there would be a grand time, with the little ones running under their mothers' feet, tumbling into the Lake, bogging in the mud and behaving much like any children, and being just as noisy.

Thirst made for a universal friendship. One never knew what would come into that crater. Often rhinos and elephants came in together, met and moved on to the water like a single family. Anything might come out of the forest, and everything. The parade was always lively but never twice the same, always fascinating and always full of the unexpected and the exciting. We seldom left it before midnight and often remained till the small hours— as long as the fun lasted.

One morning I burst into the laboratory.

"Martin, I'm fed up with those elephants," I cried.

"What's the matter now?"

"They've been in my garden again. And they've just made a mess of my sweet potatoes. And a rhino has rolled in my golden bantam sweet corn and ruined half the patch."

"By George, that gives me an idea," he said unsympathetically.

"We can get some wonderful pictures right in the garden of elephants changing their diet under the impact of civilization."

"Well, I'm not going to plant peanuts for them and I'm not going to have them around. I've spent a long time developing that garden and we need the fresh food. The elephants can just stay where they belong." I stormed out of the place and promptly made up my mind what to do.

That night we took our guns and flashlights and went down to a rise of ground above the garden to watch. Sure enough, in less than an hour, in came the thieves—nine elephants—moving along as unconcerned as you please, in single file, right for my garden. An old bull led them and behind him came mother and baby and nursemaids and cousins. The entire family had come to the feast.

The old fellow went to the boma, a wall of bush which we had planted to resemble growing trees, forming a thick barrier for animals. He paused and surveyed the wall, then began lifting out the trees with his trunk, one by one, and depositing them carefully in a heap at one side. The others stood behind him and patiently waited.

When he had made a wide enough opening in the wall, they all carefully moved through and headed straight for my sweet potatoes. I gripped my gun and felt like shooting them, I was so angry, but I decided I would give them a good scare instead, by shooting over their heads with my big .470.

I threw my big flashlight on them and they paid no attention whatever. They must have thought it was the moon. And then I laughed out loud. There was the old bull digging sweet potatoes with his tusks while the others gorged themselves. The mother had vines around her trunk and tusks, and the baby had them around his neck and over his back and tail. The baby seemed to think the idea was to get as many vines on himself as possible. He was not interested in any food but milk anyway. So he frisked around, getting in everybody's way and having a grand time.

"Martin, I think that's the cutest sight we've seen in Africa," I whispered. "I wish we could get the picture and take it back to show to children." I could hear every child in our audiences throughout the world saying, "Next time you go to Africa *please* bring me a baby elephant."

"All right, we'll try to get that picture tomorrow night."

Meantime, the old bull had finished his digging and there he stood, slowly pushing back the loose soil with a pendulum swing of one foot, as much as to say: "I'll cover these up and she won't know the difference. Anyway they've taken enough pictures of us; I guess we've earned a few sweet potatoes."

Around they turned, and again—in single file, with the old bull leading—they ambled out exactly as they had come. They never so much as touched another bed in the garden, carefully picking their way down my paths. Through the boma wall they went, and off onto the trail.

"Now what are you going to do about the elephants?" asked Martin, chuckling.

"Tomorrow I'm going to plant more sweet potatoes for them."

And that is exactly what I did. As he had promised, Martin set up his flashlight apparatus and three cameras, all around the sweet potato patch.

Next night we watched again. The herd came at about the same hour, but only the mother stopped. The others went on to the Lake. She entered the garden through the hole in the boma, as before, but she gave the cameras a close examination. She must have smelled the leather or the damp rubber covers, for she picked her way clear around the cameras, never touching the lead-wires, and began eating. As she left, she struck one of the wires and off went the flash. She screamed and scurried away. We quickly developed the picture and found that we had got only her rump, and even that was blurred.

Persistently, for several nights. Martin tried to record that sweet potato performance. He did manage to get several fine flashlight shots of the old lady, as she entered or left the garden and as she ate, but we never got the baby or the fine action we had seen on that first night. Soon the sweet potatoes were gone, and with all the activity in camp, the fires smouldering and the boys singing and calling, we were not surprised that the elephants began to give the garden a wide berth.

However, their hunger often got the better of their caution, or else they had by now become so accustomed to us that they felt we belonged there and knew we would do them no injury. Occasionally one or more of the elephants would meander right through the village, as calmly as though they were on their way to the circus, and the boys would scatter and regard them with frightened eyes.

On such a visit, several elephants stopped as they passed the boys' quarters and began to remove the fresh thatch and eat it greedily. Boys in the garden began to shout and other boys came tumbling pell-mell out of the houses, and in the uproar the elephants finally became annoyed and moved on down to the Lake to drink.

I was busy weeding strawberries in my garden one day when I looked up to see Martin standing above me on a ledge, grinding out motion picture film. I wondered what he saw in me to photograph, especially on such a hazy day.

"What on earth are you doing?" I shouted.

He motioned for me to be quiet and I turned around to see behind me, browsing along the edge of the garden, a family of elephants. My shout and the movement of the garden boys caused the elephants to move on down to the Lake, but they seemed not in the least alarmed. I knew that Martin would probably not get a picture in that light—that this would be a rare shot if it did work out. But I also knew that he could never resist an elephant.

Years before in Kansas, when Martin was a small boy, long before he had ever dreamed he would visit Africa, he would watch the big gray elephants, with their curious shuffling gait, waddle along the main street of Independence on circus day. They looked so wise and gentle, so patiently indifferent to what went on about them, so grotesquely out of place in civilization, that Martin wondered what they were really like in their native haunts.

Sometimes, when Martin took the chances he did in getting much too close to elephants with his cameras, I wondered if he hadn't forgotten that he wasn't in a zoo and that there wasn't anything to protect him from being crushed to a pulp, except luck and the chance that I would shoot straight if the animals charged.

We never sat down to our dinner, it seemed to me, that we were not interrupted by something happening. A boy was hurt, something had got into the corral or the garden, animals were coming or going. We lived in a constant state of excitement.

"I feel just like an old fire-horse," Martin used to say.

Boculy came rushing in one evening, rubbing his stomach and mumbling that he had found a wonderful small herd of elephants, several miles away and moving in our direction.

"Well, that's fine," said Martin wearily. "But they won't run away. You just get some sleep and call us early in the morning."

We started at dawn and after a walk of at least five miles, we came to the edge of a donga and saw four splendid elephants grazing below us. Martin set up his cameras and made some fine film while I took still shots of the herd. The elephants moved on down the donga and we followed, picking a nice sheltered spot to have our lunch.

As we sat there, we suddenly smelled smoke and heard the crackling of flames. A grass fire was creeping over the edge of the donga behind us. The grass in the donga was tall and dry, and before we could collect our cameras, it had caught and the flames were heading rapidly toward us. We saw that we were on a peninsula of land and that the fire had completely cut us off.

The fire was now so close that we could feel its scorching heat. It seemed to be shooting out in all directions and the smoke made a great cloud. The elephants were climbing a steep bank away from the flames.

"There's only one thing to do," Martin shouted. "Go down this slope and up that bank over there."

"But that's where the elephants are!"

"This is no time to worry about that. We'll have to take our chances with the elephants. We can't be roasted alive."

"Let's go!" I shouted over the crackling of the fire. It sounded like the lashing of some gigantic whip as the wind beat the flames against the dry grass. Martin slid down the slope and I followed.

Across the donga we fled and up the opposite bank. I am sure no two people ever climbed a hill faster than we did. I will never know how we escaped broken necks or at least broken cameras. When we finally reached the top, the elephants had disappeared. We left the fire to burn itself out in the damp forest and started back to camp.

We never shot anything at Lake Paradise if we could help it, except with the camera. We wanted to keep the place a sanctuary where there would be no undue disturbance or alarm. As a result, the elephants about us continued to come and go naturally and seemed to feel no fear.

During the dry season, as their food in the forest became scarce and the pools dried up, they came into the Lake Paradise crater and would trumpet all around us, especially during the night. We used our tree blinds at the Lake during this season, for elephants and rhino and whatever we could see, and secreted ourselves there with flashlight apparatus.

We were in a blind one moonlit evening, watching a lot of insulting baboons in the trees near by and wishing they would go away and leave the place to the other game, when we spied a long file of elephants coming down the trail. Fortunately the baboons moved away. The elephants came to within fifty yards of us and stopped. Whether it was the retreating baboons, whether they got our scent, or whether they were just cautious, we could not make out, but they stood there for nearly an hour, as if trying to make up their minds whether to leave the water they had come so far to obtain or to take a chance on the danger they sensed.

Such moments as these were exasperating. I wished I could say to them: "For Heaven's sake go and drink. We aren't going to do you any harm. All we want is to take back to the world a picture of how you do these things, and how happy you are out here in the wilderness."

Finally one of the herd advanced, taking short, nervous steps. When he stopped, his feet would keep on moving as though he were marking time, his trunk would feel the air and his tail would switch.

He returned to the herd, as though to report, then stood and looked toward us once more. Elephants always show a fine sense of discipline and respect for their leader; and in a herd, they are much less afraid than when alone. These animals now seemed waiting for the leader to make up his mind and give the orders, and they were ready to flee or to go quietly to the water, whichever he directed.

To the water they finally went, but the wise old general cleverly led them on a wide detour around our cameras, which he had evidently spotted. They drank and waded into the Lake, splashing around and trumpeting. They seemed to lose all the discretion they had shown on the trail. They had a grand time for over two hours while we watched through our binoculars, and seemed never to give us another thought. When they finished their fun, they left the crater just as quickly and silently as they had come.

In the dry season, when the game was plentiful at Lake Paradise, we did not have to go far for some of our very best pictures. Each night after dinner we would call Boculy and discuss with him the best spot for our work next day. Usually we took Boculy's advice, although even with his genius to guide us, and in spite of the quantities of game everywhere and our most careful plans, we often went for days and days without getting a decent picture.

Before daybreak one morning he had spotted a small herd of elephants grazing near by. He called us at five and we were off immediately after drinking our coffee and loading the boys.

We waited most of the day for the elephants to browse around to the windward of us and get into a good position for the light. Coming to a shady spot at the edge of the forest, we all sat down to rest and await our chance to go to work. Slowly the elephants moved toward us, and when they were only a short distance away Martin stealthily set up the cameras. We rose to move into a better position.

Out from behind a log in front of us slithered a huge cobra. It eyed us and lifted its great head, weaving back and forth across our path. Then it suddenly withdrew behind the log again. It lay directly in our path and blocked our way to the elephants. We looked about for a retreat, but in another moment there was the cobra again, and the show was repeated.

"I'll bet she has fifty of her poisonous little babies in there," I whispered to Martin. "Maybe a hundred. I'm getting out of here."

"M'baya sana" (very bad), said Boculy, who loathed snakes and feared them as much as I did. "Today better go home; very bad luck when you see cobra."

"Of all the confounded bad luck!" said Martin gruffly as we

started away. "A perfect picture and we can't get to it for a damnable snake!"

After supper Martin and I strolled from camp into the forest. A young moon was rising over Lone Tree Mountain, and every star in the heavens seemed to be shining almost within reach.

We walked back slowly under the starry canopy, without speaking. We were still thinking about the elephants and the snake.

As we reached our house a large mongoose bounded off the veranda, trailing his bushy snow-white tail.

"I hope he gets that cobra," I said.

Whenever we were out on the plains trailing elephants and came to high rock kopjes, we would stop to scout. We would take off our shoes, and Martin would climb one prominence and I another. In the rocks there was danger of snakes and it would have been just too bad if a puff-adder or cobra had struck, but our boots were too slippery and cumbersome to wear, and so we took the chance.

With binoculars we would search the countryside for game. Immediately we spotted a satisfactory herd or piece of action we wanted, we would make for it, bearing down to the leeward to avoid the elephants' detecting us.

On one of these forays, I climbed over a rock and there was a huge bull elephant just below me. He saw me at once and went into a rage. He charged, and unable to get up to me, became more furious. He trumpeted and screamed and I clambered about while Martin caught the action in the camera. When the bull subsided, I slid down toward him and when he charged I scurried up again. Martin was convulsed with laughter—he said I looked exactly like a baboon—but he was elated over the rare elephant show he was getting.

The bull found a puddle of water, rushed into it, flung it over himself, then took up in his trunk a draft of water and spouted a huge spray in my direction.

THE JOHNSON GARDEN AT PARADISE

Green onions, cabbage, green beans, radishes, lettuce beds, have come up on the left, and on the right are sweet potatoes and corn. In the foreground, the stockade of jungle bushes; in the background, the completed servants' quarters.

FASHIONING A HOME OUT OF THE FOREST

From logs and vines and thatch, the Johnsons build one of their first houses, a model for all the others at Lake Paradise.

ROOFING A JUNGLE HOUSE

Carpenters and porters putting thatch on one of the buildings at Lake Paradise.

OSA'S BEDROOM OVERLOOKING LAKE PARADISE

Flowers and vegetables and garden paths take their places beside the century-old elephant trails on the rim of the Paradise crater.

LIVING-ROOM INTERIOR AT LAKE PARADISE
All the furnishings made by Osa and the carpenters.

HOME-MADE BRICKS FOR THE JOHNSON FIREPLACES
From clays they found in the forest, they made their own firebricks.

This got to be quite a game, and since I knew Martin had enough film footage, I began playing with the ferocious big fellow. When he waggled his ears, I put up my hands and imitated him; when he screamed, I screamed; when he stomped, I stomped and danced about. He seemed to say, "Oh, if I could only get hold of her, what mincemeat I'd make of her," and "Who's Africa is this, anyway?"

I threw my shoe at him; it seemed grotesquely small beside his huge bulk as it flew. He saw it, picked it up in his trunk and gave it a great heave in the opposite direction, and then stood waiting for more. Martin said he thought I'd have that old elephant retrieving if I could just stay there long enough.

Boculy and I were making one of our rounds of the Lake Paradise waterholes one day when we started across a donga and spied a great bull elephant lying down under a tree, apparently fast asleep. It came to me that I had never seen an elephant lying down and I asked Boculy:

"Did you ever see an elephant lying down before?"

"Yes, memsahib, but always dead."

"But this one is not dead. He is sleeping."

"Yes, memsahib, but he is on his way now."

"You mean he is dying?"

"Ndiyo" (yes), he grunted as he peered at the old fellow.

I intended to find out, so I screamed. The elephant rose as though shot, staggered for a moment, and slumped down again. His ribs were showing and he seemed very nearly done in. One tusk was broken and the other was too worn to be of much use.

"Wasai sana" (very, very old), mused Boculy.

If I were like that, I would want somebody to put me out of my misery, I thought. Then, on an impulse, I raised my gun and fired. The old fellow sagged and lay quiet, as though ever so much relieved.

I had a queer feeling in my throat as I motioned to Boculy to follow me back to camp. I wondered how long that patriarch had gone up and down these trails from his feeding grounds to the water and from the forest out to the plains.

"Boculy, how long does an elephant live?" I asked.

"Many years," he replied.

"Yes, I know. Many years. But how many years is—many years?"

He grinned. "Many, many years, memsahib."

I became exasperated. "Don't you know?"

"Longer than you will live," Boculy said slowly, as he switched the fly swatter that he always carried.

"Sixty years?"

"Longer than I will live and my father and my father's father, and his father's father," was his reply.

He may not have been so wrong. Elephants do not mature until they are twenty-five years old. Left to themselves, they are thought to live at least one hundred years and it has been said that they live twice that long. They often look as wrinkled and as old as Methuselah.

"Boculy," I asked, "is there an elephant graveyard?"

He waved his hand and looked as though he wanted to say, "Are you crazy?"

The belief that there is an "elephant graveyard" to which aged elephants totter to die is, of course, mere legend. That elephant bones are rarely found is no proof of the point, for with thousands of leopards, lions and hyenas watching for meat, and with vultures and other scavengers always waiting for something to die, any carcass disappears in a matter of hours, and the bones are dragged away into the brush for further feasting.

But we have seen plenty of elephant skulls and bones in elephant country. Many of these were partly buried in drifting sand, which is probably the true "graveyard" of the elephant.

11

". . . *Osa furnished the camp with game and fish. It was strange, her talent for these arts, for she came from an inland and rather dry country. But all her ancestors were quick with rod and rifle: she always came in smiling and happy with her catch. . . .*"

—Martin Johnson

"Martin, do you know I haven't had any fishing for months and months?" I spoke apologetically, for I knew how important time was to us. "Couldn't I go down to the Eauso Nyiro by myself for a few days?"

"Why, I suppose so," he said thoughtfully. I knew he was simply trying to be kind to me while he thought up some excuse.

Presently his face brightened and he added: "I'll tell you what! You have some real trout fishing. We'll go down to Mount Kenya. We'll take one car and a driver and he can go on to Nairobi, pick up some of the things we need badly, and see how those extra tanks are coming along. We'll have a business and pleasure trip in one."

"You're the sweetest man that ever lived!" I cried as I threw my arms around him.

"And I think I'll fire those worthless Merus," he went on, undaunted, "and see if I can't find some boys down country."

We had been lax with some of the boys and they had taken advantage of our good nature. There was nothing to do but let them go, and replace them with others. Some had been just too lazy; others, who had seemed husky enough at first, had been unable to take the punishment of the weather and the work. Some were just sullen and complaining all the time.

"After this trip," Martin said, "I think I'll have a Boer trek wagon come up occasionally with flour, sugar, film, camera supplies and posho for the boys. We can't depend on occasional patrols and runners to bring what we need."

He was checking over our stores. "And we've got to get canvas covers made for our houses to catch the rain water," he went on. "I must buy more blankets for the boys before the rains come. Besides, we need a hundred small articles that we forgot the first time."

"More needles and thread for one thing," I said quickly. "What a silly thing to forget!"

Martin had discharged the forty-four Meru porters a few days before we left the Lake and sent them ahead to repair several bad places along the trail. When we caught up with them, some fifty miles from the Lake, the work was done, and Martin paid them off.

We made our first stop at Lasamis waterhole. We had made the run in record time. The sand of the Kaisoot Desert was fine and packed hard after the rains.

Immediately upon arriving at Lasamis, we set to building a thorn boma so that we could take flashlights. The waterholes showed more rhino wallows than we had ever before seen.

Martin shot an oryx and set it for bait. At eight o'clock the flash went off, and we rushed to it. There were no tracks, so we had no idea what kind of animal had set it off, but we guessed that it was a bat or bird.

No sooner had we gone to bed than a rhino came stumbling into camp, snorted and pawed the sand for a few minutes, then went away. All through the night we could hear rhino snorting at the waterhole. Then the eerie melody of night sounds re-echoed with the roars of lions. Hyenas started a ghoulish laughing that continued until sunrise.

At the first streak of light I heard the sand grouse calling. I got up and dressed, and with a boy started out after them. Martin was still sleeping.

I went by the oryx kill, and found that it had been dragged off. I saw the tracks, and I began to follow the drag. Suddenly, I came upon a beautiful big black-maned lion. The handsome old fellow was in the dry, sandy river-bed, washing himself. He would lick his paws like an innocent kitten, lie down and roll over in the sand. I was within fifteen yards of him, as I watched from behind a boulder.

"Go back and get Mr. Johnson," I ordered the boy. He slunk away and I kept my vigil behind the rock.

I thought of the black-maned beauty we had seen and missed before, and prayed that this time Martin could get his picture, for I knew what it meant to him.

It seemed an eternity until Martin arrived, with guns and cameras.

"Where is it?" he whispered.

"Right over there. At least, he was a minute ago."

The lion had gone beneath a small thornbush. Martin hurriedly set up his camera, and in a few seconds would have been ready to turn the crank, but the lion bounded out of the bush, into the river-bed, up the bank on our side, and was off across the desert. We could see him go like a streak of lightning for half a mile as he disappeared into the blue of the horizon.

"Anyway, he was the handsomest fellow I've ever seen," Martin remarked philosophically, as he put his camera back into its case. "He was even handsomer than your other black-maned friend, Osa."

Just as we started away there was a roar in the bushes. A lioness appeared, lashed her tail, growled at us, and for a minute or so looked as if she might charge. I covered her with my gun, Martin set up his camera again, but before he could turn the crank she retreated. We followed her for more than an hour as she leaped from rock to rock, finally going off across the desert as her mate had done.

The next day we had a rocky trail all the way to Merille. We reached the waterhole just before dark and, dead-tired, we pitched camp for the night. We had been stuck several times in sand lug- gars, although these experiences were nothing to what they had been on our trip up to Paradise. Martin had provided himself with long rope ladders of native rope, which we laid on the ground over the sand, and these worked like a charm.

After several days we arrived at Nanyuki and sent our boy on to Nairobi with notes to the shops, and I settled down to fishing in earnest while Martin went about employing fifty new boys to take the places of the discharged Merus. That morning Martin drove me upstream into the pines and cedars. I planned to fish the stream back to camp.

The river was stocked with the ova of brown and rainbow trout brought out from England; and although he had not said so, I knew that it was Blaney Percival who had managed this fine work, for the pleasure of those of us who loved fishing.

It was a major achievement on the part of the government to import the ova from London, at terrific expense and "shrinkage," and send them in tins on the backs of porters over this vast area and up to altitudes of 11,000 and 12,000 feet to deposit the eggs in the streams. But the "dividends" have been millions of splen- did fish and great pleasure for the settlers and the visitors from abroad.

The trout love gay-colored flies, for the insects of Africa are brilliant-hued. Most of the flies we use at home for salmon can be used in Africa for trout: the Darum Ranger, Silver Doctor, Jock Scott, Alexandra, all gave me great fishing and I took my poundage records on number six hooks with a $3\frac{1}{2}$ ounce Hardy rod.

The streams are crystal clear and cold, most of them tumbling down from high altitudes, the Mount Kenya streams coming directly from glaciers at the top. So I dyed my leaders green to make them invisible.

Because rainbow trout are cannibals and because the streams are so heavily stocked, the authorities encourage one to make large catches. I have caught fifteen from a single pool in one day and have gone back the next day and taken as many from the same pool.

The streams are gloriously beautiful—the surrounding forest alive with sound and movement, the towering cedars festooned with creepers and Spanish moss, the vines flowering into whites and pinks and blues, orchids clinging to the branches, the sun and shadows making lively patterns on the stream, the birds calling and flashing color. Beneath giant fern trees grow all the ferns known to us at home, as well as many others. Vines make fantastic patterns, and I used to swing in them as I did when I was a little girl, and often found them useful to carry me across a stream in a tough spot.

Gorgeous colobus monkeys swung about in the trees, uttering their weird, low cries. They were among the most beautiful creatures of the jungle, with their long black and white brilliantined fur.

Blue kingfishers with red beaks flashed through the sunlight and dived hungrily for little trout; black hornbill sounded their "anvils," and magnificently colored butterflies literally filled the air about me.

There in the water, beneath the dipping leafy branch of a great tree, I would glimpse a trout, lazily loafing, his nose upstream, sometimes with others about him. One whip cast, dropping the fly under his nose, and the trout was mine. I would bundle him into my creel and hear Martin say, in my mind's ear, "Boy, oh boy, are we going to have a grand breakfast! I'm ready for it now!" or, "Don't wait to make yourself look pretty this morning. Let's have the trout you caught under that big tree!" And the walk home would seem much shorter.

So well stocked is this river that on it I have caught as many as sixty pounds of brown trout in a single morning, each weighing from a pound and a half to six pounds. Sometimes, on drop flies, I have taken as many as three trout on a single cast, and I once took a total of one hundred and forty-eight trout in one day. Occasionally, I would pick out one of the huge old cannibals of eight to ten pounds.

Within one hundred and twenty-seven miles of Nairobi, in an arc to the north, and similarly to the south, there are dozens of streams which any critical fisherman would call ideal, and all are amply stocked. Among them are the Ambonia, Naro Moru, Thika, Chania, Gura, Nanyuki, Liki, Cherangani and others with equally poetic names in the Aberdare Mountains, on the Mau Escarpment, and on the slopes of the glorious Mount Kenya.

Much as he loved trout to eat, Martin never had time to practise fly casting, and whenever he went with me, he used to be disgusted with my large catches and his bad luck.

One day, I caught him on hands and knees chasing grasshoppers. "I'll never catch a fish with one of those blamed things of yours. I'm going to get some real bait the fish understand."

I took his rod and, just to tease him, said that he didn't hold his mouth right. I cast twice and, on the second, landed a trout. He was speechless and, though I knew it was only a piece of luck, he always told that story when boasting about my fishing.

Here at Nanyuki I had caught a record rainbow, weighing thirteen and three-quarter pounds. This was my favorite fishing spot, if one can have a favorite among so many.

Just as I was taking in a six-pound rainbow, I heard a grunt and swung around to see standing above me on the bank a very disheveled-looking native in shabby blanket, with his earlobes hanging down. He slid down and walked out to me in the stream and I stiffened to defend myself. With a great show of authority, he said, "Where is your kapandi?" Fortunately, I had my license and displayed it. He took it, although I was sure he could not read anything but the big red seal. He looked at me searchingly and back at the license, saluted and tore off up the bank and away. I had met my first native "Game Warden." He also asked me, before he rushed away, if I had grasshoppers in my pocket. I assured him I did not. Natural bait is prohibited by law, but I always fish with flies, for it is more sporting and more fun.

As I moved on up the stream, I startled a beautiful little bush-buck, his red coat and white polka dots reflected in the pool. He lifted his spiralled horns, eyed me a moment, nodded his head just as though saying, "How do you do?" Then he cleared the bank in a single spring, his fluffy white tail straight out behind him, and disappeared, barking and making an astonishing noise in the underbrush for so small an animal.

A huge porcupine shuffled out of my path and stood bristling at me before he fled. He would have weighed ninety pounds, twice as much as our American variety, and how the boys would have loved those quills for ornaments in their hair and ears, and to help them get jiggers out from under their toenails!

Elephants had trampled the bamboos and pushed over the trees, making a clear path to water for their totos. I was grateful for the paths they gave me and also for clearing the undergrowth for my casting.

I had left orders for the cook to meet us in a clearing and bring along a frying pan, coffee pot, two pounds of fresh butter, bread, potatoes, and a tin of good fruit. There he was, with a fine fire and a heap of coals all ready, and when the others came up, my trout were in the pan.

We sat there, in the cool crisp evening, over one of the best

dinners I have ever had, watching the sun set on the frosty pinnacles of Mount Kenya.

"Next to Paradise, the most beautiful spot in the world," said
Martin.

The following morning we were off at daybreak, but we got
caught in a drenching downpour and had to stop to cover the
things more securely with the canvases. The rain didn't last very
long, but it did its damage in the brief time. As we left the foot-
hills of Mount Kenya, the three cars got mired and we had to push
each other out of sticky mud holes all that day.

We got some good shots on the way to Nanyuki to add to Martin's already-completed several thousand feet of film showing
the dances, customs and domestic life of the natives. It was Martin's objective to record in film not only the animals but all the
manners and customs of the people of this part of the world.

One little wizened Meru chief brought in his fifteen wives to
introduce to me. Each carried a bunch of bananas and each in
turn handed her present to me, after which she stepped back and
put her arms about her neighbor as coyly as a school girl starting
a dance. I gave each a handful of sugar, after which she bowed
with great natural dignity and said good-bye.

These women are very faithful, like slaves, and must wait on
their husband's every need and whim. I have never seen a husband unkind to a wife, but the man expects obedience and gets
it, and he always respects the wife. He is as respectful to the
oldest woman among his wives as to the youngest girl.

Among themselves the women are not cattish, and never seem
to fight. They always seem to be amiable. The old "bring up" the
young wives and the latter respect their elders. The young listen
patiently while the old chatter on and give the orders. The oldest
may or may not be the "boss" of the wives. I have seen two or
three apparently in authority and have concluded that it is the

most aggressive and able who take command, with the husband's consent.

In most of the tribes a man may have as many wives as he can afford, and cares to have around. He is not as concerned about their looks as their being hale and strong, for each must help with the heavy work—planting the gardens, building the houses, carrying the firewood, caring for the children, and cooking. Women are *useful* chattels.

The more children a wife has, the more valuable she is. She is even more valuable if she can produce sons, who can become warriors and add to the family wealth and prestige. One never hears natives speak of daughters, but they are always boasting of their sons.

A baby is adored by all the wives. They have all gone through it and all help the mother. They also know the husband will be proud, and each acts as though each baby were her own, showing the same tenderness and pride in it.

There are no sissies among these women. They give birth wherever they are and without complaint. The older women attend them with utter tenderness. The mother-to-be may go on with her work in the fields, or herding, until the last minute and have only the hot sand or a bit of forest for a bed. No hospitals, doctors, twilight sleep, fuss and feathers. The children are strong and healthy, the mother does not know what she is missing of civilization, and she is up almost at once and at her work again. The women have every confidence in themselves and in nature.

In the same way—and because they have been taught to be obedient and willing—they will run for the heaviest load of dung or wood or meal and almost fight over it, for they know that by being "number one" in strength and ambition they will be first in the husband's good graces.

"That's too big a load for you," a young girl will say to an older wife. "Don't you want me to carry it?"

"Ah yah! Hapana" (Of course not), the elder will exclaim. "What do you think I am? Why, this is only a load for my little finger."

And so one sees a man walking along, carrying a swagger stick and nothing else, while the wife trails behind him carrying two hundred pounds of sweet potatoes for the market.

Men pay for wives in hump-backed cattle, goats, camels and fat-tailed sheep. And the men grow very rich. I have seen thousands of camels in one herd. Some herds are worth approximately $50,000.

Fatness is at a premium among some native tribes, and Martin was always amused watching them waddle about, wrapped around in yards of calico to make themselves look even fatter.

"Great of heart, great of mind, but the greatest part sticks out behind," I chanted one day, and Martin was convulsed.

The women's eyes were very sore, for the most part, injured by their hut fires. They build their cook fires inside the mud huts. These have no windows and only a low door, so low that one has to stoop to enter, and with only a small vent at the top. The smoke passes out through the vent in a tiny jet and meantime fills the small room. How they endure this air, I could never understand. Yet they always seem cheerful and they always smile, despite their many burdens and their woes.

The next day Martin spent nearly all the time taking native pictures, and it wasn't until late afternoon that we made for Isiolo. We had fine roads and made the thirty miles in an hour and a half, with a noticeable drop in altitude nearly every mile.

We were away again at daybreak. At the Eauso Nyiro River we lost three hours in getting across, and it would probably have been longer had not a party of Turkana natives who were camping there helped us out. They waded into the water up to their shoulders and literally shoved us to the other bank. The carburetors were full of water, but after a lot of tinkering we repaired them and camped for the night.

Eager as we were to get on, I couldn't pass up this last chance at fishing, especially in the Eauso Nyiro, the best river in British East for coarse fish.

Walking downstream I came upon a beautiful field of deep yellow snapdragons, growing on little bushes not quite knee-high. There seemed acres and acres of them, and I had a sense of walk-ing through a sea of gold. Not only did I take back my string of fish that day, but I had armfuls of snapdragons.

I knew Martin would grumble, of course, and remind me that these posies with which I planned to overload his cars would be wilted and gone by morning. But that did not prevent my planning to decorate our campfire dinner table that evening with beautiful golden snapdragons. With a fish chowder (if I caught the fish) and the guinea hen M'pishi was barbecuing and flowers on the table, this would be quite a formal meal.

My first catch, however, was not a fish. Having no sinker with me, I took a bolt and two nuts from one of the motor cars and tied them on my line. The stream was deep and swift and I needed weight to clear some reeds beneath my feet. Giving the sinkers a good whirl over my head, I threw them in. There was a terrific grunt as a huge form rose out of the water beneath me. I had hit a hippo clean on the head. He let out a roar, and, thinking he would attack, I beat it up the bank. There I paused to watch the "submarine" swim off, leaving a great wake behind him—while my boys howled at the good joke.

But the most exciting adventure is to be intent on landing a fine large fish after a good fight—to be so intent as to notice nothing about you—then suddenly to look up and find a rhino or buffalo bearing down on you. The boys would yell and there was nothing to do but shoot one's way out or scramble up a tree. I often wondered afterward how I ever managed to get up some of those trees, but under the pressure of saving one's neck wonders can be done.

Down to the Eauso Nyiro in the late afternoon to slake their thirst also came all the dainty and decorative gazelles and antelope and other plains game, and fishing here was a never-ending succession of surprises in beauty and excitement. I went off to every fishing experience knowing that I would return with something new and dramatic to write down in my memory.

Returning at night, I noted how little twilight there was. The moment the sun dropped over the horizon, a heavy curtain seemed to fall and night was there.

Everything would assume grotesque and monstrous shapes and I felt like Alice in a real Wonderland of elves. Every movement might be a hostile animal and, especially alarmed at this time, he might charge without further provocation. So I exchanged my rod for a rifle and kept my gunbearer close with a "spare" for every emergency. Despite Martin's concern for me, I felt that I was not foolhardy, however, for I knew the forest, and then—what fisherman can resist the last cast at evening when the fish are leaping and feeding on every hand?

We made excellent time after we crossed the Eauso Nyiro, and after several days of picture-taking along the way, reached our village at Paradise at eleven o'clock at night.

Even as late as it was, I rushed down to see how my garden grew. To my utter dismay, everything was ripe and rotten. Everything, that is, except the watermelons. The garden was full of them.

"Aren't you glad your father gave us those Kansas watermelon seeds?" I asked.

"What do you think?" Martin laughed. And we sat down in the middle of the patch and ate a melon in the light of the moon.

We walked along to our little bungalow, planning how quickly we could get off to a week of photographing game and a tour out-side the forest to get native pictures of the Boran whom Boculy reported to be near by. The moonlight steeped the place in silver.

The houses were all ship-shape, as though we had left only the day before, and we were delighted with the boys for having re-membered so faithfully what they were supposed to do. Martin lined up all the personal boys and gave them each a generous "bashishi."

12

". . . At Lake Paradise we expect to
get pictures of elephants such as
have never before been taken. We
will get pictures of rhino and hippo
and crocodile, as well as of strange,
remote native tribes. . . . Plant life,
insect life, reptile life, bird life,
animal life, native life—all will go
to the making of the story of Africa."
—MARTIN JOHNSON

SINCE THE TRIP from which we had just returned was primarily a
holiday, we now prepared for a camera safari. Boculy, of course,
was beside himself, for the monotony of camp always got on his
nerves. He began to select the twenty porters who would accompany us, and I had him prepare ample posho loads.

Natives aren't in the least particular about what they eat. But
we always saw to it that our boys had plenty. That is one of the
foremost secrets of keeping a safari crew happy and industrious.

On such trips I always asked Boculy to pick porters with good
dispositions as well as good backs. I can't stand grouches, and we
had troubles enough without having quarrelsome porters to be
watched and disciplined all the time. Out of the hundred-odd
natives we had at Paradise, we chose the most cheerful to go on
these safaris. And since the trips were lots of fun and a relief
from routine for the boys, they fought for the chance to go with us.

Early in the morning we set out. Boculy had called us at five
o'clock. All through the forest we expected to find elephants but
we saw none, and we went on to the Sunga waterhole to camp for
the night. As we made camp, a half-mile from the waterhole, with
the plains before us and the forest behind us, we were startled

MARTIN MAKES FILM TESTS ON SAFARI

With water cooling in chargoles, he mixes developer and makes
the best of the few supplies he could carry into the field.

MARTIN JOHNSON OUTSIDE HIS LABORATORY

Checking motion picture negative, just developed, after a camera safari.

INTERIOR OF MARTIN'S LABORATORY

All made by native carpenters from Paradise forest hardwood.

by an army of baboons. They had just settled down for the night when suddenly they spied us and started an uproar in the tree-tops. It rained baboons. They came down the trees all about us, sliding, slipping and jumping. Sometimes six or seven would pile up on top of one another. Baby baboons screamed in the tops of the trees, and their mothers would scamper up, carry them down like firemen rescuing people from a burning building. It was an amusing sight.

Next morning Boculy called us, and we opened our eyes to see ten elephants walking along about four hundred yards away. Two were so young that they couldn't have been more than three or four days old; two were about six months old. The others were full-grown cows. We immediately set up cameras, even though it was too early in the day for the light to be right for photography.

The elephants walked to the top of a small hill and stood there, silhouetted against the sky, as the sun came up. I remember how huge they looked in that light, twice as large as they actually were. It was a picture Martin had dreamed of, and turned out to be one of his best.

Presently the elephants began to amble away. "They're going to sleep in the forest," Martin concluded. "I might as well put away the cameras."

Just as he was returning the cameras to their leather cases, there was a thundering noise on the other side of the trail, which announced more elephants. We could see them, deep in the bush, but they, too, were settling down for sleep in the forest and it would be impossible for us to photograph them. Martin gave it up as a bad job.

"But the elephants are there!" said Boculy, showing his disgust.

Poor Boculy! He could never understand why we needed light to make pictures.

After watching for more than an hour, Martin—to my relief—decided to move on. The place was so dense and the going so rough that if the elephants had decided to make for us, we could never have escaped them. There wasn't a clearing for several miles. Even with Boculy guiding us through the forest, I always felt nervous and found myself wondering what we would do if the elephants charged.

Boculy was all that Blaney had represented. He was the best guide we ever had, and he fully deserved his title, "Little Half Brother of the Elephants." He could tell their size and speed and the direction of their travel by a crushed leaf or a broken branch. A few tracks would reveal to him the number in the herd.

There was quite a mystery about his birth: he said he was born near Mount Kilimanjaro, though rumor had his birthplace in the Northern Frontier. His tribal characteristics were not marked, but probably he was a Warusha. The boys all regarded him with awe.

He seemed to have no family—at least he never talked about one. When I asked about his wife he would say "Hapana" (none), and that closed the matter.

His broken jaw made him hard to understand, but there was no misunderstanding his doggedness. Often on the trail he would say, "Just a little further," then go on for three hours, until I'd say, "Nonsense, you don't see any elephants. I won't go another step!" Otherwise I am sure he would have gone on all night. He was a true nomad, and though he was only skin and bones he could be on the move all day without apparent fatigue.

He carried a light rifle that the British Government permitted him as a special honor, and he always had it with him but never used it. We had promised the British we wouldn't let him shoot.

Boculy knew the languages of all the plains and desert tribes, and he surpassed their chiefs far and away when it came to intelligence. By a sort of freemasonry, he could secure aid from them whenever we needed it. A mere look from him or a wave of his hand would drive away whole tribes from waterholes when we wanted to take possession and make pictures. What gave him this authority, we never knew.

"I think he's just a big bluff," Blaney had said. "But he gets away with it, and these people down on the plains treat him as though he owned the country. Perhaps it's that askari sweater and gun he wears. At any rate, he's no fake when it comes to elephants."

One day I asked him: "Boculy, how long have you tracked elephants?"

His face lighted in one of his wide, friendly grins; even his eyes and the deep wrinkles about them seemed to laugh. Deprecatingly, he waved his hand before his face, and looked far off as if searching for a very distant memory.

"My father," he finally said, "lived with the elephants."

I recalled that Blaney had told us that Boculy's father was one of the smartest ivory poachers he had ever known.

Boculy had no doubt "lived with elephants" since he was old enough to walk. His skill, therefore, was not so difficult to understand. The tens of thousands of footprints he had followed, his long, hard experience, explained his particular genius.

To Boculy, chewed bark meant rhino, a branch torn from a tree meant elephant, while an untorn limb picked clean of buds and leaves meant that giraffe had browsed there. Trampled grass would show him not only from the shape of the footprint what animal had left the mark, but how recently, for the blades would spring upright again in a certain number of hours and the angle of their incline would therefore tell the time clearly.

Rhino left three-toed imprints; the hippo four. The elephant, which also has four toes, left a larger footprint and scuffed a little as he walked. Boculy also insisted that a female elephant left a somewhat oval footprint, while the male left a circular one. Likewise, the spoor varied with the kind of game and helped him tell whether elephants had been there a half-hour or a half-day before.

He would pick up a piece of mud to feel the moisture, or bits of twigs and branches. These he would study intently for a few minutes, mumbling to himself and looking all about him, then he would either shake his head to indicate that it was no use, or go off like a hunting dog on some "scent" we could seldom detect. He was almost never wrong.

Boculy thought that all our building at Lake Paradise was just a waste of time and money. If we wanted animals why didn't we go on safari and stay on safari? He was always impatient to be going somewhere, and when we weren't in motion he was almost sure to be, even if it was only to go scouting around camp for hours at a time.

If we told him that we must settle down for an interval at home to catch up on our work, he often asked if he might go away on a little trip of his own. But his destination he always concealed by saying he didn't know where he was going, and he never gave us the slightest intimation of what he was up to. We were never sure that he was not off on a poaching trip, either to get ivory himself or to buy it from Wanderobos or Abyssinians, and Martin felt very worried about this, for we had pledged ourselves to Blaney and the government officials to keep him under control.

"Don't you want to take a blanket and some food?" Martin asked Boculy on one of these occasions. He never was seen to take anything but that gun and the clothes on his back.

"Hapana" (No), he replied, with a faraway look.

Then he would be gone and we would neither see nor hear of him for days. If he actually covered some of the areas he later told us he did, there would not be water for fifty miles between waterholes, but he would come back looking as fresh as a daisy, and as though he had never been away.

"What do you eat when you are away?" I asked him.

"Same as the elephants," he said, and though I couldn't imagine him climbing trees and chewing leaves, I somehow believed him.

The boys spun great "whoppers" around their campfires, and Boculy was the best of them all at this. He often recounted the story of how he broke his face, and it always held new and glorious aspects. The boys loved to hear him talk.

He told many stories about giant and freak elephants and heroic deeds, usually of himself or his hunting masters. He told "Paul Bunyan" stories about a "Rajah Elephant" of extreme cunning and intelligence and power. But we never heard him blow up a native character to Bunyan proportions.

He never showed any ill will toward the British for their punishment. He either felt he deserved it or he regarded them with awe. He even seemed proud of the British and showed a certain fellowship with them, and they respected his peculiar genius.

Apart from his knowledge of elephants, he knew all the wild berries, the best grass for thatching, the logs most solid for building houses, the wild vegetables and mushrooms, and poisonous shrubs for the camels to avoid; he would warn me against flowers and herbs (some were used for poisoning arrows), and would eat things first to prove to me that they were safe to eat.

Always he was very thoughtful. When we were on safari, he would know how glad I was to have something fresh to eat and he would have the boys gather fruit. "Give the ripest ones to the Little Missus," he would say. I was very fond of wild plums and apricots because their tartness relieved my thirst. And there were delicious red berries with large pits which had little juice but plenty of sugar, and I sucked them like candy. Also, there was a kind of large blueberry that grew on a shrub four or five feet high. The thorns were like little fish-hooks, and picking the berries was sticky business. But I never got enough of them. The figs were wormy, though the monkeys and baboons stuffed on them.

We found a shrub-like wild sage, the small leaves of which smelled like mint. Boculy said "Chai" (tea), so we dried it and sure enough it made delicious tea. I often chewed its raw leaves.

At springs we found a vine with small leaves something like a four-leaf clover or sorrel: this tasted like a delicious spinach when cooked.

Then there were wild onions—strong as garlic—which were excellent for condiments, and the boys loved them stewed with their meats.

There were no wild nuts, except the dom-palm nuts. These were fibrous, about the size of a mango, with the same-sized pit, and sweet like sugar-cane. The boys would suck on them and chew the pulp for moisture when they were very thirsty. And the elephants were very fond of them.

Bukhari, our gunbearer, was Boculy's opposite in almost every way. His face was strong and his powerful frame seemed big enough to fight anything. The combination gave him an appearance of absolute fearlessness. He had none of Boculy's nimbleness and cunning, but we always felt just as sure of him and it gave us a great sense of confidence just to have him around.

He made no pretense of being a guide, but, although he always deferred to Boculy's judgment, he knew a great deal about tracking game.

Bukhari was an ardent Mohammedan. Every morning at sunrise, wherever we were, I would see him kneeling in prayer with his face toward Mecca. Again at sunset he would say his prayers and make his salaams.

"God always listens to our prayers; we will have good luck today," he would say with a broad smile when I complimented him on his faithfulness.

He would eat no meat unless it had been "hallalled," that is, had had its throat cut with a knife before it died. This was something of a problem. Whenever I shot game "for the pot," I had to remember to have one of the porters rush out and perform this ritual promptly, otherwise Bukhari and the other Mohammedan boys would not have touched it. Furthermore, the porter who cut the animal's throat also had to be a Mohammedan.

Bukhari was as neat and meticulous as Boculy was careless. His clothes were always spotless, and if they were torn he mended them promptly. His tent, his bedding and belongings were always a picture of good order. Whenever we were on safari and came to a stream, he was always down there at the first opportunity to wash his clothes.

The boys respected him and one booming word from Bukhari was always as good as an order from us.

For night pictures we set up flashlight equipment in the forest at Lake Paradise, and one evening we arranged for Bukhari to take the cameras and stay with Martin at the waterhole while I posted myself with Boculy a few yards away on a rocky ledge, to watch and give Martin our usual signals.

Presently a rhino came sniffing down the trail. I gave Martin a low signal that there was one animal and we waited tensely. The rhino shuffled along to the water and tripped the guide wire. There was a terrific flash, followed by a great commotion at the water.

I strained my eyes and saw the dazed rhino going round and round in circles. And in front of him was Martin, holding his gun straight out and also staggering around in circles. He was evidently blinded by the flash. I screamed and the rhino stumbled off, fortunately without harming Martin.

"I couldn't see a thing," Martin explained when we reached him. "My eyes were open when that darned flash went off. But the moment I felt his hide I was going to give him both barrels."

While Martin and Boculy went scouting for elephants one morning I decided to go after meat for camp. I took Bukhari and four other boys with me. We trekked all day with no luck and started back for camp at sundown. To make better time, Bukhari took a short-cut that he was sure would bring us home quickly.

"You are just like a gazelle," he said to me as he puffed up the mountainside. "Never tired."

I was young and thin and hard as nails, and it never occurred to me to think of the rough going. I thoroughly enjoyed it.

We walked for miles, and while our direction seemed to be good, we saw no familiar signs. Finally Bukhari admitted that he was lost. The other boys were even more helpless.

It was growing dark and I knew we were in for a night of it. It was unsafe to go further and risk a bad fall or an encounter with leopards, so I climbed a tree and had the boys do the same.

"What will the master say?" they moaned. "It is so late. If anything happens to you he will kill us." They were very morose.

"Never you mind," I said. "I am the master here. You obey me and do as I say." Submissively they piped down. I had to be stern and this was good experience for them, for they would learn that they could obey and rely upon me and that I knew what I was doing.

As the hours dragged I became stiff with cold. I slept hardly a wink. Buffalo and elephant came feeding along the trail, baboons were scolding all night long and once I was sure I heard a leopard coughing not over a hundred yards away. I was never so grateful as when dawn came and we could climb down and start to move again. We walked like so many cripples for a little while until we got the kinks out of our legs.

The early morning fog lifted with the sun and from its drift we guessed our direction. Soon we struck a familiar trail and knew that we were right. About a mile farther on, we met Martin and some of the boys. He was frantic and furious. He, Boculy and the boys had been out with lanterns all night looking for us and they had not slept.

"Of all the unforgivable things for you to do!" he stormed.

"For once in my life, dear, I have nothing to say," I apologized. "Except that I'm awfully sorry to have caused you this worry."

He took me in his arms. "Well, thank God you're alive," was all he said.

On our way back to Lake Paradise, two of our boys came running, very frightened and out of breath, with the news that one of the porters had a "devil" in him and could not talk.

We hurried home to find M'pishi working over the boy.

Martin took one look and turned very pale. "Lockjaw!" he said. This was something new to both of us.

"There isn't any remedy, even if we had a doctor," he went on.

The boy's suffering was piteous. In his agony, he had jumped right into one of the campfires and was badly burned in addition to the lockjaw. Martin gave him a quick hypodermic to relieve his suffering, and sent him off at once in an automobile, with Abdulla and two others, in hope of reaching Isiolo in time to save him.

But next day Abdulla was back. They had buried the boy at Ret.

It was explained to us that the boy had had a severe headache and a superstitious porter had cut his temple to let out the "bad blood." The knife was rusty and dirty.

"He saw the sea-serpent," I heard one of the porters saying in Swahili. I swung on the speaker quickly.

"What is that about the sea-serpent?" I demanded. "How do you know?"

"Because he told me, memsahib."

It developed, as Bukhari questioned the boys, that they had been making dire predictions because this poor fellow thought he had seen the legendary sea-serpent while near the Lake one night on an errand of Martin's. The superstitious natives repeated their predictions over and over as they sat around the campfire with him. And he had developed a headache, no doubt from fear, with the awful result we witnessed.

There seemed nothing we could do to punish the boys. They actually believed what they were saying. And since we had tried to eradicate the idea of a sea-serpent from their minds ever since our arrival, we couldn't accomplish that overnight, and certainly not by discipline.

Our first tragedy at Paradise was sobering, and Martin demanded of the boys that thenceforward they check in daily for medical inspection, and he ordered Bukhari and N'dundu to keep a constant watch for any ailments.

13

*". . . I want to live at peace with
the animals, for I have the ambition
to make a picture record of the animals of Africa that will show the life
of each species from birth to death.
There are not many years left for
making such a record; civilization is
creeping into British East Africa. In
another generation, perhaps, the animals of Africa, the little, beautiful
animals of the plains and the strange,
gigantic animals, the last survivors of
the age of mammoths, will be all but
extinct. . . ."*

—MARTIN JOHNSON

"THE MAIL FROM Nairobi. The mail has arrived!"

There were no more welcome words at Lake Paradise, no more looked-forward-to event, than the arrival of the mails. These were brought to us specially by the courtesy of the government or by our couriers. To be sure, mail day occurred only once in every four to eight weeks, but Martin and I would drop whatever we were doing to rush in and go through the sack that had arrived by various stages from Nairobi.

We would tear open the letters from home and read them eagerly. Martin would get long letters from Mr. Pomeroy and officials of the American Museum of Natural History. I would pounce upon the letters postmarked "Kansas," and go sit by my-self and read them, then read them all over again. The world is a pretty small place when there is a letter from home.

There would be bales of magazines and newspapers. Copies of the *Saturday Evening Post, Cosmopolitan, Good Housekeeping, Photoplay, Redbook, The Literary Digest,* from the United States. From England came the *Sketch, Nash's, Punch* and the *Tatler.* Sunday editions of the *New York Times, New York Herald Tribune* and *London Times.*

Martin was like a boy with the Sunday newspapers. He loved the comic sections, and would spend hours following the adventures of Maggie and Jiggs, the skipper of the Toonerville Trolley, and Barney Google. American life had certainly entered our secluded Lake Paradise with the arrival of the American newspapers.

Martin was keen on the rotogravure section of the New York papers, and he would arrange the Sunday papers in order, parcel them out, one to read each succeeding Sunday, even though the papers might be months old. He would be furious if anyone broke into the periodical arrangement and disturbed this routine. The houseboys stayed away from the newspaper piles as if they were rattlesnakes stored in the corner. Martin would save those editions that he most enjoyed and go back to them from time to time and reread them as one goes back to a good book to reread passages particularly enjoyed.

"What are all these parcels?" Martin asked as he spied a pile of small boxes and packages.

"They're Christmas presents. See the mark—*Do not open until December 25th.*" I began to gather them together.

"By George! I hadn't thought much about Christmas," Martin replied.

"Well, see that you don't think about it at all until it is here. I'll have to hide these things, or you'll be into them." I wondered where I would hide them in camp. Finally Bukhari came to my rescue and hid them for me in a corner of his grass hut.

Soon after the arrival of the mail came word that Sir Northrup and Lady MacMillan were on their way up to Paradise. A runner came into our village one morning with the news. They were our first visitors.

The MacMillans, in addition to being old and dear friends of ours, had been extremely helpful to us on our first expedition. Although American born, Sir Northrup had become a British subject, was a member of the Legislative Council of Kenya Colony, and was recognized as a power in Africa.

Martin had sent Sir Northrup all necessary directions for reaching us, and they made good time on the way up, only five and a half days out of Nairobi. They arrived with four big Cadillac cars with double wheels on the back axles.

Our guests got to Paradise in the evening, just as Martin and I were finishing our dinner, so I hustled about and made them an impromptu meal, and Martin and I sat down at the table and ate all over again.

"I'm going to make you some pancakes for breakfast," I whispered to Sir Northrup.

"Good," he replied, beaming like a little boy who has just been promised a new football suit.

"I'll have to go out to the storehouse and get the pancake flour," I said. "Want to come along?"

We took the flashlight and went out to the hut which served as the storeroom for our kitchen supplies. In front of the storehouse were nine buffalo. I screamed and, as we had no guns, we ran into the laboratory. Martin and several of the boys came running, and the buffalo made off.

"You certainly picked a fine place to live," Sir Northrup remarked as we calmed down. But I knew that he loved it, and was thrilled at the adventure.

"That's nothing. Sometimes I have elephants in my garden," I said.

Later that night Martin and I took our guests down the cliffs to watch the animals drinking at the edge of the Lake. We sat down and watched the passing parade.

"This is marvelous," Sir Northrup announced after he watched the scene in silence for quite some time. "You two have more riches here than the wealthiest man in the world."

"That's the way we feel about it," Martin said.

"Yes, and the nice part of it is that you know it and appreciate it," Sir Northrup added. "I wouldn't blame you if you never went back to civilization."

The following morning we had a breakfast of good old-fashioned American pancakes.

"I rather imagined we would have pancakes." Lady MacMillan cast a reproving glance at her three-hundred-pound husband.

Sir Northrup was far too busy with his steaming-hot plate of cakes and Vermont maple syrup to reply. He was a great eater. I could almost believe his natives' boast that on safari he ate two antelopes a day and rode on four mules at a time.

So I took great pleasure in preparing six to eight course dinners for them on each of the four nights they stayed with us. I was never so happy as when I was bustling about in the kitchen preparing meals. I loved the kitchen, that's all there was to it. And I loved to see people eat and enjoy themselves. I gathered the best vegetables and strawberries from the garden, and they had never before tasted quite so delicious as when we shared them with our first guests.

Lady MacMillan was keenly interested in the garden and went out with me each day to pick the peas and beans and curly endive for our dinner. She was delighted with the way some strawberry slips she had sent us were growing.

"I want some of these watermelon seeds for my garden in Nairobi," she said. "I'll win every prize with them. I have never grown cucumbers like this from my English seeds. How did you do it?"

Lady MacMillan had by far the finest gardens in Nairobi, and she was constantly winning first prize with her blooms.

I told her how, in order to grow these melons in the proper soil, I had packed six donkeys and twelve camels with gunny sacks and had brought sand back from a long way off to make a sandy loam. The virgin soil of my garden was too rich for melons by itself. It had taken me several days to haul this sand back and forth, but it was worth it; for not only the melons but the vegetables also showed the results. I had tomatoes weighing one pound apiece, and watermelons weighing up to seventy pounds.

I was also very happy to have Lady MacMillan ask me for some of my cosmos and hollyhock seeds, and for seeds of my watermelons, tomatoes, cantaloupe, honeydew and string beans. Coming from her I considered the request a great compliment.

One night I took them both to see my storehouse. This time we took guns along as well as flashlights. And it was a good idea, too, because what should we find crouching just off the path but a leopard. I fired one shot in the air and he ran off into the jungle.

"This reminds me of the good old days when a lion would come right up to our doorstep at Juja," Sir Northrup reflected. "You are indeed in a wild Paradise."

We spent four happy days with Sir Northrup and Lady Mac-Millan. Martin and the grand old man talked about Africa, animals and photography. He was keenly interested in Martin's pictures, and was delighted with the developing room. As a special event Martin developed a movie film and Sir Northrup watched with intense interest, but admitted that this part of photography mystified him.

"These pictures are the eighth wonder of the world," our guest remarked. "You have no idea what they will mean to the world one day as a scientific and educational record."

After the struggles and hardships we had been through, those words of appreciation, coming from him, were most encouraging.

Martin and I helped them to get their cars ready. The cars were enclosed in heavy wire mesh which made them lion proof. Sir Northrup had had air mattresses and electric drop lights installed in each of the cars so that he and his wife could safari in comfort after dark. They liked safari life and were always driving off into the blue.

"We're going to come back again in a few months and we'll stay longer next time," Sir Northrup said.

"We're going to count on that," Martin replied.

Their cars slowly drew away from Lake Paradise, and we watched the caravan disappear around the winding trail. I had that empty feeling in my stomach that I always have when I must say good-bye to someone of whom I am fond.

Sir Northrup's praise made me reflect upon our work at Paradise. I felt the time had been filled with good work and much satisfaction. Our dream had become a reality. We had done our best to raise the standards of picture-making against the challenges that we had had to face.

The answer as to whether or not we had succeeded lay in the metal boxes that were carefully stowed in Martin's underground storage vault—one of the first things he had built on arriving at Lake Paradise.

Martin had been schooled in the art of photography all his life, and he had learned how to live in the wilderness; learned too, how to deal with wild people and wild animals.

We had got together a photographic equipment such as we were sure had never been available before for scientific work. We had a battery of twenty cameras, ten for motion pictures, and ten for "stills." Five of the motion-picture cameras were of the type specially designed for animal work by Carl Akeley, after he had learned the weaknesses of other cameras for making pictures of animal life. All of our cameras had been fitted with devices that would aid us in getting good results.

In order to get a special series of pictures from which scientists might study animal motion, we had two Akeleys mounted together so that two films might be exposed at one time and by one set of controls. One of the cameras was timed to make the usual sixteen exposures to the second, but the other was timed to make sixty-four exposures to the second. When the film taken by the first

A CAMEL SAFARI TO THE PLAINS

Osa leads the caravan into the N'groon Mountains, making pictures of elephants which have left the forests during the rains.

HIPPO HERD TAKES A MUDDY BATH

On the Eauso Nyiro River, the Johnsons make a fine hippo close-up on one of their short safaris.

ELEPHANTS ON THE KAISOOT DESERT

An elephant family, with a tiny baby near the end of the line, ambles across the scrub country as they leave Lake Paradise and the rains.

PINNACLES AND SHOULDERS OF MT. KENYA

One of Martin Johnson's finest pictures of this beautiful mountain on the Northern Frontier, which rises to a height of 17,040 feet above the plains.

camera was projected it would show the animal's movements in natural motion. But the film taken by the second camera, projected at one-fourth the speed, would give "slow motion" pictures that would permit a close study of every movement.

We had a third motion-picture camera fitted with four lenses of different focal length which Dallmeyer of London made for us, mounted just as similar lenses are mounted on high-power microscopes. When we first went out to Africa, we lost many good pictures because of the time it took to change lenses, but during our four years in Paradise, with the new equipment from Dallmeyer, we could change from a short to a long-focus lens, or vice versa, in a fraction of a second.

Though long-focus lenses are notoriously hard to use, Martin had had years of experience with them and had learned how to handle them. The secret of success was a very simple one. The lenses and cameras had to be mounted so firmly as to eliminate the vibration that made "shaky" and "fuzzy" negatives. We got good results with the twelve and seventeen-inch lenses. They brought the animals we were photographing close and to full screen for the audiences who would see the pictures.

Other lenses—wide-angle lenses, portrait lenses, and very fast lenses for forest work—enabled us to meet all photographic emergencies. Martin had devised a "fire-department" camera for use along the road. We had often missed many a picture while traveling from one place to another simply because of the delay in getting the camera out of its box and setting it up. This one could be set up and focused before you could say "Boculy."

And we had a series of cameras operated by electric motors. We could place them in the open where the animals grazed and lead a wire to a tree or a blind half a mile away. With these we could also get pictures of the shy and rare animals that stayed in the forest and rarely ventured into the open.

It would take sixty thousand feet or more of negative a year to record our Lake Paradise experience. We had already made many miles of film. We had left no stone unturned, no avenue unexplored, and I was proud of helping Martin make what I hoped would some day prove a valuable addition to the knowledge of the world.

14

". . . Sometimes we have spent the whole day walking miles and miles after elephants and have come home to find that a fine herd had called on us, and we could have made a fine picture by staying at home and not moving a step . . ."

—MARTIN JOHNSON

"TODAY LET'S GO to Wistonia, elephants or no elephants," I suggested. "It's so beautiful there by the waterfall."

I knew that Martin would be wanting to take elephant pictures, with the sun rising clear and bright. There had been no elephants at Wistonia for days, but I loved the place and wondered how I could persuade him.

He frowned, then brightened and slapped his knee, in the way he did when a bright idea struck him.

"All right, honey. I need to get those butterflies, and this will be just the day to do it."

Wistonia waterhole was a favorite spot for both of us. It was near Lake Paradise, the trails were good, and we had made some of our best pictures there. It was everything one dreams of for sylvan peace and beauty, and that is why we gave it the Swahili name which means "extreme loveliness."

We gave names to all of the waterholes we frequented most. Usually Swahili names, because they were so descriptive or poetic and because the boys could identify them when we gave directions.

Translated into English, they were: "Lotus pool," for the lotus and lilies; "Grandfather," for the big bull elephant who came

177

there regularly; "Martin Johnson," for the place where he first saw an elephant in 1921; "Boculy," for a favorite of his to which he had led us and where we invariably found elephants, and many other names.

Wistonia was, without doubt, the most beautiful of all. From the steep fifty-foot-cliffs surrounding it, showed beautifully tinted rocks, ranging in color from rose red to deep volcanic blue-black. Beyond the outlet to this gorge was a peaceful valley half a mile in length, carpeted with red flowering pom-poms on long green stems, a sort of African heather, tiger lilies, wild gladiola and little white flowers of several varieties.

The waterfall was a thin bridal-veil spray which fell from the cliff above into a wide, clear pool. On one side was a grassy bank and on the other a mass of boulders grown over with moss. And upon these rested butterflies of every conceivable hue, when they were not filling the air with their color. The pool emptied into a racing brook that skipped down the donga in a succession of little silver rapids until it disappeared from sight.

Though it was my favorite, Wistonia was only one of many equally beautiful spots about Lake Paradise where, for centuries, the springs and tumbling waterfalls had been carving out drinking pools for the elephants and resting places for us to enjoy. Powder blue lotus with yellow centers filled the pools; clumps of black-eyed susans grew up the banks; orioles, finches and warblers chorused everywhere, and thousands of butterflies and moths ranged in color from glossy black with purple polka dots to the most delicate of mauves, blues and golds.

At one of these waterholes we built a tree-top blind from which we could watch the game and make flashlight pictures.

No sooner was it ready than Martin, always eager to get a picture, suggested that we go right out and give the blind a trial that night.

"But Martin," I protested, "see those clouds? It's going to rain. You'll ruin your cameras."

"All right, Mrs. Killjoy, you stay here. I'm going out alone," he said, knowing perfectly well that I wouldn't let him go alone, for he could never stay awake and I always wanted to help him and felt it was my duty to be with him.

"M'baya sana" (very bad), said Bukhari, as I looked to him for support.

But Martin was getting his cameras ready, so I collected my things, including plenty of blankets, a mattress, two thermos bottles of coffee and some sandwiches, two good woolly sweaters and woolly socks. I knew that those blankets would be welcome, for at Lake Paradise we were at an altitude of about 6000 feet, where a heavy dew always fell after sundown and the cold was very penetrating.

Arriving at the waterhole, Boculy and I traced the most numerous tracks with our flashlights. Martin set his cameras at various angles accordingly and focused them. The cameras we covered with black rubber hoods, not only to conceal them but also to protect them from the moisture. Then Martin attached his flashlight apparatus and strung his release wire to the tree in which our blind was made.

Meantime the boys had tied together a rude ladder of poles, sticks and vines, and up this we climbed some fifty feet, attaching the wire as we went. The moon kept appearing through broken clouds and Martin had a good time kidding me about my rainstorm.

"Why, this is going to be a perfect night," he said. "You wait and see."

After laying our mattress and blankets, we spread tarpaulins over our heads and then settled down to being as comfortable as two people can be in a tree house. Our boys climbed down and went back to camp. We gave them instructions to come back for us at sunrise.

At about nine-thirty, more than twenty elephants came to within a few feet of the tree and stopped. The old ones were sniffing the wind nervously. No doubt the eddying currents of the forest gave them our scent, but they could not get our location. They circled around their babies and stood there. We hardly breathed, hoping that they would soon be reassured and move into range of the cameras. But they did not move, except to mill about that spot. For nearly an hour they stayed there.

Martin gripped my arm and pointed to the waterhole. Beyond, a leopard was coming down a side trail to the water with an easy, loping gait. He stopped and began giving the low consumptive cough so characteristic of his kind.

At once there was a terrific hullaballoo from baboons which had up to now been quiet enough and apparently asleep in near-by trees. They are the leopards' prey and they now sounded as though each and every one of them was being eaten alive.

Elephants hate baboons, and our herd at once stampeded at this annoying din. In a few moments they were gone.

"Gosh, if we could only get all of that on film," Martin said ruefully.

When the leopard had drunk and left the pool, and the racketing baboons had settled down once more, Martin fell asleep. Soon he was snoring peacefully. But I was wakeful, as I usually was in a blind, and I sat watching the clouds drift across the moon until I felt that I was moving on my platform through the moist jungle.

An hour passed, and I heard, far off, a crackling sound which grew nearer and louder until I was sure there must be buffalo coming. They are anything but dainty, and although they weigh much less than elephants they make ten times the noise.

They were not coming rapidly, so they must be feeding, but at last they began to straggle down the trail, their hooves scraping and rattling on stones. The buffalo continued to come until the trail was choked with them, and I wondered if there would be enough water in that pool to fill so many huge tanks.

Packed as close as sardines in a can, they rubbed and jostled each other, and drank with terrific noise. It was enough, at least, to wake Martin.

"Holy smoke," he whispered. "Must be two hundred. And all on the wrong side of the water."

When they finally left I expected to see the waterhole dry as a Kansas creek in a drought, but the water was still there, reflecting the moon.

Martin fell asleep again, but still I sat listening. The forest always seemed alive to me, and the imminence of something just about to happen kept my pulse going and my nerves on edge.

Now the clouds were gathering and I knew my predictions were coming true. Soon there was a flash, a clap of thunder, and a terrific downpour began. I was sure it was a cloudburst. The rain beat in upon us. I wakened Martin.

"I'm frightened," I whispered.

"You're all wet, but that's nothing to be afraid of."

"It's not that. I don't mind being wet. Listen!" I huddled in the blanket.

All around us we could hear the crackling of branches disjointed by the wind and rain. The storm was playing havoc in the forest. Near by a tree crashed to the earth and the noise echoed around us.

I was completely miserable. Little drops of water trickled down my neck and rolled off my nose. Overhead the tarpaulin sagged with gallons of water. I tried to keep warm, but it was impossible.

"We've got to get those cameras," said Martin.

Then the tarpaulin caved in, dumping a deluge over us and drenching us to the skin. I was so furious I began to cry with rage, as I climbed down the ladder after Martin to collect the cameras.

Back in the blind, we sat down on sopping blankets with the rain still drenching us. We could not go home. There was nothing to do but take it.

"Those plates will surely be gone. Just as well I didn't get any pictures," said Martin as he did his best to wrap up his precious equipment. I could visualize him toiling over the cameras tomorrow, taking them apart, cleaning, oiling and greasing them, and painfully polishing every lens.

"I wonder," he sighed, "if the public will ever know what it takes to get these pictures."

I rummaged for a thermos bottle and tried to pour out a cup of hot coffee, but I was so cold that I was trembling all over and could scarcely hold the cup. Martin put his arms around me. We huddled there together all through the night.

"Just like a couple of baboons," I thought aloud.

The storm passed with the coming of dawn. The clouds dispersed, the sun shone through and steeped the forest with rays of mellow gold.

This routine was too exhausting to continue. We could not work all day and sit up all night in a blind. So Martin often used a device by which the animals would take their own pictures while we slept in our beds at home. By stretching wires across the trails and connecting them to our flashlight apparatus, the animals would trip a spring and release both the flash and the camera shutter. Next morning we would hurry down to collect the plates and develop them.

Oftentimes a booming flash down at the Lake would awaken us and, too curious to go back to sleep, we would take our guns and flashlights and go down at once to remove the plates and reset the cameras. Then, we would rush to the laboratory to see what we had caught.

There were no end of disappointments. A bird in flight would trip the wire and we would have nothing. Or we might have only a rhino's rump as he backed into the scene. Or the tail of a genet cat or mongoose or the blur of a bounding bushbuck. But every now and then there would be some choice picture to reward us for all the trouble, and one of these made us forget a hundred failures.

We had to go out early in the morning to take in our equipment. The cameras were set high enough to be out of reach of hyenas, but there was no way of protecting them from the baboons, who are so curious they can't leave anything alone.

Baboons swarmed over the Paradise country, and they were always somewhere about, in the trees or scrambling over rocks, drinking at the Lake or feeding in the fig trees. They were both a nuisance and a constant amusement with their bad manners.

In the forest one day, I bumped into a big baboon. He seemed struck dumb with surprise and shock; he looked me over carefully and nervously, and then decided he didn't like my looks. He seemed to recognize in me a member of his species, but thought me not nearly as good-looking as himself. Perhaps he thought me a "white" baboon.

He started making wry faces at me. I retaliated by making the same faces at him. He would stick out his tongue and screw up his face and slap himself on the chest in a rage, and I would do the same. He fell to his hands and knees and hopped about, and so did I. He stomped about, and I did too. Unable to contain myself, I began to laugh and he scampered away. I had apparently won the hideous-face contest. He climbed a tree, jumped up and down, shook the branches, squeaked, grunted, barked, smacked his lips continuously and rapidly hurled every baboon invective he could think of.

Baboons were always getting into my garden. One day I even spied a big fellow in the tomato patch, stuffing all he could stuff into himself and having a wonderful time. He saw me and hobbled away, with a tomato in his mouth, one in each hand and in one foot, and one under each arm! Baboons were very greedy and always seemed hungry. Full of nervous energy, they were always flea-picking, or what is really a search for the salty scales on the skin. All monkeys crave salt, and the scales are a salty tid-bit, not the proverbial fleas they are supposed to be.

One fresh morning I walked down to the Lake and had just located a nice patch of mushrooms when I heard a crash and snort behind me. I whirled about, expecting to find an elephant. There stood a large rhino. He was furious. He pawed the ground, and swung his head to and fro. I knew that he was going to charge.

A rhino doesn't wait around and think things over the way an elephant does: he is too instinctively mean and short-tempered. Almost before I could jump for a tree the ugly fellow started for me. Luckily I found a low branch. I climbed as high as I could. After a lot of pawing around and snorting, the old scoundrel finally decided he was outwitted and left.

On my way back I climbed down through some dense growth at the water's edge. Just as I emerged I heard a thud and the breaking of branches a few yards away. I glanced up at once and found myself looking into the beady little eyes of a huge elephant. He was just as surprised as I was. Maybe more so!

"Don't move!" the native boy with me whispered.

It was a useless warning. I couldn't have moved had I wanted to. I was rooted to the spot. The curious thing was that Martin on the other side of the Lake had happened to pick up his binoculars at that precise moment and he saw me through them. There was nothing he could do. Anyway, he knew me well enough to realize that if the elephant came for me, I'd have gone up a tree like a cat. Many a time I had been treed by rhino or elephants within ear-shot of our house, and I had had plenty of practice at tree climbing.

The elephant didn't seem a bit angry or worried. He waggled his ears and switched his tail about, and just stared. Finally, he decided to see what I would do if he went away. So he backed into the forest a few yards until he was out of sight. That was my cue to go. I quickly slipped away along the shore. A few minutes later I looked back. The elephant had returned and was drinking quietly without even looking up.

Martin tried to keep an eye on me most of the time; nevertheless there were times when he had to leave me with an exacted promise not to stray far from the camp unless Bukhari or another gun-bearer went with me.

I didn't think his concern was warranted, but I would have been pretty disappointed in him if he hadn't felt that way. And every time he said something about protecting me, I felt mighty proud of his affection.

Actually, I felt just as able to take care of myself in Africa as in Kansas; nevertheless I took Boculy or Bukhari with me if I went outside Lake Paradise, just as a matter of good sense. I knew that each of them was thoroughly dependable and would lay down his life for me if necessary. They continually watched out for animals and would let me take no unnecessary risks.

When Martin buried himself in his laboratory for days, I grew lonely, and I had to do something besides gardening. So I took long walks into the forest to gather plants and orchids, or just to hear and see the animals that I loved. And occasionally I did short safaris on my own to the near-by mountain waterholes, to help Martin fill out some gap in the picture record.

In Lake Paradise itself, Martin said that we had more excitement and goings on than the best six-ring circus on earth, and that it was not dull for a single moment.

Down in our front yard, baboons were almost always moving about, babies riding their mothers "bareback" and doing a kind of rodeo and other antics. There were kudu and Abyssinian bushbuck dashing in and out of the forest glades or down to drink. There was game of all sizes, and the forest was always full of visible or invisible life. Birds of all kinds darted in and out of the trees and drifted up from the Lake in flocks.

From our kitchen extended our back yard, an open glade at the top of the crater, reaching back to the forest. Here elephants often came out and paraded before our fascinated eyes, or browsed about unconcernedly.

At night the forest world seemed more than ever awake, with all sorts of movement and alarms which continued from dusk to daylight. The animals paraded down to the water and back again, and we never tired of watching from our cliffs or lookouts.

As we became more accustomed to having elephants pass by us at a few feet, or stand beneath our lookout almost close enough to touch, we grew bolder. We began to talk to them, and even threw pebbles onto their backs. Usually they would make quite an uproar at us, but I think they soon accepted us as just one of those petty annoyances of life in the jungle, and guessed that we were harmless.

"You've done everything but feed them peanuts," said Martin. "What a life! Nothing but circus all day long and it doesn't cost a cent!"

15

". . . The camels have a mean and dirty look. They are cranky and stubborn and dumb. Their language is simply disgraceful . . ."

—MARTIN JOHNSON

"THE RAINS ARE due again, Osa. And when Boculy says they are due, we can expect them any minute."

"I know. That means the elephants will be off for the plains."

I hated to think of leaving Paradise again. We were already in our second year here and it seemed to me that we were hardly settled. But I knew that this meant we must leave it for several weeks if our work was to go on.

The elephants left the forest during the rains, for they could not stand the sound of water dripping on leaves and stones. This was our great opportunity, for we would be able to follow and photograph them in good light and in large herds. In the forest they were always scattered, and photography was difficult because of the lack of satisfactory light.

"How long do you think we'll be gone, Martin?"

"Better plan on at least three months' supply of food."

"I'm glad we have plenty of butter. I counted twelve pounds today, and tomorrow we will churn six more. I'll have it all salted down right away and put into jars and paraffined. And M'pishi has eight dozen eggs in salt water; we ought to have ten dozen to go." I spoke with pride, as I thought how good they would taste out there on the desert.

187

"I'll need fifteen boys this time for cameras alone. Boculy will help you pick the boys, the camels and the mules, and Bukhari will help you do the loads. All our usual tents and camp equipment and the copper stills, Osa, for this is going to be one of our biggest jobs."

For the next few days the camp hummed with excitement. All the boys loved safaris and now they chanted and shouted as they packed the loads, tied and tested them.

"Hi-yah, you old cry-baby!" yelled a porter as he passed a camel. "Tomorrow you will have something to cry about when I load three hundred pounds on your back."

At dawn, with the birds singing everywhere, and the boys left in camp yelling good-byes, we set off for the plains with what looked like a young army.

Fifty camels, two saddled mules, nearly one hundred porters and camel boys, and our personal servants, made an imposing company, and I wondered if I had enough of everything until we should return.

As we turned around the bend below the village, the last good-bye was from a company of baboons, who chattered and scolded us as usual. They were headed for the Lake and I suddenly remembered that my tomatoes were just ripe. I hoped that N'dundu, whom we had left in charge, and the shamba boys would see these baboons coming and be ready with their sling shots.

On these safaris out on the plains it was impossible to use cars, as water was scarce and the soil boggy. We, the boys and the camels carried on our feet great clods of mud, sometimes weighing four to five pounds.

We did a wearisome ten to twelve miles a day at most, in slow stages, while the elephants could do much more. We carried sticks for support. It was something like tight-rope walking. The camels slipped and fell, so the boys carried all the breakables. It was hard going, and Martin paid a special bonus to the boys who carried these precious loads.

Often we were caught in the rain. Then we would have to stop and cover the cameras with tarpaulins and sit among the rocks. There was nothing else to do; we just had to put on our raincoats and sit it out. We would see elephants moving in the distance, but following them in a heavy rain was impossible.

Plodding along behind our caravan on good days, I reveled in the vivid greens and beauty the rains brought, in birds singing and flashing their gay color, in game birds drumming up from cover, in the sweetness of the air, the mountains of clouds, the great rainbows and golden sunbursts. It was a relief from the forbidding heat that usually beat upon the Kaisoot.

Occasionally, we came upon fields of white lilies and tiger lilies, "morning glories" that bloomed all day, and miles upon miles of brilliant canary yellow poppies.

As we traveled, the camels grazed on low shrubs and salt grasses. But many shrubs are poisonous to them and the drivers would press on until they saw food that was satisfactory for their animals. This meant that, weary as we were at the end of a day, we often had to walk on for miles and miles to find proper food for the camels.

In the dry season, or with good going, we might do thirty miles a day. In camp we would have a good dinner and Martin would give me a paper. It might be six months old, but its news and its funnies and fashions were as exciting to me as though it had been bought that day. While he smoked a fragrant cigar, we would read ourselves to sleep.

Then we often heard the camels screaming in panic, and they would lash about and tumble against our tent ropes, threatening to pull the whole tent down upon us. They were made panicky by hyenas that came stealing in to tug at some bit of leather or a fragment of food left at our campfires. Being tied, the camels were more than usually nervous.

When it was dry, there was always, in addition to the camel food problem, the urgent need of water in an almost waterless land. With such great loads as we had to move, it was difficult to carry a sufficient quantity of water for our drinking and baths and for the camels to drink, and thirst was a hovering threat and fear. We remembered a sad experience on our first African visit when our boys almost went mad for need of water.

The fresh water of Paradise was a joy in contrast to the alkaline waters of the desert and plain. The boys called the springs "sweet water," and Martin called Lake Paradise "our cup of sweet water."

On safari, we *never* seemed to have enough water. After a rain, the streams and washes went dry almost immediately, and we had to use muddy waterholes where rhino and elephants and other animals had been. Often we had to chase them away. We took the water, mud and all, and when distilled it was as good as new and we could use it for cooking. We also used alum to clear the muddy water which we had to draw from rivers and pools, but it gave the tea a horrible taste.

As we traveled along, the tinkle of the wooden bells of the camels was like music. The tread of the camel is as silent as night, and there were only the bells to break the complete silence of the safari. It was hypnotic. Walking, I would fall into its rhythm, and riding, would succumb to its lullaby, by night and by day. This is one of the most unforgettable and pleasant of my memories.

I preferred to walk than to ride. I mounted one camel for a picture and became so seasick I thought I should never finish the ordeal. Martin said it made him seasick to watch me.

Camels can carry a load of three hundred pounds. We used native "saddles" of wood, especially adapted for packing, and tied on the loads with thongs and jungle vine ropes. The animals carried two large barrimals of water each and these were a marvel-

OSA AND HER
PET GIBBON, KALOWAT

At her feet is a greater bustard which she has bagged.

OSA'S PET CHEETAH, MARJO

One of her most beautiful pets, presented to Osa by Blaney Percival and carried on the expedition from Nairobi.

YOUNG LION CUB CLIMBS A TREE

An extraordinary photograph made by the Johnsons on one of their lion safaris.

ous help over the volcanic slag and where we were two to three days from water.

Camels are cry-babies. They wail when they kneel or rise, when you load them, pull them, and, sometimes, even when you look at them. They bawl about everything they do, especially if it is work. No matter how gentle you are with them, they are always sorry for themselves, from morning to midnight. In a caravan, they wail as they walk, gruff tones of the adults mingling with shrill tones of youngsters, and with one hundred of them in a pack or a line that makes for considerable noise.

The leader of our column on safari, an old "Ship of the Desert" who was in his prime, was a special objector. He was in good health and well treated; he had no sores or diseases and was always well fed; yet he invariably started the day with a long lament. He would grind his cud, moan and groan and grate his teeth. At night, when the boys tied one of his legs back against his hip, as with all the camels, to prevent his running away, he would sob and wail until we could hardly sleep for his complaints.

In the morning when his native keeper came along to load him up, he invariably snapped at the man. When the load was put on the saddle he groaned some more, as if the pain of it were unbearable. And when he got the order to rise, he would snort and cry as if he were being beaten. In the meantime, the other camels were trying to out-groan each other.

On safari, if charged by a rhino, or at almost any other opportunity, the camels might go wild and buck about and scatter their loads to the winds, especially if they were not well broken. A camel, having thrown off his load, would stand about looking very unkempt and stupid.

Sometimes on safari, I'd get so weary I couldn't keep up. I would sit down and weep and get over it, take a rest and eat some chocolate and revive. Martin would miss me and stop the safari and wait, though he was often irate at not making camp on time. Despite occasional fatigue, I was in fine shape and able to take it.

In camp at last, our porters would have the tents pitched in a jiffy. I was always amazed at how quickly and with what good will the boys would rush about to make us comfortable, no matter how worn out they were.

While we were unpacking, our personal boys made a quick fire and hot water for tea. As soon as this was ready, we sat and sipped it while the boys continued unpacking.

By the time we had finished our tea, our baths were ready in our individual tents, if water were available. To step out of a tub and into fresh, clean garments was like starting life all over again at the end of a hot, dismal day. Then I would rub my face thoroughly with a good dose of cold cream, followed by a skin tonic, because the water was too hard unless I could gather rain water. There was very little room for luxuries in our equipment, so I appreciated these few all the more.

And Martin appreciated my never letting down on my appearance. "Go along, honey," he would say. "Take your time and put on your lipstick. I love it, and it goes well with your brown skin. You look as if you were dressing for dinner on Park Avenue instead of Elephant Row."

As the reddest sun I have ever seen glowed on the horizon, long purple shadows crept over the plains and everything, even the air, became rosy. Then night fell suddenly; there was no twilight. On our little table had been laid a snowy white tablecloth and the hurricane lanterns were lit. I fussed around and arranged napkins and dishes at each place. Cleanliness was my obsession, and I knew, as every housewife the world over knows, that an attractive table adds as much to the meal as the food itself.

As we took our seats, I served hors d'oeuvres, which were sardines in some one of a hundred disguises. Then came a simple soup from our ample stock of canned goods—or M'pishi would make us a fresh soup from guinea fowl, partridge, antelope or gazelle, to be followed by a roast with vegetables. A sweet of some sort usually topped off the meal. Every man seems to love a dessert, and Martin felt a dinner was never complete without some sweet. We kept a well balanced diet, and we took our time over our dinner, relaxing after the tension of the day. Martin would smoke his cigar and we would enjoy the sounds of birds and animals settling down for the night and the sight of the sky lighting up with stars.

In order to get decent water, we caught the rain off our tents. We could not drink it because of the green dye from the cloth, but we used it for baths and for hair washing.

We set up a canvas bathtub. One day, longing for a bath and feeling too hot to bother, I jumped into the water without looking carefully. Thorns stuck through the tub. I screamed, thinking a scorpion had got me, and then the tub collapsed.

The days were very hot. I was in my bath one day when over the edge of the tub came a six-inch scorpion that looked to me like a small lobster. I screamed and went over backward and Martin came running and killed the scorpion.

So it was that we had good reason to shake our boots and clothing every morning for scorpions, spiders, small snakes and night adders. I never, myself, rolled down the flaps of our tent. We always had the boys do this carefully, for vermin seek the warm cozy spots at night and the boys insisted that their eyes were quicker than mine to detect the small dangers. As Suku would say: "Little Missus, don't put your dressing gown on until I have shaken it out. For perhaps the great father in the sky or the devil down beneath has put a scorpion in there."

As we were plodding along on safari, we suddenly saw our boys stop, break file, and toss off their loads. They scattered on the run, as though something were about to strike them. Near by was a cluster of vivid green trees. Into these they ran and madly began cutting twigs.

"They are cutting 'brushi,' M'sahib," said Bukhari with a grin. "See, how white my teeth are. I use this brush, Dukani a Mungu," he added, meaning "God's store. Everything free."

The boys cut each twig short, removed an inch of bark, and chewed the end until the fibres spread; with these the boys gave their teeth a high polish. I had them cut me fifteen brushes; I chewed them and found them remarkably successful. They tasted something like slippery elm.

The elephants seem to like the leaves of this tree. "That is why they have such white ivory," said my chief boy solemnly, as though he had discovered a great truth.

Otherwise the natives would never use a toothbrush, although I offered them all the equipment and urged them to take this care of their teeth.

On safari, porters would stalk along all day with these tooth-brushes of the jungle in their mouths, chewing away at the ends, like an Indian and his betelnut, and every now and then they would take the brushes in hand and briskly polish their teeth. Generally, our natives had magnificent teeth, strong and firm and evenly formed.

Boculy had been scouting and reported finding great elephant herds moving toward the Irreri Valley at the foot of the N'groon Mountains. We gave him a Meru boy and sent him off to watch the animals as we hurriedly broke camp to follow.

That evening we met Boculy on his way back to us and I had never seen him so tired. He said he had seen the elephants and had sent the Meru back to guide us.

While we were speculating on whether the Meru was lost or had gone to sleep somewhere, the boy came dragging in, completely exhausted and begging for water. We gave him water, but slowly, for it was terribly hot, and then made a bed for him in the shade.

Boculy soon picked up and looked as spry as ever and we laid our plans and went on. Soon we saw tracks of elephants everywhere and could then make out great herds, moving off among plains game of every kind.

That night we set flashlight cameras in the Irreri sand river on a trail where elephants had watered the night before. We made a lookout for ourselves on top of a high bank where we could clearly and safely see the entire sweep of the river bed.

The moon came up extremely bright and in the crisp air we were glad to have our blankets. We watched until after nine o'clock with no result when suddenly Martin exclaimed:

"Great guns, see what's coming."

There, about a hundred yards away, came an elephant procession, a score of them. They were not on the trail where our cameras were set but were coming straight down the middle of the sand river, making no sound, and hurrying as though they were very thirsty. In the bright moonlight we could see every detail of their figures, but their legs seemed very long and their ears larger than any I had ever seen.

Directly in front of us they stopped and started digging with their trunks, pawing the sand back with their feet.

"Why don't they go down there a hundred yards to open water?" I whispered.

"They must know what they're doing. See that!"

Several of the herd were pulling down dom-palm nuts while the others dug. When one of the diggers grew tired another would take his place, showing perfect team-work.

As each hole deepened, the elephant's legs went down and down out of sight, and ultimately his head, the hind quarters sticking awkwardly out of the hole. Sand would be blown out of the elephant's trunk in a heavy spray.

After about thirty minutes of this hard work, the elephants began to blow out water with the sand and they soon began to drink, but it took them a long time, for the water came up slowly. One would drink for a time, leave while another took its place, then go back and nudge the other away with his tusks and resume drinking.

One old female with a tiny toto was very grouchy. She worked at her digging alone and trumpeted if any other elephant came near. The toto was constantly getting in her way and she would stop and nudge it back. When she had the hole about four feet deep, the little fellow tumbled right in and she had to get it out with her trunk. Then she gave it a good slap. Then the toto insisted on having his dinner and she had to spank him again.

Discouraged, the toto wandered off to where another elephant was digging. This elephant, a half grown male, was annoyed and jabbed his tusks against the baby, making it squeal. The mother, mad as could be, came running over and gave the young bull a jab with her tusks and he screamed and ran away. The mother then coiled her trunk around the toto and led it back to where she was digging. Another elephant was there, drinking, but she promptly drove it off with a trumpet and a stab of her tusks.

After about two hours, having satisfied their thirst, the elephants began filling their trunks with water and throwing it over themselves. The old mother doused her toto and gave him a thorough bath. Then they all moved on down to the open water and sprayed themselves again and splashed about. We could hear other herds near by, trumpeting and breaking branches, but no others came to our spot.

At about midnight they all started back down the river bed in the direction from which they had come, in single file and hurrying as though they had to keep an important engagement somewhere.

Of all the exciting experiences we had on this safari, our encounter at Irreri was the most fun and the most memorable.

Life in the jungle had almost as many small dangers as it had large ones. Out on the Kaisoot Desert on this safari, I found a cobra in a food box in the stores tent, as I lifted the lid. I froze and slowly backed off, and ran out of the tent. Then the boys came with sticks and knives and killed her as she reared to strike. We had our boxes on logs to avoid white ants, so I now had all the forty boxes taken out and the logs carefully removed and we cleared the entire stores tent. There I found twenty small day-old cobras! And those babies were just as poisonous as the mother.

The boys loved such excitement: it provided conversation around their fires for weeks after the event. And how those cobras grew in size and ferocity and the boys' heroism correspondingly! They strutted about and gave the snakes a thousand killings. Whenever I could steal up to the fires and listen unobserved I did so, for I needed the Swahili and here was always a good story.

One evening Martin listened to the porters singing and shouting at their fires.

"What are the boys so happy about down there tonight?" he asked.

"I just went down and overheard them," I replied. "That rascal Bukhari has been up to his tricks again." I told Martin that they were discussing an old Boran chief who had come up that day to watch the camera.

"What is the Bwana doing?" the chief had asked Bukhari.

"He is getting all the animals in that little box," was the reply.

"How many can he get in there?"

"Oh, mingi sana! (very many). Every one you've ever seen!"

"All in that little box?"

"Sure," said Bukhari, now beginning to expand his story. "I've been in there, the mem-sahib has been in there, lots of chiefs too.

Why, the master captured them and let them go again after they had been in there a while."

As Martin began to take pictures of the other natives, the old chief became more interested and more astonished at the fact that the natives did not disappear.

"How can he put them in the box, if they are still outside?" he asked.

"Oh, he takes them in and lets them out very fast. He had them in the box but you didn't even see. Were you asleep?"

The old Boran's eyes popped as he reflected on the wonder. Then he surveyed Bukhari's great bulk, down to his large feet, and grinned incredulously.

"But surely not elephants," he said.

"Why certainly, elephants—tusks and all."

"Ah, wei-wei nasima rongo." (You tell me lies.)

"If you think so, come and I'll have the master put you in the box," and Bukhari drew him forward.

Terrified, the old chief shrank back. But as he moved to go, Bukhari caught him and whispered:

"The master can do everything, just like the British. He has many more boxes of many kinds too. We have to be very good to him."

"Yes, yes," mumbled the chief. "What can I do?"

"The master likes sheep," said Bukhari slyly. "Why don't you give the Missus two sheep?"

The laughter at the campfire rose to a new high.

"The best lamb I ever tasted," we could hear Omanga shout, and all the boys yelled, "Ai, ai, ai."

16

". . . Our friends think we're having a tough time out here, and I suppose it isn't any bed of roses by some of their standards, but to Osa and me it is Paradise in every way. We are doing the work we want to do, living in the great sunny, healthy out-of-doors, enjoying good food from our own garden, accomplishing what we believe is useful and important work, and we feel richer than anyone we know . . ."
—MARTIN JOHNSON

"DO YOU KNOW what day it is tomorrow?"

Martin looked up from his porridge, a little puzzled.

"Sure, it's Tuesday."

"Oh, shoot! You mean you don't know tonight is Christmas Eve?"

His eyes widened. "By George, if we stay out here much longer I won't even know what year it is. By that time our money will be gone and we won't be able to get home. We'll have to stay here and live on the fat of the land."

Then and there I made up my mind that I would give him a Christmas surprise such as he had never had before.

I had my mule, Lazy Bones, saddled, and with Boculy and three boys I started off to shoot our Christmas dinner. Although I knew how Martin felt about my going off alone, he would be busy in his laboratory and wouldn't miss me.

For some unaccountable reason Lazy Bones was very irritable. It was quite unlike him, because he usually had a sweet and gentle disposition, and I wondered about it. I dismounted, and carefully examined his legs to see if he had been hurt. I looked at the saddle, but everything seemed in order, so I mounted once again. We rode

199

along the trail and still the mule fidgeted, and seemed greatly disturbed about something.

As we came to a steep ravine, Lazy Bones suddenly stopped, then bucked. I hung on for a moment, then lost my grip and went over his head into the stones along the ravine. I landed head-first and was dazed for a few minutes. When I opened my eyes, Boculy was standing over me with a canteen of water.

"Did you hurt your head?" Boculy asked, his eyes popping.

"I got a little bump. But I'm all right. It's Lazy Bones. What's the matter with him?" I asked.

Boculy shook his head. The mule was standing beside him, peering down at me with big eyes, looking very forlorn and sympathetic. I think he was trying to explain to me what was wrong. The native boys said it was a puff adder that had frightened him. But I had had enough riding for one day, so I sent him on home with one of the boys leading him. Later on they reported that they had found a tick the size of a shilling under his saddle blanket!

We pressed on, and the boys spread out and watched for birds. Suddenly I spied a long, feathered neck showing above the grass. It would be just the thing for our Christmas dinner—a giant bustard. I raised my rifle, and fired. There was a short rustle, then no movement save the slight sway of the grass in the warm afternoon wind.

There lay the giant bustard. Thirty-five pounds of delicious African turkey. I held him up. He was a beauty. The feathers of his tail were spotted, his handsome chest a pearl-gray. His long beak and the proud little white pompom crest on his head were splotched with red where the bullet had entered. As I looked at him, I realized as never before that there was more joy in shooting with a camera than a gun. But this wild African turkey would taste mighty good on Christmas Day, so with two native boys carrying the prize, we turned back along an elephant trail.

As we emerged from a bit of forest, Boculy suddenly grasped

my arm. We stood motionless, hardly daring to breathe. Ahead, at the top of a ravine, was a leopard. He was sprawled out majestically in the golden grass among the tiger lilies, sunning himself. I raised my gun and slipped the safety. The leopard lifted his handsome head towards us, stared for a moment, then sniffed and gracefully slid away into the grass.

But that wasn't the end of our adventure. Just as we neared the entrance to Lake Paradise and our little village, we heard the unmistakable crunching sound of elephants. Boculy listened for a moment, held up one finger, which indicated that there was just one animal, and promptly fell to his knees. I followed suit, and so did the native boys.

We began crawling off on a detour, just as the elephant came into view. He halted, got our scent, looked in our direction, and began "rocking," which I knew to be the prelude to a charge. When we looked again, the elephant was quietly feeding. He must have thought us baboons, for I am sure that is how we looked as we crept along through the grass on all fours.

At the edge of the crater we met Martin. He seemed very worried. He had his .470 rifle under his arm.

"Osa, where in heaven's name have you been? I saw an elephant wandering up from the Lake and I was afraid you might meet him."

"We did meet your elephant," I laughed, "and what's more we met something else."

"Something else?" he snapped.

"Yes. Our Christmas dinner. Look, Martin! We're going to have a feast that will equal all the Christmas dinners you've ever had back home in Kansas."

"Equal? Why, Osa, I bet it will be better than any Christmas dinner back in Kansas."

Martin looked at me delightedly as the boys helped me lift the bustard.

"Just hold that pose," he said. "I'm going to get the camera and snap you—standing there and holding that bird. And we'll get Lazy Bones into the picture too."

"Hurry up!" I shouted to Martin as he focused the camera, and as the boys helped me hold up the prize. "This bird is heavy. It's almost as big as I am."

Of course, there was a little matter of cooking the thirty-five pound bird for the Christmas dinner.

First of all, the barbecue pit had to be prepared. The pit was about three feet deep, four feet long, and three feet wide. I had the boys line it with stones which were fired to a white heat, then covered with moist earth.

Then I cleaned and rubbed the bird with olive oil. Of course, there would have to be stuffing. What is a Christmas dinner without stuffing! And wild mushrooms from the forest would be just the thing to put in it.

These preparations completed, I stuffed the bird, sewed him up, rolled him in banana leaves, then wrapped him in a damp cloth, plastered with clay. He was then ready to be placed in the pit, and the pit filled with earth and a layer of coals on top. There I left him to cook for eight or nine hours, a process of steaming in his own juice—a "natural" fireless cooker.

What else could we have to make this a Christmas dinner without precedent? Our two-acre garden would solve that.

I went to the garden to get a couple of bunches of celery. This had been one of the problem children among my garden family and it was amazing what lovely white and tender stalks we now had.

In the forest, where I went to gather asparagus, I found a clump of beautiful stalks, which for some unknown reason the baboons hadn't touched. I was just about to cut them when a cobra raised its head out of the center of the cluster, ready and poised to strike. I screamed and the native boys, always on the alert, killed it. I particularly hate snakes, and the incident upset me a good deal, but not for long. I had too much to do.

Finally my menu was complete:

```
┌─────────────────────────────────────────────────────────┐
│                                                           │
│              CHRISTMAS DAY MENU SPECIAL                   │
│                    LAKE PARADISE                          │
│                                                           │
│                          *                                │
│                                                           │
│                      ANCHOVIES                            │
│              WILD BUFFALO OXTAIL SOUP                     │
│                (with garden vegetables)                   │
│                  WILD ROAST TURKEY                        │
│                      (bustard)                            │
│               WILD MUSHROOM STUFFING                      │
│        WILD ASPARAGUS              CANDIED SWEET          │
│        (Hollandaise Sauce)            POTATOES           │
│                   CELERY HEARTS                           │
│        MIXED GREEN SALAD      WATERMELON PRESERVES       │
│               STRAWBERRIES AND CREAM                      │
│                       COFFEE                              │
│                   NUTS & RAISINS                          │
│                                                           │
└─────────────────────────────────────────────────────────┘
```

I draped Spanish moss to look like bows over the fireplace, and above our chintz curtains at the window. In the forest I had found a bush laden with small red berries. It wasn't holly, of course, but I tied little bunches of it together to make wreaths and hung them all about the house. And, little by little, things took on the atmosphere of Christmas.

Lake Paradise was an Eden for every sort of flower. I gathered armfuls of them and arranged the room and the table until we looked as though we were having a real party.

There were tiger lilies from the plains, sometimes with one red and one yellow blossom on the same stalk. And orchids which would have cost a fortune in America bloomed on the trees in the yard. There were clusters of heatherspray, wild yellow poppies, wild gladiola, carnations and cosmos. There were no poinsettias, but we most certainly could say "Merry Christmas" with a house full of flowers.

And then it was Christmas morning at Lake Paradise.

Overlooking the great desert, I felt as if I were living on the roof of the world, as if I dwelt in a wind-swept tower, never before inhabited by man.

It was about seven-thirty when I called Martin to announce that our Christmas dinner was on the table. He came into the room, and for a few minutes he just stood there and stared at everything.

"Osa, it's wonderful!" he cried. "Watermelon preserve, too!"

"This beats that Christmas dinner we had in London. The Savoy hasn't anything on you, Osa."

We said no more but just pitched in and ate. I had never before been so proud of a table, and I had done it all from the jungle. When we had finished, Martin pushed back his chair and came over to my side of the table. He took my hand in his. I looked up at him. Neither of us could say a word. It was one of those times when no words could convey our feelings.

We went into the living room. By this time night had fallen. Stars shone in the sky; the moon sailed into view, cold, distant and serene. It poured a smooth river of silver light into the garden and left the forest in shadow. The same moon would be shining down on Kansas this very Christmas night. Time and space seemed close. I could feel the brisk chill of the African night, as the cool breeze stirred the chintz curtains at the window.

After we had finished coffee, Martin suddenly jumped up, nearly knocking over the tiny coffee table.

"Osa—the presents!" he cried. "The Christmas presents!"

I hadn't forgotten about them. Bukhari, who had kept most of the presents hidden under a pile of straw in his hut, had brought them in before dinner.

Martin was as excited as any small boy expecting a new bicycle.

He went over to the table in the corner where I had carefully arranged all the gifts and began to look at the various boxes.

"Holy smoke! What a lot of them! We did pretty well for ourselves, I think."

He was busy unwrapping the packages. There were ever so many, all sorts, sizes and shapes. Packages from our friends all over the world—packages from friends we didn't even know personally—packages that had arrived at Paradise many, many weeks before Christmas, some even months before, all carefully marked: "*Do not open until December 25th.*" There were our own special surprise packages that Martin and I had prepared for each other—things bought months before, ordered from America or Europe.

"What's this?" Martin was opening a small box. "It's from home—from Kansas."

"It's from your father." I had noticed the Independence postmark on the brown wrapping paper.

Martin turned to me. "Why, Osa—what's the matter?"

"Nothing."

"Nothing! Now, you can't fool me, honey. You were thinking about something. I know what it was—Kansas! When I opened that package from Dad."

"Yes, I was thinking of home. After all, it's Christmas, you know, and it *is* nice to think of home at Christmas."

"I wonder if it snowed in Kansas this Christmas, Osa. Remember how all the kids used to get out their sleds and go coasting down-hill? That was the best fun in the world."

I laughed as I thought of all the things we used to do as children back in Kansas during the Christmas holidays—those happy childhood days in Chanute when my brother and I would hitch our little yellow sleds to Mr. Jerome's grocery wagon, and go gliding along the avenues of snow, shouting with glee as his chestnut bay trudged through the deep drifts, and clapping our red mittened hands to keep warm. I shall always remember the trees, burdened with snow, and the doorsteps of every house in town chocked with the soft white stuff. The trees were crisp, sparkling, and white, and the air on Christmas morning quivered with the pealing bells of the Episcopal Church on Main Street and the music of the early morning carolers. I thought of the houses in Chanute, delicately frosted, with their gables and chimneys. Why, we hadn't hitched our sleds to an old grocery wagon at all on Christmas mornings; we had hitched them to the Star of Bethlehem.

I could hear Martin speaking. "I remember . . . I remember . . ."

Yes, "Remember!"—certainly one of the loveliest words in the English language.

After a bit, Martin lit his cigar, and we sat by the fireplace. Every flickering flame was a memory. I could see the store windows in Chanute, Kansas, brightly lit. Everything one could dream of had found its way to the counters of the stores. There was Main Street, hung with garlands and wreaths. And, right there in the middle of Main Street, stood an enormous Christmas tree, shining with colored lights and hung with ornaments and red and green ribbons. Santa Claus had come to Kansas!

And he was here in Africa, too.

Martin puffed away on his cigar. I looked up at him, and he smiled. He rose and came over to me.

"You know, Osa," he said, "I think that we must be the two happiest people in all the world."

"I'm sure of it, darling," I said.

"What do you say if we go out and take a walk?"

I got our coats, glanced at the mountains of Christmas cards and packages—from home, from Sir Harry Lauder, Mr. Eastman, Chic Sale, Mr. Pomeroy, Will Rogers, Mr. Wilcox, and many others. There's nothing in the world quite like knowing that your friends haven't forgotten you.

OSA AND BOCULY EXAMINE FRESH ELEPHANT TRACKS

Elephants have left their footprints in the mud outside the Lake Paradise crater.

OSA BRINGS HOME THE DINNER

A lesser bustard, or wild African turkey, and a
fine guinea fowl, "for the pot" at Lake Paradise.

A LION MAKES HIS KILL

Having broken the zebra's neck, the lion holds his quivering prize before beginning his feast.

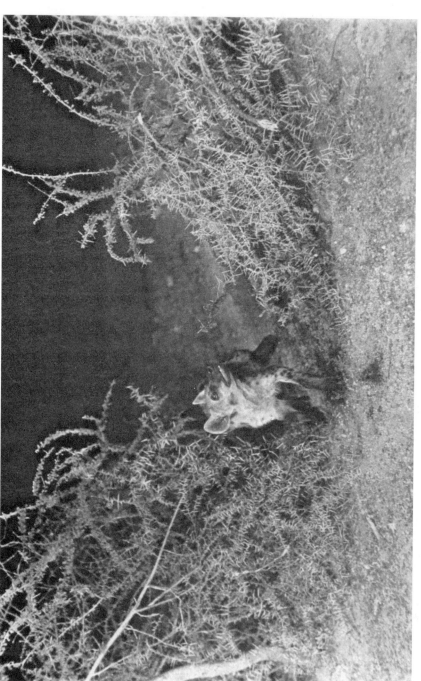

A SCAVENGER MAKES HIS OWN PORTRAIT

Laughing as he trips the wire setting off the flashlights, a hyena steals into Lake Paradise.

The scene was peaceful and lovely. We could see the black outline of the forest. The Lake was alive with moonlight, and Martin and I watched in silence as the animals came to the water to drink—elephants, baboons, rhino, leopards, and buffalo.

We heard the sounds of the elephants as they cracked down branches, lumbering their way through the denseness of the forest. We saw them at the water's edge, listened to their trumpetings.

As the animals wandered about, the ducks and the birds flew up from the surface of the Lake, and we heard the quick frightened beat of their wings in flight.

I huddled into my coat, and took Martin's hand in mine.

Stretched out before us, surrounding us on all sides, was a primeval world. I felt very close to the beginning of life.

As we looked up to the peak above us we saw a star twinkling at its very top like the star the Three Wise Men followed to a manger in Bethlehem.

We felt that here at Lake Paradise, deep in the heart of Africa, we had really found the timeless peace on earth, goodwill toward men. I nestled closer to Martin. Neither of us spoke. And we sat there into the dawn.

17

" . . . *At first we built our blinds so openly that they were advertisements to the game to stay away. Osa said, 'Even the natives run!' The animals saw our monstrosities of stone and trees and were at once panicked and would not come back for days or weeks . . ."*

—MARTIN JOHNSON

"Bedelia, Bedelia, I'm going to steal you."

I COULD HEAR Martin singing in his laboratory. Just why, from all the songs that had ever been composed, he chose "Bedelia" for his favorite, I never knew. But I knew that he was happy.

"Osa," Martin called, "come here. I want to show you what we got last night."

I took the negative and saw, crouched there in the full light of the flash, a beautiful leopard, gracefully posed, with every facial expression and marking of his coat clear and distinct.

"That's the best picture we have made at Paradise." Martin was bursting with pride. "And I've finished all the developing and we're going on safari in the morning!"

I was just about to tell him I had planned to spend the day in my garden. I had intended to keep my eye on Mumbora who was going to bake bread and biscuits. And there were the new curtains to be put up in the guest cottage. Well, they could wait.

After all, these safaris were the only means of getting our work done. But I began to wonder if our home would ever be "home."

Martin picked the various locations in which we were to work according to the season of the year and the kind of game we were after. Elephants were almost always to be found at Lake Paradise, but we had to go down to the plains and desert to get lions and other game. Some of our best and most interesting work was done around the waterholes.

During the dry season, the game, which had scattered far and wide through the rainy months, came to the waterholes in thousands, for the scorching heat dried up all but the largest springs and pools. Nowhere does the sun seem to be hotter than in Africa. Out there in the open we were exposed to the full blast of it and the temperature would shoot up to one hundred and twenty degrees in the shade, with very little shade from sparse acacia and mimosa trees.

We couldn't shut off the heat, and we were glad to have all the sun there was for photography; so we just made the best of it. Our blinds were built wherever the camera demanded: in a treetop, on a rock kopje, or on the ground as near to the waterhole as we could make it without scaring the game. We took along thermos flasks, blankets, pillows, and whatever we could manage to make ourselves as comfortable as possible. And because we often had to stay there and swelter for days and days without getting a single picture or until we got the shots we wanted, we took plenty of newspapers and magazines. The magazines were months old, but they kept our minds occupied and they also kept us from talking, which we dared not do lest we frighten the animals. In some places safari ants and scorpions were so bad that we couldn't lie on the ground and so took camp chairs in which to rest when we weren't at the cameras.

Our ground blinds were built of whatever was most inconspicuous—rocks in a rocky landscape, thornbush in bush country or open plain. The animals were hard to fool, so we made the blind look as natural as possible, setting the trees and brush to make them look as though they were actually growing. We gave ourselves a roof, if we could, or we stretched a blanket or tarpaulin inside the blind to give us shade.

Sometimes the boys would start cutting down thornbush and would get themselves covered with stinging black ants. A little black puff-ball hanging to a thorn branch meant an ants' nest, and sometimes these would still be on the brush after our blind was built. Then the ants would get into our clothes or drop down into my hair and give us a lively day. When the ants bit me I wanted to scream, but knew that if I did, there wouldn't be any game. We had to get pictures, so I let them bite and at night doused myself with ammonia, though I often looked as though I had the measles.

The boys also dragged thornbush down to the waterhole and filled in the depressions, so that we could keep the game out in sight and before the cameras. We would let this remain for a few days, so that the animals gradually became used to seeing it. Then we would crawl into the blind early one morning and wait for the light and the animals to be just right for beginning our photography. It was tedious work and it called for a maximum of patience and for steeled nerves. I think it is the most tedious work I have ever done, sitting there by the hour and trying to be as silent as the tomb.

Our schedule was to get up at dawn, for we had to reach the blind before sunrise. The boys were supposed to call us, but we never took a chance on them, for they loved to sleep. Oftentimes *we* had to wake the boys. We always set our alarm clock for four-thirty.

"Please go away and let me sleep!" Martin would yawn when he heard the clock. Although we never stayed up late at night, and would go to bed as soon as Martin had smoked his after-dinner cigar—no later than nine o'clock—it seemed to us in the morning that we had hardly shut our eyes when four-thirty would come 'round. And when it rained, or we had a holiday for any reason, nothing seemed better than to be able to roll over at dawn and go back to sleep.

M'pishi would make a quick breakfast for us while we were dressing. Even on safari, breakfast was a big meal for Martin, and I tried to have enough supplies to give him some variety. He liked his porridge and pan muffins, and I used to carry tinned kippers and tinned sausage whenever I could.

"Give him plenty of good things to eat, darling," Grandmother had said to me when I married him. "He's a big man and he has to have lots of good food and that is surely the best way to keep a man happy."

"Is it going to be hot cakes this morning?" he would ask as he splashed himself with cold water at his little basin in front of our tent. "Or some of Grandmother's baking powder biscuits— the big ones that a man can dunk in his coffee and enjoy?"

"Not *this* morning. You're going to get a surprise—a scrambled ostrich egg, just for you."

While Martin was checking his cameras and film, I would help the cook put up a good lunch, just as if we were going on a picnic, and load up the porters and hurry them off. Then we left orders with Suku when to send the boys back to the blind for us that evening, and since he could not read a clock, we set the alarm again for the proper hour.

We had to reach the waterhole before the sun came up so that the game would not see us going into the blind. Sometimes we would have to walk miles, for we couldn't camp near to the water-holes, and even if we were using our cars, we would leave them at a considerable distance and walk the rest of the way so as not to frighten the game. Often we would take separate water-holes ten or more miles apart, so as to speed our work.

My first pictures were anything but prize shots. Waterhole work required a great deal of panning—or moving of the camera —for the game would not group themselves into satisfactory compositions, but were constantly moving about. My panning was atrocious, and I got animals with no heads or a head and no body, or would cut up the groups badly. Or I would get a lot of beautiful sand or sky—but no animals!

"I'm going to make a comedy film of your shots sometime," Martin howled when he developed some of these. "They will be the world's best."

But as time passed, and I learned the tricks, I sometimes had the luck to get good pictures on a day when he had not been successful, and this pleased him very much.

Our early morning walks to the blind were exhilarating. The air was full of fragrance, even on the desert, and everything was a delicate soft grayish-blue color, contrasting with the blinding brilliance that would soon follow. That was the finest time of the day. Nowhere in the world have I heard so many beautiful bird-calls. Hundreds of thousands of birds seemed to be singing and whistling at once. On the clear air I could hear the faintest coo of the doves or the squeaky voice of a baby partridge. As we walked, birds flew up all about us and out of every bush we passed and beat the air as they whirled overhead.

Oryx, zebra, and plains animals would be browsing in small groups and were very alert and easily startled, for this was still feeding time for the lion. These animals will not drink at water-holes during the night unless they are desperate for water, and they are always on the move, for every tree, bush and clump of grass may hide a lion or leopard. Their lives are in constant danger. Except for the cats, only the rhino, elephant and buffalo dare to drink during the night. From the distance we could usually hear the roar of a lion announcing that he had made his kill, and sometimes we would see one stalking zebra or antelope.

Having reached the blind, the boys would help to set up the equipment and then close the opening with a pile of brush and would walk back to the cars or to camp. The blinds were usually heavy enough to keep us secure against anything but rhino or elephant, but once we were closed in, we would have had a hard time getting out without the help of our boys. This seemed to me a great risk, especially when I was all alone in a blind, but Martin insisted that this was the safest and best arrangement, so that is the way we left it. Many a time out there alone I was scared to death—more of the possibility of having some hostile natives or Wanderobos come along, than of the game.

"You're not going to take my little girl out there again!" declared my father heatedly, when Martin told him about this. "You know what I told you when you married her! Tramps on a railroad are bad enough; but she can't take these risks and I won't have it!"

"Don't you worry; she can take care of herself," Martin always said proudly.

So that the animals could not see us move about inside the blind, we hung a blanket over the back wall. Except for the camera openings, the walls were closed, though we had peepholes and sometimes a "window" that could be opened if necessary. Even our cameras were camouflaged in greens, yellows and bronzes to conceal them. We had to be constantly on the alert, except at noon. If we were to take our eyes from the waterhole, we might miss our choicest picture. The animals were very quiet unless they stampeded. They would steal down to the water and, since we were twenty-five yards or more away from them, we could not hear them drink.

We had changed the technique used on our first expedition to Africa. Then we had been satisfied to get animals on the run. That was exciting and dramatic, but it was not what we wanted. We wanted to photograph them as they actually lived their family and individual lives, just as though we were not there. So *we* now did the hiding and tried to keep them entirely unaware of us.

Martin would become drowsy with the heat, and he always

worked so hard that I liked to see him rest. So I tried to keep awake and be on the lookout. He used to jolly me about being his "little watch-dog," pinch me on the cheek and thank God for a woman's curiosity. Then he would start reading a magazine and fall asleep.

When animals appeared I nudged him, and as he usually jumped up and made some exclamation, I would cover his mouth with my hand before I woke him, to shush him in advance.

"How do you expect me to keep the animals here if you snore like that?" I would whisper.

"You feed me too well; that's the trouble." Then he would begin to grind out film and comment on the picture he was getting.

"Doggone! Isn't that beautiful—those zebra in the cat-tails, with the umbrella tree overhead and the little plover at the water?" He had an unerring eye for beauty, and his pictures always had in them a perfect sense of composition.

Very little game appeared in the morning, unless it happened to be a hot day. Normally they would come down in single file, but on a torrid day they would rush to water in herds or groups.

The zebra came first. They were the most timid of the lot and would stampede away at the slightest sound, with a quick nervous switch of their tails and clattering of hoofs. The oryx stood off at a distance, watching the zebra, and when all the excitement was over and the zebra had settled to drink, they would come slowly within camera range, moving with grace and assurance. And then would follow the other antelope and gazelle.

The buck impala trailed behind the zebra in single file, their harems of more than a hundred wives following close. I have seen a single buck with a family of as many as two hundred wives and children. These would wait at a discreet distance while the buck came down to see if the coast were clear. He would take quick little steps, stopping every few feet to lift his beautiful head and scan the landscape. Then, after he had scouted thoroughly and assured himself that the waterhole was safe, he would go back for his wives and babies and gallantly escort them to the water.

The giraffe stood off in the distance for hours before hazarding a drink. Then some curious and venturesome baby pushed ahead and its mother had to follow, for she had no means of restraining it and would not dare to let it get more than a few feet away from her protection. The other giraffe gradually came up behind her, but were always ready to run at the slightest camera sound or other disturbance. Tick birds clung to their backs and were a great annoyance, for they might fly up at any noise, however harmless, and the giraffe then clattered away.

Whether they stood still or galloped with that disjointed gait of theirs, the giraffe were models of dignity and grace, and I watched them endlessly. Their tails switched continuously with a slow and rhythmic motion, as if they were being blown back and forth by the wind. All giraffe seemed to look down upon the other animals with haughtiness and scorn and to mingle with them only because they had to do so.

Through the binoculars I watched them twitching their noses and puckering up their funny mouths as if to say: "There's something wrong down there. That's a queer looking contraption beside the waterhole. What is it?" Sometimes the whirr of the camera seemed to fascinate them, and instead of running they just stood there and looked our way, as motionless as statues.

Just as aristocratic were the ostrich, and even more comical. With heads held at an absurdly high angle, and tripping along as though they were walking on hot coals, they made straight for the water, without looking to one side or the other. They seemed never to admit that they so much as noticed the other game. Then they drank long and deliberately, scooping up the water with a low, level push of the beak that made them look as though they were ducking their heads. And just as snobbishly they walked away.

The game made a wide path for them, for the ostrich have very sharp claws and erratic and murderous dispositions. A single kick of those powerful legs would knock out or rip open anything but an elephant or rhino.

Ostrich were always a good show, and of course I couldn't resist the babies. The youngsters were bald and featherless, with scrawny necks and toothpick legs, and they wobbled around, trying to walk a straight line. The mother ostrich would strut along, paying no apparent attention to the flock that toddled behind her, but if a hyena or other enemy showed up she was after him like a streak. Other hens followed, ruffing out their plumes and tripping about like a ballet. And the cock, in his splendor, would be among them, preening himself and prancing about as though he couldn't stop showing off for an instant, although the hens made straight for the water and paid not the slightest attention to him.

Quantities of birds flocked around the drinking places, completely oblivious of the game, whatever it was. Great flocks of doves, grouse, partridge, vulturine guinea fowl, cranes, snipe, wild ducks, Egyptian geese, and others kept things in a lively state. The haughty secretary bird, wearing her beautiful head-crest at a rakish angle to the rear, walked quickly to the water's edge, took dainty little sips of about two drops each, raising her head each time to see if she were being attacked. The greater bustard, equally proud, and wearing a gorgeous pom-pom at his throat and a full and feathery crest on his head, made a grand entrance. He stood, lifting his polka-dotted wings and his long tail for all to admire, and then walked right into the water and drank as though he would never stop. Kavarando cranes danced about madly and kept up a continual flirtation and a jittery song: "Oh-ha-a-a-a-! Oh-ha-a-a-a!"

Most comical of all was Mr. Warthog. He was amusing, but no joke to fight with. The other animals treated him with respect. He trotted in with his wife and ten little razor-backs in single file, each with his tail straight up like a flagpole. They not only drank but plunged in and wallowed. The other animals all looked disgusted at this; promptly they walked away and would not attempt to drink the roiled water, but waited until the pig family had left.

As we learned to recognize animals that came to the waterholes again and again, from their peculiar markings or disfigurements, we gave them names. "Here comes old scramble-stripes," Martin would whisper. Or it might be "The Uzee" (the old man), or "Mr. Unicorn" (an oryx with one horn), or "Granny Twiga" (the old grandmother giraffe). Seeing our friends among the herds did a lot to relieve the monotony of the heat and the long hours of breathless waiting.

In the blinds, we lifted our feet and put them down as if we were walking on a creaky floor. When there were leaves or stones, we would lay down blankets to step upon, and we were always careful not to brush against each other. When I wanted to say something to Martin, or he to me, we would wink or make a gesture in our own eye-and-sign language, or whisper cautiously. But after it was all over and we had got a good picture and the animals were gone—chattering baboons would have been no competition for either of us!

About one in the afternoon, I would get out our lunch basket and we would eat inside the blind. We usually had two thermos bottles of hot coffee, game sandwiches (sometimes breast of partridge, for Martin was very fond of it), stuffed eggs, American sweet pickles, and a tin of tomatoes which we ate and drank as the coolest thing we knew. Martin would smoke a cigar and read, for there was little else we could do, and we would relax and try to catch forty winks.

That was noon hour in the blind. The sun was directly overhead and we nearly suffocated. We kept on our helmets and spine-pads for protection, even if we had shade, and we covered the cameras with an umbrella or tarpaulin. Often, at noon, we would catch

sight of a beautiful animal or group for which we had been waiting for months, and we would try to photograph it, but this was impossible due to the shimmering heat waves, and our developed
negatives were usually spoiled.

From two-thirty to four o'clock, the game would come back to
drink, and at four o'clock we got busy again in earnest, for the
light was then best. Sometimes the dust, which the animals had
kicked up all day, would be so heavy that it ruined the light, but
we learned to judge this pretty well.

Animals won't perform for the camera like Hollywood stars.
And to catch them doing what we wanted them to do might take
weeks, months or years. They would do the most interesting things
when we least expected it and consequently were unprepared.
Later, we would watch for them to repeat the action and might
never see it again.

In Hollywood, too, any amount of light can be had in an instant to illuminate any subject or angle. But if our sunshine failed
us, as it might for some reason at any minute, we had to stop work
and wait until the sun made up its mind to help us again.

From four until six, we worked like beavers, watching every
move the game made and selecting the unusual specimens or
groups and the most interesting action. Then, about six o'clock,
we would decide to call it a day and Martin blew a blast on his
shrill police whistle to call the boys. They would come running to
open the blind.

We had to carry everything home with us, even if we were coming back the next morning, for hyenas would steal anything that
had leather on it, and sometimes even other articles. Baboons
were so curious that they would get into everything, and they
were as destructive and mischievous as a gang of bad little boys.

One blistering hot day at Chobe Hills, I lay in the blind waiting
for something to happen. Martin had gone off to another water-

hole. The day dragged out with no luck. In the late afternoon, I spied plains game coming up from the distance—zebra, oryx, gazelle, giraffe. But they lingered, on the alert, as if fearful, and I wondered if our blind frightened them or whether they got my scent, when I suddenly saw a long line of natives approaching from another direction.

The natives went to the waterhole, slaked their thirst and filled their gourds. They were so strange-looking that I went out to meet them. They proved to be Merus on safari. They were quite frightened, and I could not understand them nor they me. The women suddenly went into a huddle. Then they brought me a burnt sweet potato and some burnt corn and bananas! They seemed to say, "Poor little girl! She is lost out here, she will surely starve." Though I knew that they needed their food, I could not have refused it.

Often at these waterholes we met Wanderobos, the wild men of the Northern Frontier. They live deep in the forest and are seldom seen, for they come out only for game, water and wild honey. They are pretty hard on the game because they kill elephants, giraffe and other animals for meat and skins, and they make the neighborhood dangerous with their poisoned arrows, set in traps. So the government runs them in whenever they are caught, scares them thoroughly, and tries to teach them better ways. We have often seen them scurrying off into the bush or up the side of a cliff, wiry and agile and bushy-headed, their inevitable bow and arrow always in hand.

Their poisoned arrows and traps were a menace to our own safaris and we were often stopped by them. We never knew, when coming up to a waterhole in their country, when we might press against a branch or step against some vine that would release an arrow, and the arrows might be set in several directions. The porters were always wary: they would stop the safari in its tracks with a shout at the merest sign of trouble. The traps were particularly a problem in thick forest. Here again Boculy was a great help, for he knew how the arrows were placed and he could "spring" them from behind or by cutting vines or tossing poles in ahead, or by beating the trail.

The arrows of the Wanderobos are poisoned by the venom of a scorpion or cobra, or by the milk of a poison bush mixed together with honey or gum. The merest scratch of such an arrow-point will mark an animal for death, usually within a few hours, depending upon the poison used. The animal is paralyzed or else he goes mad, froths at the mouth, tears out of the herd and dies. But the meat is not affected and is perfectly edible, so we were told. At least the Wanderobos eat it. They cut out the part around the wound and eat the rest, and they also drink the blood.

The Wanderobos wear no clothes. They usually travel alone or in very small groups, and scatter and run for all they are worth at sight of a stranger.

We have often seen their campfires, but on going to the fires have found the Wanderobos gone. We have found shallow sleeping pits, not unlike gorilla pits, which they have dug beside their fires and filled with mattresses of twigs and leaves. Generally they prefer caves for shelter. They have no huts or villages and are the perfect nomads, living as near to the original savage state of man as is probably possible today. Our porters would see their fires and shake their heads and say, " 'Mbaya sana" (very bad). The boys feared their stealth and cunning more than their strength. However, they never stole from our camps, probably because they are so shy about any contact with strangers. Very likely, too, they have no wants that their hunting does not satisfy.

As we were walking back to camp from our blind one evening we came upon a tiny native boy, not more than six or seven years old, herding his sheep and goats back to his father's manyetta for the night. He carried a little spear that would not have hurt a thing, but it was his badge of importance. He was to become a warrior and he must be a brave one.

As we followed him, the sun set and there in the dusk, not thirty yards off the trail, we saw a herd of more than twenty elephants.

The toto began to sing at the top of his little voice, and went right on without a quiver. We stopped behind some bush and watched, ready to shoot if necessary, for the wind blew directly to the elephants and they could not miss his scent, and they most surely saw his flock. But the toto never faltered. He went straight on, bravely singing his song, to keep his spirits up.

The elephants went on feeding and seemed to pay no attention whatever. Either they sensed that he was a little child (and I have always given the elephant credit for such intelligence) or else they were just too hungry to care. Or it may have been merely the toto's good luck. In any event, we saw him turn off over a rise of ground and disappear.

18

*". . . Osa does not like rhinos and
I am sure that when we are safely
back home and she has a nightmare,
it will be a rhino she sees coming up
the fire-escape. . . ."*
—MARTIN JOHNSON

"FARU! FARU! RHINO! Rhino coming!"

N'dundu stood at the front of our safari column, brandishing
his gun and waving back to us wildly.

The safari halted. Thick bush closed in all about us and we
could see nothing, but the camels were already beginning to buck.
I stood ready with my gun while Martin walked forward.

Then, straight out of the bush, half way up the line, a huge
bulk plunged into the safari. Camels lunged and ran. Boys scattered and shinnied up trees. There was so much confusion that
the rhino was gone before we could see him clearly. But he was
soon back again. There was a shot, and as I ran forward, I could
hear Martin scolding.

"Don't you ever do that again, you fool! Do you want to kill
me?"

"But Master, the rhino was charging."

"Well, you did a good job of it, for once." He turned to me.
"He got the rhino, but when I saw him aim that gun my way . . .
whew! It's a mistake to give any of them guns."

Our safari by now was a complete wreck. Crates and boxes
thrown off by the crazed camels were strewn about everywhere;

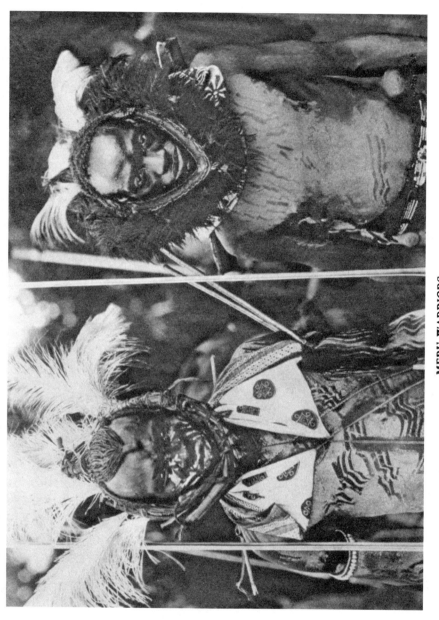

MERU WARRIORS

Two native warriors wearing head-dresses of ostrich feathers. Their war paint of red, white and blue is made of earth and berry juices.

OSA TURNS A RHINO CHARGE

With her screams, Osa startles two charging rhinos and they run away.

OSA AT HOME ON SAFARI

Before starting off for a day in the field, she checks her
guns thoroughly to be sure they are ready for action.

camels were running away, with their keepers in pursuit; our porters, chattering like mad, were trying to collect their wits and their baggage. The result was that we had to pitch camp and spend the evening reorganizing ourselves.

Often rhino charged our safaris, and it seemed that wherever and however we met the beasts the meeting was always violent. Rhino are always looking for trouble and for a chance to murder, not only human beings but every animal as well, and all the animals hate them. They are nothing but gangsters and are certainly Africa's public enemies number one.

Rhino go to bed with a nasty disposition and wake up in the morning in the same frame of mind. They never associate with other animals and seldom travel with their own kind, unless with a mate or a baby. Of all the animals in Africa, I dislike the rhino most. And what is more he seems to know it, for he is always chasing me up trees.

"There goes my little boy scout, climbing trees again," Martin would howl as he saw me swing up on a branch to get away from one of the monsters. But I noticed that he was just as quick at it when one of them came his way.

When I went fishing, I was always likely to run into a rhino, because I often got into thick bush and my only path would be a rhino trail along the river bank. There I might find one of these animals asleep, or scuffing along toward a drink, or a female nursing her baby, and I was always on the lookout.

On my way back to camp one evening, after a day of fishing at the Eauso Nyiro River during a safari we were making for rhino pictures, I rode my mule Lazy Bones and was telling N'dundu and the boys who walked beside me about my first encounter with a rhino. I became very excited and the boys were listening intently. The headman was completely absorbed. He kept saying, "Ndiyo (yes), M'sahib," and nodding his head as his eyes watched me.

Suddenly I spied a real rhino and yelled, "Faru iko!" The boys only laughed, thinking I was just being dramatic, even when I leaped off Lazy Bones and took aim with my rifle. I had literally to drag one of them behind a tree, as the rhino made for us and slid past. Fortunately, the beast charged on down the trail.

Rhino often finish a charge like that, as much as to say, "Well, I gave them the scare of their lives. I really ought to mash them, but I'll let them off this time."

Almost everything they did seemed to me to be a little crazy. In the heat of the day, when they wanted to sleep after browsing all night and wallowing in a mud hole all morning, they would not pick a nice big tree near by and lie down there. Instead, they would walk to some rocky hill or mountain, perhaps fifteen miles away, climb up among the volcanic slag and boulders and find some tree about the size of a beach umbrella, only half large enough, and flop down there to snooze. One big rhino under such a small tree looked ludicrous, yet oftentimes there were two! Frequently we had to climb up there in the roasting heat to get their pictures, and this didn't make the idea seem any more reasonable to me.

About four in the afternoon, rhino start feeding. They break small limbs from the trees and chew the ends into a pulp. Thorn-bush and scrub are their favorite foods. They also peel the bark off trees with their horns. They enjoy leaves, but I have never seen them eat grass or any other food. Like a horse, the rhino chews a long time on his food and then spits out the fibre.

On the Northern Frontier there are no white rhino. The principal difference between the white and black species has always seemed to me to be that the white rhino looks blacker than the black rhino. The different soils around Lake Paradise, however, gave us rhino in all colors—red at the N'groon Mountains where the beasts rolled in the red dust and wallowed in the red mud at waterholes, black at Lake Paradise from the black cotton soil, white on the plains from the white alkali dust and the soda pools.

Rhino wear mud packs to keep away the flies. Perhaps this is where the natives learned the trick of putting red earth on their bodies, mixed with castor oil, the smell of which would surely keep anything away.

Whenever we pitched camp at night, we would always order the porters to build a shelter of poles and grass for the cook to use as his kitchen, and beside this a work-table made of smaller poles tied together with jungle vines. On his work-table, the cook would place his aluminum pots and pans, to keep them clean and away from ground pests. In good weather he and the boys preferred to sleep in the open around the cook's fire.

One night we were wakened by a terrible racket. We rushed out of our tent into the bright moonlight and saw a rhino tearing out of camp. The boys were already up trees. For fear he might come back, I got my rifle and fired a few warning shots into the air in the rhino's direction.

The cook had seen the rhino first and had started running across the plain. He now came back, somewhat sheepish but still scared. The rhino had noticed the bright aluminum in the moonlight, so the cook thought, and had charged for it as the most attractive target on the landscape.

Blaney Percival had told us that a rhino had come into his camp and charged his campfire and stomped it out. But we usually found that a good fire would keep them off. We always had fires burning all night, especially when we were in big game country, with elephant, rhino, lion or buffalo about.

To keep these fires blazing, I had the porters bring firewood each evening as they came in from the field. Each porter we left in camp during the day also had a share of firewood to bring in for his chore. And two porters each night took their turns as watchmen, patrolling for animals and keeping up the fires.

"And I don't want you coming in the middle of the night to call the Master or Missus," I would warn them. "I want to sleep tonight." For they would wake us at the slightest provocation.

We had a real scare one night when a rhino came right into camp and snorted up to the tent where Martin and I were sleeping. I had a double scare, for when I woke I had been dreaming about rhino. I hated them all and was so angry that I jumped up and grabbed my gun and ran screaming out of the tent, which was a very foolish thing to do. The rhino had gone off to some distance. He stood there for a few moments trying to make up his mind whether to wipe me off the earth, then snorted loudly, wheeled and ran away.

I saw that the fires were all out and the sentries had evidently been asleep. That was the reason we had rhino invading us! I gave the boys a good dressing down, and I instructed Bukhari that from then on there would be fires every night and it was going to be hard on any sentries I caught asleep. I felt that Martin had enough to do to take care of his cameras and that it was my job to give him every protection and comfort possible, and at least a decent night's rest after a hard day in the field.

Tents were always a great temptation to the rhino. The cloth bleached out in the rains and the sun, and on moonlight nights they shone like beacons across the plain. One night a rhino charged right through Bukhari's tent, taking it along with him and leaving Bukhari safe in his cot. An ugly rhino wrapped in one of Benjamin Edgington's creations must have been a funny sight to the other game, but it was not so funny to us, for we were out a costly tent which we badly needed and which could not be replaced.

At the waterholes at night, we were always sure of at least one good rhino fight. They locked horns at the slightest provocation, or for no reason at all, and gored each other terribly. Nine out of ten rhino wear huge open wounds or scars from these fights. Some of the gashes are as large as dinner plates, and I am sure these must contribute to the animal's ugly disposition.

Usually the fight was over a female. And the females seemed to enjoy the rows, even to encourage them. A coy two-ton lady would rub against the side of one of the big fellows and trot around in a silly way, then go over and rub noses with the other male. Then the trouble would start. The males would paw the ground, race at each other, clinch and whirl around in circles, snorting like locomotives. Sometimes a fight would last the entire night and completely wear us out watching it.

Trying to get flashlights of one of these encounters, Martin and I set up an elaborate arrangement of cameras at a waterhole and secreted ourselves in a thornbush blind. Soon a rhino and his mate appeared, sniffed around for a while and then gave our cameras a wide berth, although the wind was right and they should not have got our scent. They went off to the edge of the pool. In a few minutes another male appeared and in no time at all a fight was on, completely out of range of our cameras.

The fight ended abruptly after about twenty minutes, and the rhinos came back and went off up the trail down which they had come. But they met other rhino who were coming down to water. Instead of fighting the newcomers, all stopped and seemed to have a sort of conference, then the new arrivals came down the trail and skirted our blind and cameras, just as the others had done. They also stormed around for a time and went off without giving us a picture. We concluded that the first rhinos had somehow warned the others and that perhaps there was some real fraternity among them after all.

"Rhinos never attack man unless they are provoked," Blaney had once said. Therefore I was very amused when Blaney was charged by a rhino one day as he drove serenely along in a car, with no intention of provoking anything. Even though he shot into the air and finally shot the rhino on the horn to divert him, the beast tore into Blaney's car and ruined the radiator.

"Must have been something wrong with that one," remarked Blaney, very perplexed.

We never shot rhino unless we had no other choice. Our business was to get pictures, and when a rhino did charge the cameras we shot into the ground, into the air and all around him, trying to scare him off. Sometimes I would shoot one at the base of the horn with a solid nosed bullet which would ricochet off and not wound the animal, but would give him a good headache for a couple of hours. Frequently the rhino could not be frightened. We learned from long experience to tell when he wasn't bluffing and meant business. Then it became a question of his life or ours.

In addition to our feeling against killing, it cost us fifty dollars to shoot each rhino, and several times that amount for each elephant; so using our lungs or firing in the air to scare them off was an economy.

At Lake Paradise one afternoon we were photographing a mother rhino and her baby. This is always dangerous because any mother animal with a baby is jittery and will charge on sight, and the rhino is particularly suspicious.

Martin had risen from the ferns in which we were concealed and was cranking the camera. The baby spied us, ran under its mother, then out again, and the mother, now thoroughly alarmed, began looking for us.

"Look!" I whispered suddenly.

Martin turned quicker than a shot. There, walking straight for us, was a big bull rhino, his head lowered and his two horns aimed straight at the camera.

I grabbed my .465 elephant gun.

"See if you can turn him," Martin shouted.

I shot over his back, screamed, shot at his horn. On he came.

I knew Martin was making a good film of the rhino, and probably thought this was one of those familiar false alarms. I didn't think so, however, and I was right. The rhino stopped, snorted and charged. At twenty-five feet I aimed and shot for the brain. The great brute fell.

"Martin, does this day mean anything to you?"

"Why, yes, of course. This is the day we ship film."

"Oh-h-h-h!! Well, I'm not going to put the paraffin on your old tins today. I'm going out, and you can ship film without me. Bukhari! Get my guns!"

Martin's eyes widened in perplexity.

"Where are you going?"

"I'm going out to find a rhino, and I hope he charges me!"

"Osa, what's the matter?"

"If you don't know, I'm not going to tell you. If our wedding anniversary means no more than that to you, I don't care what happens."

And off I went, so upset I wanted to weep. I actually wished I could meet a rhino or an elephant right there in front of his eyes so that he would be good and sorry.

Like all families, we had our little tiffs, but we agreed on so much that the differences were always over very inconsequential things and were quickly made up. However, two persons are bound to get on each other's nerves occasionally with daily association for so many years.

Perhaps Martin would row with the boys and boss them around, or impose some severe discipline in a way that seemed to me extreme or unnecessary or bad-tempered, and I would put on a huff, hop on my mule Lazy Bones, call my gunbearer and an extra boy or two, and start for the forest. Sometimes I would make use of the opportunity to do some real errand such as going out to gather watercress, wild asparagus or flowers. Again I would go in whatever direction the mule started to take, just to get away. Invariably, when I returned I would find that Martin had been looking for me and was very worried, and this gave me both a certain feminine sense of triumph and drew me to him, for he was the kindest man on earth.

M'pishi might run out and say that the master had been searching for me and had questioned him, that he had told the master I had gone to the forest, that the master feared I might be harmed and had sent M'pishi after me. Would I come back, for "Big Master very worried."

In the same mood, Martin would flee to his laboratory and work off his anger or emotion on his negatives. Or make believe that he was doing so, at least until he got hungry.

We were camped on the Eauso Nyiro River, and Martin had gone out scouting for rhino with Boculy. I felt as though I wanted fish chowder for dinner and this was to be my day. At Paradise there were no fish, so whenever I was on safari near a fishing stream I did my best to catch a supply for camp. Martin and I left camp about the same time and we traveled a mile or so together before I branched down to the river, riding my mule Lazy Bones. N'dundu and Butoto were with me. I had gone perhaps a quarter of a mile when I spied a rhino coming after us at full speed. I knew Lazy Bones could not carry me and outrun the rhino, so I jumped off and tried to race with him. But he stopped dead and balked. I pulled and yanked at him, but he wouldn't budge.

"You fool!" I screamed at him. "You're crazier than a rhino!" And I left him there and off I ran.

Martin was still in sight. The two native boys were close to my heels, and the rhino was not far behind them. I fired twice, but in my excitement missed. Butoto scrambled to the top of a big ant hill.

Martin had heard my scream and had started back on the run to meet me. His boys followed him. Lazy Bones was terrified, and sped past me so fast that I wished I had stayed on his back. Martin was still too far off to shoot the rhino, so he fired into the air, and he and the boys started yelling for all they were worth. With all the shooting and shouting, the rhino's ears probably ached, for he wheeled and disappeared in the long grass near the river.

I was furious with fear and rage. It seemed as though we were having just one too many rhino scares.

"I'm not any too fond of them either," Martin said as he held me in his arms. "Anyway," he added, chuckling, "just come running back to papa when you get into danger, and be sure to bring the danger behind you. This would have made a grand comedy picture."

I was just recovering my sense of humor when I examined my gun and found that N'dundu had placed only four cartridges in the chamber that morning instead of the regular charge of five. I realized to what serious consequences this might have led if I had been out on the field and had counted on the usual five shots when in reality there were only four. I lost my temper and lit into N'dundu. I shouted to Martin that he was to be discharged. When small details become matters of life and death, we had to know that our boys could be counted upon. After the set-to with N'dundu he disappeared, and did not show up at camp all that night. In the morning Martin found him waiting outside our tent. The boy was so sorry that he actually cried.

"Well, I'll forgive you this time, N'dundu, but it must never happen again," I said finally. And from the look on the poor fellow's face I was sure that there would be no repetition of the incident.

The boys were not in the least malicious, even though they were often as prankish as children. At times they referred to us as "Mama" and "Papa," and whenever one scratched or cut his finger, he would come to us and say, "I am your toto; I am sick. Please help my finger." We would give him a bandage and he would leave full of genuine gratitude. All things considered, I think we understood them pretty well.

Occasionally the boys or I would find animal babies. We promptly returned them to their mother unless she were dead, in which case I would invariably adopt the babies as pets. The boys would bring in these tiny animals, saying: "Here, Mama, are two fine leopard totos," knowing I would enjoy mothering the little things.

So I acquired at Paradise from time to time, and kept until they went back to the forest, a lion, a leopard, two baboons, two mongoose, an aardvark, a fox, a genet cat, a baby elephant, a Tommy gazelle, several ostrich and a flock of guinea fowl.

Our gadgets and supplies were of the greatest interest to the boys and other natives, and whenever we encountered a native safari on the desert, the chief or the most inquisitive among them would ply our boys for hours with questions about us and our magic.

"Yes, and the master has a powder that he mixes with water," said Boculy to a Samburu herder one day, describing our cement. "Then he can turn it into rock, in any place or shape he wants."

The Samburu looked very astonished. Suddenly his eyes lit up and he asked if he could have some.

"What will you do with it?" asked Boculy. "You have rocks enough on the plains."

"But I have an enemy," the Samburu confided. "If the Master would bring me some of his powder, I would put it in my enemy's waterhole and stop it up so he would have no water and all his stock would perish."

My most thrilling rhino adventures seemed to come when I was out alone, or perhaps they seemed more exciting for that reason. When we were on safari to the plains waterholes, there were literally tens of thousands of game birds about, and often I used to go out before breakfast and watch them come down in fluttering clouds to the springs for water. If we were short of food, I took a few home for Martin's breakfast.

As I was taking one of these before-breakfast strolls just outside camp one morning, I saw a large flock of partridge. I flushed them and fired. Out from behind a thornbush came a snorting rhino. I had only a 20 gauge shotgun, which was no match for this huge beast, so I turned and ran for all I was worth, with the two-ton colossus lumbering after me.

Reaching camp, I screamed, and Martin came out with a rifle. There stood our cars in a group, and the rhino charged up to them. Seeing that the automobiles were not afraid of him, and probably alarmed by the strange scent of rubber and gasoline, he gave up. He backed off and trotted away, stopping occasionally to snort and impress upon us that he wasn't really afraid.

Martin burst into laughter. "You're a fine one, he said. "You go out to get me a partridge for breakfast and you come home with two tons of rhinoceros."

On safari at Lasamis, we found what seemed to be the very capital of the rhino country. The place was one of the most barren and desolate I have ever seen. Hundreds of natives and a number of whites who had died of thirst were buried here, and piles of rocks had been placed over their bodies to protect them from hyenas.

Every day we counted scores of rhino here. In the bed of the sand river we found three of their waterholes with a wide and much-traveled trail leading down to them, and here we decided to spend a night and see what pictures we could get with flashlights.

Selecting the best of the waterholes, we made a lookout on the rocky bank, above the trail. The moon shone very bright: in its reflection on the sand we could see everything clearly.

We decided that Bukhari and I should keep watch while Martin and Boculy went down to the trail with the cameras. They set up the equipment and then lay down in the sand only a few yards away to control the flash apparatus. We had agreed that we would not talk, but that I would give warning whistles. If rhino came straight down the trail toward them, I would give one whistle; if on the left, two whistles; if on the right, three whistles. If rhino came from the rear, they would get my scent and I would have to take care of them.

Down the trail toward Martin came one rhino, taking little goose-steps, kicking rocks and pebbles as he scuffed along, sniffing and snorting and making himself very important. I was so excited that I had a hard time getting my mouth in shape, but I finally got out a low whistle. The rhino stopped, turned off the trail and went down the river bed to another waterhole.

We waited nearly two hours. Then a pair of rhino showed up. They were evidently thirsty and were moving along briskly. The wind was right, so they could not get our scent. I was just ready to whistle when they also turned off the trail and went down the river bed. We had forgotten to cover those other waterholes with brush and for some reason the animals were avoiding us.

Every rhino has his favorite waterhole. It may be a vile mud-hole, and he makes it muddier by wading and wallowing in it, but for some reason he regards that water as sweeter or more attrac-tive; he is about as reasonable in this as he is in other matters.

Then a mother and a big toto came up behind me. She got our scent and scurried off, the lumbering baby at her heels. I wished that I could make all rhino afraid of me like that.

I turned to see a big bull rhino making straight for Martin. I whistled. The rhino moved suspiciously toward the cameras. Mar-tin pushed the buzzer and off went the flash. The rhino fled. I could see Martin setting another flash and I began to feel that the system was working.

No sooner had we settled down once more than a rhino came up from the left. I was just about to whistle, when I saw one coming from the right. I didn't dare whistle for fear of confusing Martin, but I had to warn him. Then I saw another rhino coming from the left, and another, and before I could reflect, there were nine rhino around us. I was frantic. I feared that if I screamed, Martin would be alarmed on my account and run right into one of the beasts.

Then the rhino began to attack each other. I pictured our cameras ruined and Martin stomped to a pulp. The fight went on for what seemed hours, though I suppose it was only a few minutes, and the rhino suddenly ran away. Then I heard Martin speak and never had his voice seemed so sweet. He and Boculy were climbing up the bank.

"Wasn't that exciting?" He put down the cameras and gave me a kiss. "Boy, some of those were beauties!"

"Beauties, my eye!" I said. "They had me scared to death."

"I was all primed to get the best rhino fight in history," he went on eagerly, "but I was set for a close-up and they wouldn't come within camera range."

"You have no business doing things like that, with those rhino fighting all around you."

"Why, Osa, there wasn't any danger. Boculy and I were following everything they did with our binoculars. Out there on the sand in that moonlight, it's as bright as day."

"Well, I'm going to bed," I replied, weary and unconvinced. "It's almost morning."

He took my hand and we walked slowly back to camp. Grevy zebra shone white in the clear light and they scattered as we passed. The desolation gave the place an eerie atmosphere and Martin's arm around me felt especially comforting.

Martin became very lively as we reached camp. "How about developing that shot we got tonight?" he suggested. "I'm not a bit tired. We could have some hot cakes and then go to work."

I was too nervously exhausted even to answer. I fell into bed without taking off my boots, pulled a blanket over me and was instantly asleep.

19

". . . Your headman is as a rule faithful and humble and admiring. But he makes two demands of you. The first is that you must be a good shot. The second is that you must never run away. If you live up to those demands . . . when he returns to Nairobi after a long safari, he can tell boasting tales to an admiring circle of town natives. But if you fail to live up to what your servant expects of you, then he is a marked man, a laughing-stock for his fellows. . . ."

—MARTIN JOHNSON

WHEN WE WERE at home, there was always plenty to do. I ran the dairy where I made butter provided by the cows we bought from the natives. How clever of Grandma, I thought many times, to have insisted that we bring the butterchurn. I put it to good use churning ten to fifteen pounds of butter each week. I also made some moulds and when there was time I made butter patties to dress up the table.

There were no fish in Lake Paradise, but I shot quail and guinea hen on the trail and kept the table well stocked with fresh meat. I loved to cook and prepare dishes that would make Martin's eyes pop. My greatest reward was when he would scan the table and say: "Oh, boy! Oh, boy!" Especially would he be delighted if we were having corned beef and cabbage or floating island pudding.

With the work we were doing there were always loads of clothes to wash, and it was not easy to organize our laundry force. The porters who helped Suku could never understand why we should want to wash clothing; they thought that carrying up so much water was just a waste of energy. I tried to explain but gave it up as a bad job. "Never mind *why* you have to wash these things!" I said at last. "Just go ahead and wash them and don't use too many soap suds!"

Even so I had to watch everything on wash-day. The boys liked to use one cake of soap for each garment. They loved to see the bubbles, and they had some sort of notion that a garment couldn't be cleaned unless they rubbed the bar of soap on it for a very long time. Once we received a shipment of soap flakes from America. These completely confused the boys because the flakes would disappear before they could be rubbed in.

They were curious about our great supply of canned goods. Naturally, they couldn't read signs on the tin cans of food, and one day I left a can of scouring powder on the kitchen shelf. The dining room boy thought it was salt and placed it in our salt tin. He also filled the salt cellars with it. I baked bread with it. The cook flavored the soup with it. At dinner time things were very exciting for a few minutes.

I kept a special eye on the commissary, not only to be sure we didn't lose things but because we had to measure our stores very carefully. I had to plan ahead months in advance because I couldn't run around the corner to a grocery store if something ran short. I kept inventory of the stock, and every time I took down a can of evaporated milk or any other canned product I would check it off on the stock list.

But life was not all domestic. While Martin managed the moving picture cameras I used a Graflex or Speed Graphic to get still pictures. Moreover, it was my job to cover him in dangerous spots and break up a charge if the game came through. In the field Martin relied on me and I relied on him. We were interdependent in every way, mentally and physically. I was his wife, his partner. The most important thing in my life was to know that I could be of help to him.

Knowing how much Martin relied on me kept me on my toes. Once a lion charged while Martin was taking pictures. He bore down on us with swift powerful springs. Martin continued to crank, confident that I was covering him. At twenty-five feet I fired. The lion dropped, dropped so close that Martin could touch his mane with his toe. I sighed a great sigh of relief. Neither of us said a word. But Martin winked—and that wink meant everything.

Out of the waste petrol tins we made all sorts of household utensils: the boys cooked in them, we carried water in them, we made flues out of them. Martin even made me a tin boat for the Lake.

"But, Osa," he said, "never go out in this cockle-shell without a blown-up tube around your waist. The marshy edges of that lake are too dangerous."

Two weeks before, we had found rhino horns sticking out of the mud. They told their own tale. We fastened a rope around the horns and pulled the dead rhino out with the aid of six camels and all our boys. We had to keep our water supply pure.

There must be fish in the Lake, I thought at first, for I had seen little beetles and pollywogs breaking the water and birds feeding, and I fished for a year before I gave up. I used pin hooks, small hooks, large hooks, every size of hook. I tried meat, dough balls, worms from the garden, large green worms from the tomato plants, grasshoppers and every kind of insect. But I never got a bite, except mosquito bites from the air. I finally was forced to admit that Blaney was right, as usual. There were no fish in Lake Paradise.

I sounded the lake but never succeeded in reaching the bottom. The boys swore that it was bottomless, and finally I was almost willing to believe it.

Martin said that I worried him and he used to watch with binoculars from his laboratory, but thought that this was a good way to work off my fishing zeal and keep me at home!

A BULL ELEPHANT CHARGES
Turning back from the retreating herd, a huge elephant puts out his fan-like ears
and prepares to charge the Johnson cameras.

A TREETOP BLIND AT LAKE PARADISE
Where ground blinds gave them no camera advantage, or were too insecure or
easily detected, the Johnsons built blinds in trees to photograph elephants and
other big game.

AN ELEPHANT FAMILY ON THE PLAINS

Feeding on long grass, the elephants are moving to shelter from the morning heat.

ELEPHANTS CROSSING A SAND RIVER

One of Martin Johnson's greatest and most unusual pictures, made at the Merille River. Elephants seldom go into the open in daylight, or provide the cameraman with such a choice background and composition.

I often took my little black toto along, and he was always sure at the beginning that I would catch a fish that day, but when he got hungry he would assure me that there were really no fish there and we had better go home.

"What do the birds feed on here?" I asked the boy.

"Fish," he said. "Yes, I have seen them eating fish."

Later I would say, "But there are no fish here, are there?"

"No," he would assure me. The porters were always agreeable and would "yes" me into doing what they were sure I would do anyway.

Some of the boys swore I would fall into the jaws of the sea-serpent. The natives had many superstitions, and this "sea-serpent" at Lake Paradise was one of them. I never could get an exact description, but was told it was a very evil thing of the devil, like a crocodile, but with a huge body and neck like a dinosaur, and an enormous tail reaching across the Lake and "as high as the cliffs" (which were one hundred and twenty-five feet or more).

The animals were all the friends of this sea-serpent, unless he took a dislike to them, but *all humans* were his enemies. He lay in the Lake every night with his head protruding, and any human being who saw him would promptly die a horrible death. I could never get one of the boys to go down to the Lake at night: they would go anywhere in the forest, but not to the water. So any errands at the Lake after dark, Martin and I had to do ourselves. And when we went almost nightly to the cliffs overlooking the water, the boys could never understand why we didn't drop dead. "Didn't you see the serpent? Aren't you afraid of dying?" they would ask.

When my boy was bitten by the puff adder, the other boys swore he had seen the serpent. The serpent had put the curse on him, which accounted for his great agony.

When Martin's flashlights did not work they were sure that it was because of the serpent.

"Oh, hush!" Martin always said when they later brought it up. "Watch your talk!" Which, translated into strict Swahili, was the equivalent of "you're crazy." But they only walked away muttering and were never convinced.

Their superstitions were endless. When a buffalo charged me, and I had to shoot him, the boys became very grave, gathered special leaves from the forest, put these in my hair, crushed the leaves and rubbed them over my forehead, gathered other herbs and crumbled and sprinkled these over my hat. With it all they made a great show of offering thanks to Allah.

"God's medicine," they said.

The boys had many strange ideas and tall stories. One day two porters caught some baby partridge. I asked how they did it and they said they had just whistled and held out corn and the birds came to their hands. They were very solemn and would not change the story, though I questioned them seriously. Finally, Bukhari began to laugh and said that they had of course taken some posho and made a little trap and caught the birds. At that the boys broke down and also laughed, but would not admit the truth. They seemed to love to tell whoppers and I think they actually grew to believe them.

They had their own way of saying things. They called ice "water that goes to sleep." They called my touring car "Chocolate." They called Martin's shredded wheat "Rat's nest." When I punctured a tire on my car, they said, "Your car has a sore foot, M'sahib."

They loved to jolly me and play childish tricks to see what I would do. I had warned the boys that any noise was taboo while I was fishing. My dad in Kansas had taught me as a little girl that if I wanted to catch fish I had to be quiet, and so I had always practiced the utmost caution.

One day, three of the boys were fishing with me at the Eauso Nyiro River. I was catching nothing. One of the boys began to sing in a low voice and suddenly he pulled in a fine fish. An-other boy across the stream began to whistle and he hooked a fish. The third began to talk coaxingly and he got a fish. Only I, with my silence, caught nothing. "You see, you must make music or talk to the fish here if you want to catch them," they said solemnly. As they continued to pull in fish, I began to think there must be something to it, and though I was reluctant to change my tactics, I began to sing, talk, whistle and coo, and caught a total of nothing. That evening they had a grand time over this and I heard them telling at their fires how they had fooled the Missus.

They liked fat-tailed sheep, and when we were on a fishing trip and met natives with sheep, they would say, "M'sahib, you must have some sheep-meat for bait. Here, only the crocodiles eat fish."

I used to talk to the boys in Swahili about their families. "How does your wife look?" I asked one of the boys. "Is she tall? Is she short, like me?"

"Oh, no. Maridadi sana (very beautiful) and big and strong," as he measured wide with his hands and smiled approvingly.

It was not an easy matter to keep our boys clean, in spite of regular inspections and our constant orders that they take care of themselves. However, they were very critical of a white man who was not meticulously clean and well dressed. Bukhari and our personal boys had learned to be very neat about their persons and their belongings, but the others were hard to discipline.

Among these was Ouranga, Martin's camera boy and laboratory assistant. He came into the laboratory one hot day and stood beside Martin.

"For Heaven's sake, Ouranga, go and wash yourself! Here, take this bar of carbolic soap and give yourself a good scrubbing."

"But, Master, I wash my face and hands every day. I think white man washes too much."

"Listen! You go down to the Lake and give yourself a bath all over." As he pushed the boy out of the door, he added, "You smell!"

The boy stopped and looked at Martin pityingly with his great brown eyes and said innocently, "Bwana, to the black man you smell too. On safari, the animals charge you but they do not charge us; you smell bad even to the animals."

"Well, you keep yourself clean." Then Martin's diplomacy revived. "See here, Ouranga, if you keep yourself clean I'll give you a handsome present when we get back to Nairobi."

And he did.

The boys were our constant amusement and exasperation. Although they would all dip into the same posho dish, they were not always friends. They were forever "squealing" to the little-big boss, and I would have to take time out, often preciously needed for work, to make peace. My extreme punishment was to threaten to cut their shillings, whereupon they would at once make up. This would not make them lose "face," for one could not be blamed for giving in to save the funds he needed for himself and his family. Actually, whenever I had to invoke this penalty I found some means at the end of the month to restore the money on their solemn promise not to misbehave again, and they usually kept their promises. None of them was malicious, and I felt that they were all like children who are best disciplined when shown the way and treated with understanding.

But we had to maintain a strict discipline, which extended all the way from proper hours for meals and going to bed, to personal cleanliness and order. One rule which Martin promptly laid down at Lake Paradise was that there were to be no native women in camp, for we had the same problems as an army and trouble enough as it was in keeping our boys at work. One of our Buganda drivers, however, whom we had sent for supplies, suddenly appeared with his wife. He had left our precious things at Isiolo in order to cart her and her goods hundreds of miles. There was nothing to do for the sake of discipline but immediately to discharge him and put him out of camp, turning him and his wife and baggage over to a camel caravan for return to Nairobi.

The boys were extremely kind always, and their affection had an unspoiled simplicity. When I had my one and only illness during our first days at Paradise, the cook came to me daily with tea, biscuits, fowl and the things that I liked, and when refused admittance, he would sit down on his haunches and frown: "But she must eat. Doesn't she like my food any more?" The boys would sit about outside and, as though I were dying, they would murmur: "Did God take her away?"

They had a name for every white person, and because they were very critical about cleanliness in foreigners, however unkempt they might be themselves, they would remark: "He's just like a pig," if anyone were not meticulously neat. But they would call him "Maradadi," or "pretty-boy," if he were scrupulously dressed!

Martin they called "The Master Who Makes a Row," for he had to give most of the orders and he told the boys off if they were remiss about anything. Sir Northrup MacMillan was "Big Stomach."

A good master was "Bwana Missouri," while someone they disliked would become "Bwana M'baya" (bad master).

Another was "Lazy-lazy" because his manners were slow and deliberate; another the "Man with the Little Voice" because he was so quiet; or "The Laughing Man," "The Long Man," "The Little Man," "The Good Man," and anybody's son was invariably "Toto," which literally meant small child.

Native servants have a sort of unwritten union or caste system. Each does a special service and nothing more. The cook will not wash, the wash boy will not drive a car, the driver will not take care of belongings, one's personal boy will not cook, a

...er is of high "caste" and will not stoop to ordinary labor ...ringing in firewood or other services.

...he boys were always telling cock-and-bull stories about the ...ame. One had to watch them. They would rush in with yarns of a great elephant herd, "mingi sana" (many, many)—"tracks just fresh." We would rush breathlessly out with cameras, walk for hours and find nothing.

"Where are the elephants? Where are the tracks?" Martin would demand. They would say they thought the tracks had looked fresher or had looked like more. Or that the elephants had once been there, even if not so recently. They were just like children, eager to be "big boys" and make a hit with the Master.

They were apt to steal occasionally, but by and large they took very little. Our cooks did take more sugar and tea than I allowed, but I indulged them—I felt that the items were trivial and knew that the boys loved these things and that stolen sweets were probably sweeter in Africa than anywhere else. I knew, too, that the sugar and tea gave the boys pleasure, of which they had little enough.

For the most part our boys were extremely honest. I think many masters are too rigid with them. Some place their stores under lock and key and watch them constantly. I never did this; I simply told the boys that if they wanted sugar or anything, to ask me; that they wouldn't have to beg, for I'd give it to them. But they were not to take it without my knowing, for that would make me "very sick in the heart." I know of one man who charged a boy with stealing a few ounces of sugar, when the boy was actually innocent. His employer wrote him a terrible kapandi, which took the boy years to live down.

As a rule a boy will not steal from his master, and our boys seemed to take a personal interest and pride in us. We gave them every attention and reward we could without offending the local standards. We watched after their health, gave them good food and comfortable huts, and did our best to keep them cheer-ful. Whenever they had done a very hard day's work, I gave them a special ration of tea and sugar, their chief delicacies, especially if it were cold or rainy or disagreeable, and they were quick to respond to the smallest kindness and appreciation.

They were, however, given to taking our Flit guns. We could never keep a supply. What they would do, after we left them, with no Flit to flit, I often wondered. And our mosquito netting they seemed to love. When we found them taking anything of real value, or something likely to affect the discipline materially, we became very severe and held "court," and imposed fines by cutting salaries or deducting shillings from the culprit's pay, which we restored as a reward at the end of the trip.

Our chief boys were extremely loyal, and among their little gestures of artfulness and politeness they would come to me on safari and say, "A man is here with vegetables; would you like to have them?" I knew the boys had no vegetables and no doubt wanted some, so I would buy the lot, take what we needed, and parcel the rest out to the boys as a present.

They had no conception of age, as we know it. To them a person is either a "toto" (very small child), or "manomi" (man), or "uzee" (old man).

They were always talking to me and I encouraged them, for it improved my Swahili. Full of humor, they invariably "reacted" in speech to whatever happened. If I went out for meat for camp and came back with none, my cook would say, "What's the matter, M'sahib, are your eyes tired? Perhaps you have been working too much," or something equally sympathetic and inquiring.

Suku, my houseboy and personal servant, was a rare one. He would not eat game because "all wild animals belong to God." The same was true of birds. He stuck to domestic animal flesh, which he said belonged to man.

Suku was very small and active. In addition, he was resource-

e took him on light safaris, for then we could carry only
all company, and he would do almost anything that came
, from washing and ironing and mending, to driving a car or
ooking the meals. He would pitch or strike camp, bargain with
the natives, and keep the stores and "books," or carry a load if
required. This did not mean that he lacked pride. On the contrary, he took a great pride in a good job well done and in our
comfort and success, and was quick enough to see that just as we
did everything, so must he if our work was ever to be accomplished.

"You must get a big salary from the Master," he said to me
one day. (The average white woman in Africa, as the natives see
her, is a woman of no work, provided with all necessary servants,
and is merely her husband's hostess.) "You take pictures and
act in them, drive a truck, cook, mend, wash clothes, fish, and
even shoot the meat for camp, and are a 'big game hunter' for
the Master. He must pay you very much."

He was mystified by the money we spent, for he came from
Meru, a trading post and government center, and knew exchange,
and especially the cost of cars and equipment. "Does the white
man have all the shillings? God must have forgotten the black
man."

Money was quite an obsession with him. He was very ambitious
and acquisitive, and very keen to know what people in America
received in salaries. He was astonished when I told him.

"But, in America my maid has to do all the housework, for
I can't afford two servants, and she does more than ten of you
do in a house here, so she is worth ten times as much," said I.

And then Suku was satisfied and completely understood. "Ah,
yes," he reflected, "she does more than one thing, so she gets
many salaries."

"What is America? Who does the work? Any black people
there?"

I told him of Harlem, of the colored folk who went to schools and engaged in business and the professions, and his eyes grew very large.

"Any elephants and lions in America?" He could not seem to understand why not, and thought it must be a very queer place, probably like the desert. When I tried to tell him about the few lions and elephants we did have in the circus and zoos, he got thoroughly mixed up, and that night I heard him telling the boys at the campfire:

"American men must be wonderful. They keep lions and elephants in a big house. They make lions sit on chairs and tie knots in their tails.

"And the elephants make a dance like we do around the camp fire," he added.

"Ah-h-h-h, ah-h-h-h," I heard Ouranga laughing, "you are telling stories. The white man can pick shillings off the trees, but not make lions sit on chairs."

I asked him about his family, as I did all the boys, and we were always chattering to one another about their domestic matters. Suku said:

"I have only one wife—she is a wonderful worker—and I have three children—boys. She builds me a nice house, sows my seed, cares for my cows and sheep. Some day I will be very rich. She and the totos do everything so I can go on safari and make shillings."

He liked sugar, tea, rice, and bright-colored socks (even if they were footless), wooly caps, shoes, red blankets (for show), mosquito netting, but he thought the rest of our equipment mere luxury and quite useless.

"When you go back to America, will you bring me a bicycle and wrist watch?" We got him a wrist watch, but we could not figure out how he would use the bicycle on safari or at home.

"Have you any totos? Who will you leave all your money to?

,ur mother and father living? Have you any brothers and
.s? How are your 'old' people? Are they rich?" he would ask
, endlessly with insatiable curiosity.

He loved the wooly caps we bought him and saved some for his
totos. Suku would, like other boys who affect them, wear a cap
all day, regardless of heat. He would even wear the ear, cheek and
chin flaps down in the hot sun.

He was a drowsy boy and would invariably fall asleep unless
I set him to watch something. Even when riding in the car, I
would ask him to watch for animals or to help keep an eye on
Martin's car just behind, but he would soon loll over on my shoulder and I would have to poke him awake. If he rode in the back,
he would be sound asleep even over the bumpiest roads.

When I received a letter from my mother, he asked what she
said and looked at the packages she sent me.

"Tell her Suku said hello," said he.

Months passed. Letters came from Mother. One day he said
solemnly, "Mama not good. Suku says hello and she never an-
swers."

He thought it a pity I had no children. "You could make them
work and you wouldn't have to work so hard," he reasoned.

If Martin looked glum, he would say to me: "You haven't fed
the master well; his stomach is hungry."

M'pishi was almost as curious as Suku about the wonders of
America.

He wanted to know what work we did. Who was my cook? Did
we get lots of grouse for dinner?

When I told him that the dishes washed themselves, he rubbed
his head and looked at me sidewise as though he expected me
to do some magic then and there.

"Where do you live in America?" he asked.

"On a mountain," I told him, "just the same as here. But the
mountain is all one house and many, many people live inside."

He could not believe that.

"Do you walk up?"

I explained about elevators, which seemed to him a pure fairy tale.

"But why do they all live in a mountain when there is so much room?" he asked as his eyes swept the plains and the far horizon.

Another time he inquired, "What kind of stove do you have in America?"

I described my beautiful gas range.

"But no wood?"

"No. I push a button and have a fire."

"No matches? Where does the fire come from?"

"From the ground."

He shook his head. "Then it belongs to Mungu. Mungu gives the Americans everything."

If the porters developed a dislike for one of their number, they would begin to gossip. He might merely be refusing to divide his food with them, or some other trivial thing, but the gossip would grow until they had made him into something evil; then they would gather one night at the campfire and hold "court" and decide to try to bounce him by complaining to the master.

Martin invariably told them to "go jump in the lake," or something equally impatient. They would answer, "All right, but you will see. You will have nothing but trouble." And we did, for if they didn't make it, they would blame every trouble on the "victim." We failed to get pictures or the weather was bad or the animals ran away or our water ran out.

"You see," they would say, "he is the cause; he is unclean, bad; bad blood is in that boy; you will never get anywhere until you get rid of him."

But these complaints would suddenly disappear when the boy

thing really good or gave in and submitted to whatever they were demanding of him.

we had specially bad luck at any point, however, they would gin to wag their heads and search for the boy with the bad blood, like a bunch of old witch-hunters. "Somebody here has bad blood," they would swear, and usually look knowingly at the one they suspected.

Boculy often used this device to "sink" anyone he disliked and, since he was so jealous of his post, anyone he suspected of becoming a rival for his place with us, or for our esteem. Yet he could be equally generous on the other extreme, and sometimes he was right.

Boculy continued to dislike N'dundu, our assistant headman, and blamed everything on him. We had taken N'dundu because Blaney said he had fought with the British against the Germans in Tanganyika during the World War and was reputed to be a fine gunbearer. But he was cocky and irresponsible and I cracked him over the head with my rifle one day for his insolence, which broke my gun stock and made me very unhappy, but had the effect of making him more reasonable. Boculy began to hatch tales against N'dundu to dispose of him. Boculy swore N'dundu was unclean: his feet were unclean, his heart was unclean, his thoughts unclean, the animals "smelled" trouble when he was near and God was displeased. Boculy was probably jealous, but finally we did have to dispose of N'dundu for other reasons. Again in a mysterious way Boculy had proved to be right after all. He was a strange wise man, but along with his own peculiar wisdom he had as many inconsistencies as anyone else.

Boculy polished his cartridges every morning as we would polish our shoes. He was always rubbing and polishing his gun, but only on the outside! The barrel of the gun was so corroded I would have been afraid to shoot it for fear of its bursting. Our gunbearers offered to clean his gun for him, but he always scorned them and said it was in perfect shape, though they knew the truth. This gun had been given him by the King's African Rifles, and rumor was that it had saved his life several times, which probably accounted for his affection for it, though not for his neglect.

One day at camp outside Paradise, a boy came in to say that he had seen a native caravan with sheep and goats and cattle not far away.

Soon Boculy came up and solemnly announced that he was having trouble with the porters, and asked me to hold court. I agreed, and he brought me about ten porters who all looked very dejected.

"What is the trouble?" I asked, prepared to hear about a fight or a theft.

The headman rose and made a speech, saying that the porters were all becoming ill and could not work. They complained of very bad stomachs (their stomachs were very mad at them).

"But I have given you plenty of the choicest meat, just the things you have always liked. What more can I do?"

"We are eating too much game meat," they argued, "and our stomachs are refusing to let us work on nothing but game meat. We must have some mutton, and now there are sheep near by."

I considered this very seriously and asked Boculy what he thought. He agreed that the boys were right. He had actually heard their stomachs rumbling like an elephant's. I called Bukhari and he too thought that there must be something wrong with the diet, for even his stomach had been giving him trouble.

So I found Martin and told him, and he laughed loudly.

"The rascals!" said he. "They want a feast, and then they will surely be good for nothing afterwards."

But, as though we believed them, we held a long parley that night, and finally gave the order to purchase a supply of the animals.

the feast, they all worked well for a day, then sagged
and asked for more feast.

See here!" said I. "Enough is enough! The big Bwana works
ay and night on game meat, and his stomach isn't mad at him.
You can work too, and don't try to fool me any more!"

"Ndyio" (yes), they said, and went contentedly back to work.

Wherever he comes from, the African native knows Mungu
(God). Whether a thing is good or evil, he seldom speaks of the
devil, but always of "God's will." If a hail storm comes up, he
says, "God is throwing rocks at us." If it thunders, "God is angry."
If it is a beautiful day, "God is very happy."

There was an eclipse of the sun while I was making a meal.
Said M'pishi, the cook, "God has shut off the light. Shall we go
back to bed?" He was absolutely serious.

Along with their religion, some of the tribes believe implicitly
in their witch doctors, no matter how absurd the "magic" may be.
One day a witch doctor came into camp. He looked wild, with
a skin around his loins. Martin hired him, out of curiosity and
because he thought he would make good entertainment. It was
raining heavily and the witch doctor boasted he could easily stop
the rain. So Martin gave his permission.

The old fellow gathered eggplant and jungle vines, and made
a bundle which he carried aloft and waved around in the air
with one hand, rattling a gourd with the other. He danced up
and down and howled and yelled. The boys were all deadly serious and apparently believed in him earnestly. This went on for
over three hours. Suddenly we had a cloudburst. Our tents and
cots were awash, and that night we had no fires. The "doctor"
left camp surreptitiously, and the boys were disillusioned when
they had to sit around eating cold food.

"O ti" (oh, my), was all Boculy could say as he shook his
head and grimaced.

"He was not the child of God," said another, defensively.

20

". . . It's terribly hard for the tenderfoot because he thinks it ought to be hard. But the more you work in the wilderness, the more you realize that trying to accustom one's body to the hardship is all wrong; the right thing is to temper and adapt the hardship to one's body . . ."

—MARTIN JOHNSON

THE FOLLOWING EXCERPTS from my diary at Lake Paradise are presented with the thought that they may impart a compact, swiftly-paced picture of our day-to-day life.

Lake Paradise, December 21, 1924

It is so beautiful everywhere we go, even outside the immediate Lake area for one hundred and fifty miles in any direction, that we have decided it is all Paradise! Every safari we make out into the plains is full of beauty and interesting experiences. While I am always glad to get back here to the comforts of our little home, I never regret leaving on a new trip, for I know that it will all be happiness.

We will have to be going away again soon, for the rains are heavy and the game is going down to the plains. There are so many places we enjoy that we may make a long safari and take in as many of them as we can, all in one trip.

If anyone had told me a few years ago that I would be making a home in the jungle, hundreds of miles from anywhere, and would be as happy as we are here, I could not have believed him. And it will probably be impossible to make our friends at home understand.

The rains have washed the air and brought up the flowers and a thousand fragrances. With Boculy and Bukhari, I walked around the crater as far as we could go and still get back for dinner—about

.iiles in all. The rim of the crater is thirty miles around, and
i would have walked it all had there been time.

.e trees are bright green, and the silvery Spanish moss everywhere
.s the forest a brightness and movement that is more than ever
.iimating. It is always full of life, however. Today we saw elephants,
some of the few that have not yet gone to the plains; and several
rhino and buffalo. And a little Abyssinian bushbuck and her faun,
both in bright reddish brown coats with white polka dots. The bushbuck looked at me, trembling all over, and then scampered away,
their bushy white tails spreading out like fans behind them.

The trails around the rim are very irregular and give you a good
workout. In and out of the forest, through dongas and up their steep
sides where elephant trails and footprints are often a great help,
and over logs and boulders these trails wind. And just often enough
—to keep you from forgetting that you are tired—you have a brush
with game or catch a clear view of the Lake or of the Kaisoot Desert
for a rest and reward.

Lake Paradise, January 9, 1925

Martin jollies me a great deal about "having a way with animals,"
and I think he believes it. But no one can ever be sure about any animal, let alone a wild one, and there is no "way with them," except to
be always on the alert and to molest them as little as possible.

Animals are curious—and some much more so than others. If they
are in a friendly mood, they like to look you over at as close a range
as is safe. Elephants, rhino, buffalo, lions, giraffe, the plains animals,
will often steal up to within a few yards without charging, especially
if you are in a motor car, so that they get the scent of rubber and
gasoline and do not make you out. But a little movement and they
will charge or be gone in a flash. If advances are going to be made,
they want to make them; and that is just as true of pets as of animals
in the wilderness.

If a wild animal has been wounded by some person, he is much
more likely to charge the next human being he sees. And even if he
has been gored by one of his own kind, he is more likely to be bad-
tempered than pleasant. Long memories in this respect are no monop-
oly of the elephants.

Heat, humidity, and weather conditions generally affect animals
just as they do human beings, or at least similarly. Many times I
don't blame animals for being mean-tempered for I feel the same way
myself. All I ask is that they don't take it out on me, for I want to be
left alone just as much as they do.

STREAMLINED ELEPHANT CHARGE

A huge tusker lays back his ears and begins to rock as a preliminary to charging the Johnson cameras.

BAKING BREAD IN THE OPEN ON SAFARI

Osa shows Mr. Eastman, an expert cook, how it is done.

When an animal gets to be so mean that his bad disposition is chronic, the rest of the family or the herd throws him out. This is a pretty sad state for an elephant or almost any animal, for he has a much harder time getting his food and he is in much more danger having to shift for himself. When he grows old and his tusks or his teeth are bad, or he becomes crippled in some way, he has a really bad time of it. But once he has become marked as a "rogue," no animal will take him in. He is then a real outcast. I think some of these lonely animals really go insane and that, no doubt, is why they do the things they do to native villages; for sometimes they go berserk and tear into a group of huts and wreck everything they can reach, for no apparent reason whatever.

On Safari, Logga, February 8th

These safaris take much more planning than an ordinary hunting trip, where food and ammunition and clothes are the only stores to carry. The cameras weigh a great deal and have to be handled with extreme care, and we also have to carry duplicate equipment to guard against loss and accident, including extra springs, crank-handles, magazines, clamps and parts.

The job our porters seem to like most of all, except eating and sleeping, is blind-building. They know they will not have to work too hard at this and will be given ample time to do it. And how they slow down to a walk! We select a spot at a waterhole and send the boys out for brush. One brings in a branch, another a handful of reeds; and we have to jolly them into making some speed or stand right over them until the job is completed.

Meanwhile, they have to stop and wipe imaginary perspiration from their brows, especially if we are watching, or they think of the funniest stories to tell each other, at which they double up with laughter and further delay the work.

On Safari, Logga, February 11th

Last night we slept out in the blind. Nothing but a leopard came down. He fooled around for half an hour and then went away without giving us a good picture. But crickets came in billions. I have never heard such a din. Beginning shortly after dark and continuing until long past midnight, there was such a racket that Martin and I could scarcely hear each other talk. The sound was so continuous that I began to wonder if there were not something wrong with my ears and whether they might go on ringing like this the rest of my life. I began to long for a moment's silence. Then it came. The silence lasted for about an hour, when suddenly the tree frogs started up just as bad a racket. When morning finally dawned, our nerves, were on edge. We were so jumpy that we were ready to bite each other's head off. But after a good walk back to camp, some hot coffee and a good breakfast, we were ready for work again.

For days we have been seeing big game, but they have remained in the forest through the day and our night pictures have been nothing to boast about. But we have made up for this in gorgeous safari material and Martin has made beautiful bird and butterfly pictures.

The rains are so unseasonal and disappointing for pictures that we are going back to the Lake. It is beautiful out here on the plains and all a part of our Paradise. I love it whatever the weather, but it will be good to be back in a bed again and to see my flowers and pets and get into some fresh clothes.

Lake Paradise, March 3rd

After dinner, we take a walk to the forest or over to the cliff, or if we are very tired we sit on the veranda and watch night fall over the Lake. There is always life at the Lake, whatever the hour, and in the evening birds in great numbers are usually leaving the water to go to roost. They give the air a constant movement and color. Night comes swiftly and the animal calls increase until we have a tremendous symphony of jungle sound all about us. It throbs through us and we seem to become a part of it. I can feel my heart keeping the beat of it, and its rhythm lulls us to sleep.

Below our veranda is a natural clearing with great trees standing about. We have named this Paradise Park. Practically all the trees have had their bark rubbed off by elephants. And since they are bare for as high as fifty feet, I suppose that elephants have scratched their backs here for fifty to a hundred years.

Lake Paradise, May 12th

Alaki, our Boran mule boy, was kicked in the hand and stomach so badly that he is going to be laid up for a while.

Runner from Marsabit tells us to be on watch for Habash raiders from Abyssinia. They are poaching ivory near Lake Rudolph. Killed thirteen askaris scouting for them. We aren't worried, but will cross that bridge if and when we come to it. Martin says I've always been wanting to see a Sheik and maybe this will be my chance.

Sent cabbages and vegetables, a jar of cucumber pickles and three pounds of fresh butter to Marsabit to the D.C. by his runner.

One mule died. Leopards got two of my chickens last night. Kalowat ate some of my toothpaste and is acting queer. Planted two more rows of green beans.

Lazy Bones was drinking at the Lake today when baboons came up and began chattering at him. He gave them a terrified look and instead of retreating up the path he had come, he started around the Lake. The baboons followed, about one hundred of them in all, barking and screaming—parents, children and all, with babies riding their mothers' backs. Lazy Bones ran faster and faster, all the way around the Lake, hotly pursued. Exhausted, he ran to his corral and one of the boys let him in.

Martin and I rocked with mirth as we watched this show. "Just as good as a rodeo or Western movie," he said.

My corn is ripe and I feed Lazy Bones choice ears of Country Gentleman or Golden Bantam. He loves it, and whenever he sees me heading for the garden, he tags along like a little dog. I don't want him getting into the garden for I know he will eat everything in sight, so I have the boys come and hold him. He stands, watching my every move, until I come back with an ear of corn. Then it seems to me that he almost wags his tail in delight.

Lake Paradise, July 6th

Lazy Bones has become very fussy and refuses to carry anyone but me. Today Martin hatched the idea of putting him to some use, carrying water up from the Lake. I protested that I thought it a shame to do this, for he had enough to do carrying me around, but Martin said it would be light work and it would take only a few hours a day. Besides, he pointed out that the mule has little else to do but eat and sleep anyway. So the boys took Lazy Bones to the Lake and hung two barrimals of water on him. He promptly began bucking and raced around the Lake, stopping to buck and kick every now and then. Finally he got the barrimals off, turned and gave one of them a fine swift kick, puncturing it. The boys ran to save and repair the barrimals as Lazy Bones walked proudly back to camp. Martin admitted that making him work was hopeless. I think Martin was really more concerned about his barrimals than anything else, for they are the property of the government and are very hard to get.

Martin has been made a Deputy Game Warden by the government, with power to arrest ivory poachers or other offenders. Before, I was secretly hoping we might see some of these Abyssinian bandits, but now I hope we don't, for Martin will surely try to carry out his duty. I don't mind shooting it out with elephants or rhino, for I know what to expect, but I hope we don't have to fight a score of these ruffians, even if they can't shoot very well. We haven't heard any more of the poachers about whom the D.C. at Marsabit warned us.

Lake Paradise, August 7th

Another runner from the D.C. at Marsabit came up today with a note that Abyssinians are poaching ivory to the West. He is going after them and he warns us to be on the lookout.

The Boer trader who brought our supplies up from Nairobi last month went on to Moyale and has not been heard from. We liked him. He was a gray-haired man, rough and typical of the old South Africans, a big cowboy type, six feet two inches tall and powerfully built. He was said to be an excellent shot. The runner says the D.C. has proof that the Abyssinians got him.

Lake Paradise, August 15th

So many animals sleep during the day, or remain in the deep forest where photography is impossible, coming to the waterholes only at night, that we are forced to use flashlights to get pictures. This means that we have to sit all night in a brush pile or perched in a treetop where we are not only pretty cold and uncomfortable, but exposed to leopards. And it is hard to stay awake, for our days are full of work and we are often exhausted. Then the animals often get our scent and shy away from the waterhole, and we spend the night without getting a single picture.

Here at the Lake we can at least sleep in bed. But when the flashlight goes off with a boom, we are too excited to wait and usually get up and take a gun and rush down to get the plates and reset the cameras. Then we go into the laboratory and develop and if the picture comes out well, we forget that we are sleepy.

Last night we sat in a treetop blind across the Lake with a flashlight set up on the trail. At the foot of the tree we set up a small tent where we could rush the cameras in case of rain. About midnight a rhino came down from our rear, touched the tent, sniffed at it and backed away. He got a whiff of us, but could not make out where it came from and circled around us for nearly an hour, then went away. Bright moonlight and we could see him perfectly. About two, a couple of hundred buffalo came noisily along the trail and went down to the Lake but missed the flashlight apparatus. Nothing else came, because of a hundred or more baboons in the trees near us, who sensed us and kept up a continuous racket. By morning, I could have wrung every one of their necks.

Lake Paradise, August 29th

Martin is ill. Temperature according to my thermometer is one hundred and three degrees. Hope this is not a return of his old malaria which he hasn't had for years. Gave him powders to make him perspire and rolled him in blankets and am doing best to make him comfortable.

One of the boys came in this noon and said one of the porters had died suddenly. Can't find out what happened to him. He was all right yesterday. Since Martin is ill they asked me to help bury the boy. I couldn't help thinking how I would feel and what I would do if anything happened to Martin away off here. We took the boy out in the forest and the boys dug a shallow pit and covered the body with rocks, to keep away the hyenas. I asked them why they didn't make the grave deeper, or cover it with more rocks. "Never mind, Little Missus," they said, "his heart is gone to God."

Kalowat has a jigger in her toe. Sent her out with Bukhari to have the boys extract the jigger. She cries and whimpers like a baby whenever they do this, but likes all the attention they give her.

Gathered a lot of red pom-poms and arranged them around the bedroom, for Martin is very fond of them.

On Safari, Lasamis, October 1st

Today we saw a lion sitting right on top of an ant hill. The light was bad, but we tried a picture. What a shot it will make if it comes out well!

They dote on fresh pork and often hang around the ant hills looking for an easy dinner. Wart hogs use the abandoned ant hills for refuges and they are good safe ones, but Mr. Lion waits around, hoping that in the evening the old razor-back will come out to prowl for his food. Then the lion has only to make an easy spring and he has nice juicy chops for himself and his family.

Leopards also like pork, and they frequent the ant hills for the same reason.

But the wart hog can put up a good fight, if he has half a chance. His tusks are keen and he knows how to use them. He is one of the most pugnacious creatures on the plains. He trots along with a comical egotism and self-assurance, as though he were just as big and tough as anything in sight, and as if he dared anything to tackle him. He is so ugly I should think he would scare off almost any but a very hungry adversary.

I saw a little wart hog go after a leopard that attacked him recently and not only fight to the finish but completely wear out the leopard. He left him exhausted and very badly cut up. That leopard won't trouble the little pigs for a long time, I am sure.

On Safari, Eauso Nyiro River, October 7th

Today I discovered five fine hippo. This was at about eleven A.M. and I knew that they would sun themselves through the noon hour, so I sent one of my boys back for Martin with a message to him to rush down with the cameras in the hope of getting some good afternoon pictures.

While waiting for the boy to return, I went scouting with Bukhari and a camera boy, and found a rock kopje that was alive with hyrax, the little "rock rabbits," but the light was so bad I could get no decent pictures of them. Except that they had dark brown fur they reminded me of cottontails back home and were just as nimble. The father would come out to look at me, sit up like a chipmunk, with his forepaws in the air; mother would follow him and sit alongside; then the babies would come scurrying out and sit up in line. At my first move to get out a camera, they were gone. Family after family went through this routine and through the glasses I could see them screwing up their noses and faces, trying to sniff me. They shook with nervous excitement. We have tried again and again to photograph them; some day we will succeed.

The boy arrived at camp to find that Martin had gone to a waterhole. This meant that he would have to walk two miles to get Martin and two miles back, and then two miles more to me. So he and some of his cronies decided to save themselves all that trouble and to cook up a story. He came back to tell me that Martin would not come. He must have known how stupid this was and what he was letting himself in for, if he had had a brain to think.

Tonight Martin was furious when I told him what he had missed. He gave the boys a big lecture and fired the boy who lied to me and sent him off to Isiolo. The other boys who were in on the story he fined three shillings each. They won't do that trick again, for they are all very frightened. And when I hear Martin talk like that, so am I.

Martin was also upset because at the waterhole he had seen nothing but a stork and a couple of secretary birds for his long wait, and his cameras are full of dust and will have to be cleaned.

On Safari, Eauso Nyiro River, October 13th

While we have been at the River, I have made up for lost time fishing. I've caught a big variety and enough whitefish to keep the boys stuffed. Yesterday I caught over one hundred pounds of whitefish and catfish.

Perhaps I have eaten too much, for last night I had a terrible nightmare. The Eauso was alive with fish and I grew tired of using a line so I tried simply lifting them out with a stick. Sure enough, I landed the first one as easy as you please. He was a nice silverfish, about eighteen inches long, but no sooner had I landed him than he began to grow. He was soon three feet long and then six. Then he turned into a crocodile and opened his hideous mouth to swallow me. I threw my cigarette into his mouth, which must have burned his tongue, for he let out a roar like a lion. His eyes flashed and he lashed his tail and made for me.

I swung into a tree to get out of his way and he placed his forefeet against the trunk and glared at me. But he was growing and growing and was soon walking around the tree and standing higher than where I sat.

Then I saw that he was the sea serpent from Lake Paradise. His neck had elongated and his body had grown enormously. His long tongue flashed out like a snake's and fire began to come out of his nostrils. The boys were right, I decided: I had defied their superstition and here the serpent was coming to devour me. He crawled closer and closer and I yelled for Martin.

"What's the matter, honey?" I heard him say.

I was sitting up in bed. The moon made a patch of white light on the floor of the tent. My heart was pounding like a hammer, goose bumps stood out all over me and I was cold as ice.

On Safari, March 25, 1926

Rained all last night though this is supposed to be the dry season.

Humadi admits that he was foolish to try to capture the baby rhino to add to my pets. He said he didn't know a toto could be so strong. He wants a stretcher, groans and carries on and thinks he is badly hurt, although there is nothing the matter with him but bruises. He has made a pair of crutches and manages to keep up with the rest of us. Another of the boys has hurt his foot and can scarcely walk. We are all covered with mud and are a sorry looking lot.

The boys are famished for meat. The game is so scarce I haven't been able to supply them. Our food rations are also low: potatoes are gone, milk is gone and there are only a couple of tins of fruit left. But we have lots of posho and if the boys can live on that so can we.

Our Boran camel boys dress in one piece of camel skin that has been softened. They carry another such skin which serves both as a saddle blanket and a tent, but it is very small and funny, and they never pitch their tents until it has started to rain. When the rain is on them, they set up three sticks, throw the skin over these and crawl in. The space is hardly big enough for a cat and sometimes their legs and bodies lie out in the rain, with only their heads sheltered.

On Safari, March 30th

Rain has given us a bad time with camera supplies. We have built big fires to dry things out, but the humidity is so great the dampness penetrates everywhere. Martin thinks he will have to throw away at least two thousand feet of film and several dozen plates, and we haven't too much stock on hand. Hope the fine film Martin has been making is not ruined. Rained all last night and water came into our tents, but we had prepared for this and had all our cameras and clothing up on logs. Places that were dry stream beds a few days ago are now roaring rivers. It is hard to realize that this is desert most of the year.

Tried to follow some elephants when the sun came out, but going was too thick and with mud up to our ankles we couldn't keep up with them. Baboons tore up a two-hundred-foot bank under which we were passing and loosened rocks and we had to run for it to save our necks and the cameras.

On Safari, April 4th

The Boran tribesmen spend their lives accumulating camels, hump-backed cattle, sheep and goats, but except for drinking the fresh blood and using the sour milk, they do not seem to know what to do with their property. The cattle and camels are never worked and the natives never eat the meat, so the herds grow to enormous size. A single village may have fifty people in it and five thousand or more animals.

The natives are a worthless lot. And their ignorance and cruelty is evident in the way they treat their cattle, branding them with horrible cuts and burns. Some of these wounds take a year to heal and some never do, but fester from the countless flies and the dirt. Some animals have one ear cut off; other have their ears cut to threads.

The Boran cannot count above twenty, but they know every animal they own by sight. A man may have a thousand animals and if one is missing as they come into the lion-proof boma at night, he will know it.

The women are far better looking than most of the native women of East Africa. They have small and almost European features, but their skin is dead black. Their feet are small, despite their having to walk constantly all over the desert and plains. Their hair is bobbed, and if it were not for the filthy one-piece skin they wear, they would be quite presentable.

The men are tall and straight, with good skins and rather effeminate features. Both men and women have perfect white teeth.

When we want beef, we have a hard time bargaining. These people have no use for money, but they demand thirty shillings for each ox, and must talk it over among themselves for a day or more before they will close the transaction. Then they demand, in place of the money, marduff, an unbleached muslin, for they cannot use and will not accept coin.

Lake Paradise, June 15th

Martin removed, cleaned and repaired Delco engine and fixed our pump. Elephants came up to our stockade during the evening, reached over and took Lazy Bones' fodder and had a good feast, then walked away without troubling anything else. Some of the boys saw them, but didn't interfere for they were afraid of starting a rumpus. Heard elephants trumpeting around our camp all night.

Caught up with my darning and mending.

Abdulla finished putting the cars in order and carpenter repaired the garage.

The moths are the largest and most beautiful I have ever seen, and they come in all colors. However annoying the African insects may be, they are beautiful to watch. The beetles are gorgeous, in a wide variety of colors and patterns, and if we were not so busy with elephants and a thousand chores I would spend all day studying them.

The place is alive with birds: flamingoes, heron, cranes, wild ducks and geese, paraqueets, hornbills, soft-throated thrushes, starlings, weaver birds, bulbuls, eagles and nightingales, wood ibis, blackbirds, wagtails, white-necked raven, swallowtails, Maribu storks, hawks, doves, pigeons and all the game fowl.

On Safari, Ret, November 7th

An old rogue lion tried to get into our corral early this morning. We were making an early start and I heard the commotion and ran out to scare him off. He charged and I had to shoot him. He ran nearly seventy yards and just as I was going to give him another shot, he fell dead. We found a bullet through his heart. The vitality of the

King of Beasts is tremendous and this makes his charge all the more dangerous, but I have never seen such a performance as this.

Blaney told me about an elephant that had charged for nearly two hundred yards after it had been shot in the lungs.

These experiences prove how essential it is to hit in a vital spot on the first shot, and how dangerous it is only to wound the animal and further provoke its murderous intentions.

On Safari, Kampiatoonia, December 18th

Last night we sat up until after midnight in our blinds, but no game came to the pools, so we assumed we had built the blinds too close to camp. Then it rained, filling all the pools, so that we doubted game would come today, and took Boculy's advice to go to a nearby valley where he was sure we would find elephant and rhino.

Boculy never seems to get tired and today he walked us for three hours up and down hills and over rough stones until we had to call a halt. We were passing so many filled pools that we knew the whole place was heavily watered and the game would not be searching for water, and we were on a wild goose chase. Boculy, always philosophical about everything and never willing to admit his judgment was wrong, as it seldom is, said:

"When the rain comes, the game all goes."

"Then let's go where the game is," I said.

"But it will not be there," he replied, in deep thought. Which is typical Boculy logic.

He has three standard explanations when we do not find game. The trouble is due to "Business caused by you" (if we scare the game); "Business caused by rain" (as today), or "Business caused by God," which covers all the other reasons in the catalog. I have never yet heard him say, "Business caused by Boculy."

When he has made up his mind that we are not finding game for some reason, he gives it up for the day, with a shrug of the shoulders, and will not look further.

If he has gone off alone and found game, he often returns and stands in front of us and says "Tayari," which means "Get ready." No matter what we are doing, even if we are in the middle of a meal, he wants to go at once, and if we do not rush right off he sulks, as though his last friend had deserted him.

Lake Paradise, April 7, 1927

Martin sent for Boculy and ordered him to get all the native boys up after dark to see some of the best still pictures we have made while here. We have shown these to some of our personal boys from time to time but wanted to get the reaction of the porters. We had each boy come up to the light while Martin and I showed him the pictures.

At first they didn't even know how to look at them. They acted like very young children, holding the picture upside down and sideways, until I explained how to look at them. I even had to persuade some of the boys, by pointing to their hats or clothes, that the pictures really were of them.

When their eyes finally became adjusted to the three dimensions, the boys just went crazy. They laughed and laughed, and all wanted prints to send to their wives.

21

". . . *You can romanticize all you will about the lives of animals. You can picture them as living the life of an idyllic Garden of Eden. But if you do, you must ignore facts, as you must ignore facts if you want to make a romantic picture of the noble savage who, in reality, is not "noble" at all. The life of the plain and forest is a cruel life. It is a life of hunting and being hunted. The only law is that of the survival of the fittest."*

—MARTIN JOHNSON

"MARTIN, FOUR LIONS! Look through these glasses . . . right out there under the acacia tree!"

"Boy, isn't that a sight! All males and every one with a fine mane!"

I scanned the plain for others, but evidently these were alone. Four bachelors living and hunting together. One yawned and rolled over sleepily, as we watched, and lay there with his four paws in the air. One was licking another's face, and then affectionately rubbing against him. The fourth was sitting down and looking very bored. They all seemed so nonchalant that I concluded they had grown up together from babyhood, as often happens, and were now a practiced and contented "gang" or pride.

One by one each yawned and ambled off to the shade of a bush and flopped down to sleep. We retreated to have our lunch and had the boys keep an eye on the lions. Hours later we went back to the spot and found them still asleep. All but one. He was stretching and yawning and shaking himself awake. Then, just like a housecat, he smacked one of the others playfully with his paw. The other leaped up as though very angry and for a few minutes we were not sure that there was not a genuine fight on. But it was all in fun. They wrestled and pushed each other around for a few minutes and then, evidently hungry, began to scan the plain.

The tussle had waked the two other lions and now all four trailed off in the direction of a soda swamp near by. We followed and watched closely through our binoculars. The cats drank at the pool and then began stretching again as though doing their morning exercises. The swamp was several hundred yards long and shaded by acacia and grown up with tall light-green reeds, cat-tails and creepers.

Game began to appear on the plain, slowly heading toward the swamp. Three of the cats slipped into the reeds and disappeared. The biggest of the four walked slowly to the end of the swamp nearest us, and then he also slid out of sight into the grass. I wondered what one of them would do if he disturbed a sleeping python. Such swamps were favorite hiding places for these snakes, which lay there to seize unwary gazelle or baby animals foolish enough to stray away from their mothers.

Nearly an hour passed. A small herd of common zebra, trailed by scattered Grevys, had been edging toward the water. They paused while one of the leaders walked ahead. The little pony stopped every few steps to sniff and peer about. At last he reached the pool and after standing there for long minutes, began to drink. Suddenly he started, and ran.

Close on his heels was one of the lions. The zebra were now all running like mad and spreading out fan-shape over the plain. Three lions were after the lone zebra, driving him toward the end of the swamp, nearest us.

There we saw the fourth lion waiting, crouched in the grass. ·They were playing a "system," then! As the zebra came up, the big lion bounded on to the back of the poor creature, and with a quick thrust and jerk of his paw, drew back his victim's neck. The

zebra reared with a throaty death bark, and as he fell the other
three lions pounced on him in a milling pack.

The lions stood there for a moment as though getting their
breath. Then they stood with their forefeet on the carcass and
roared as I have never heard them roar before or since. The
vibration seemed literally to shake us—and the earth. It was
something to remember! And all within earshot would know that
the King of Beasts had made his kill and that he was undisputed
master of the jungle.

Perhaps the only animal to dispute the mastery of the lion
is the elephant. He is equally kingly although, being a vegetarian,
he lets the lion and all other animals alone. The lion likewise,
except when he is hungry and goes after a zebra or antelope for
food, displays the same aloof dignity, completely ignoring other
game, and is entirely self-sufficient.

There are many marks of similarity between elephants and
lions. Neither is afraid of anything in the animal world, for each
is far too powerful and intelligent to have anything to fear from
anyone but man. A lion will attack man more often than an elephant, however, because he has a highly nervous disposition and
probably because he is more frequently molested by this two-
legged creature. Martin and I respected lions and elephants equally,
and never tired of observing their habits.

While a lion is not always on a rampage, as is commonly
believed, and will usually behave if left alone, one never knows
what to expect. Consequently, we were always on the alert. If
one is traveling on foot, his chances of being attacked by a
lion are increased; but if he is driving in a motor car, he is quite
safe. The lion smells the strange rubber and gasoline, which apparently do not smell like anything good to eat, and he therefore
pays little attention. However, lions have charged even our motor
cars on general principles, and once I had to shoot a huge old
grandfather who didn't like our looks and came for us. I shot as

he sprang, and he fell across the hood with one foot through the open windshield all ready to do damage. He was an old "rogue" lion, covered with fighting scars and with one eye gone.

A rogue lion is something to watch out for. He develops such a bad disposition that even his own family can't stand him, and they banish him from the pride to shift for himself. This doesn't improve his good manners, for his self-importance is damaged, and he becomes all the more vindictive. He has to hunt alone, which is neither easy nor fun, and this makes him even grouchier. If he goes up to another lion or group of lions, they smack him and send him scampering. If he tries to share their kill, they light into him and give him a good beating. Month by month of this solitary living makes him more and more of a menace to the natives, and he may meet and kill off many of their sheep and cattle until finally some native hunter organizes a group of warriors and they hunt him down and exterminate the old fellow.

We were on a lion safari from Lake Paradise and were scouting outside our camp in the N'doto Mountains. We were struggling up a rocky ravine one morning when we spied a lioness on the opposite slope, lying outside her cave. She had three little babies, which were not more than a week old and were climbing all over her, giving her a busy time. She finally saw us and bristled. Knowing what a lioness with cubs could do, we kept on going!

At the top of the ravine we concealed ourselves, and stopped to watch her. One baby was on her back, digging his tiny claws into her fur—which she didn't seem to relish. Another stood in front of her and went *phat!* as he cuffed at her, and then tried to attack her whiskers. Her tail was moving constantly, probably out of nervousness over the strangers she had just seen, but one of the cubs thought it was for him and he seized it and bit it. She turned around and growled and the little fellow dropped her tail and backed off, thoroughly surprised and scared.

Suspicious as she was, though she could no longer see us, she did not move. As she lay there, the morning light on her mane threw a sort of halo about her head, and she made a glorious picture of jungle motherhood. The babies were quite fat, but as we looked at her through the binoculars, we saw that she was dreadfully thin. No doubt she was afraid to leave her babies to go out and hunt food for herself. We watched her through the day and she did not leave her home once. Finally I said to Martin:

"I'm going to get her something to eat. She looks starved and there isn't much game in here. I just can't stand to see her like that!"

"Well, they usually take care of themselves, these lionesses," Martin argued, "and we are out here to make pictures—not to feed the animals."

But he finally gave in and we walked until I found an impala which I shot. We called the boys, who half dragged, half carried it back to the entrance to the donga. We left it in a hurry, for we didn't want the lioness to charge us, and then climbed back up to watch what she did.

When the lioness spied the meat, she stood for a few minutes scanning the place, suspiciously, but her hunger got the better of any fear, and with a leap she was down a fifteen-foot bank and off to the entrance of the donga. She pounced on the carcass, ripped open one of the legs and began devouring the meat, proving to us that we had been right about her state of starvation. She was nearly famished. At last, she began dragging the carcass toward the cave. She would pull it with her teeth for a few feet, and then take it in her forepaws for a few feet.

Up the side of that ravine she dragged it. Now and again, very tired from the effort but reluctant to leave her prize, she would stop and pant for breath, her ribs showing through her coat. Then she would look up at her babies and tug away again. When she

TURKANA CHIEFTAIN ON NORTHERN FRONTIER

He is wearing a coiffure of his ancestors' hair, matted with mud, and decorated with ostrich feathers. In his ear is a new piece of jewelry which he cut from a cracker tin. Osa gave him.

FULL-MANED LION
Osa makes a close-up of a fine specimen, camouflaged in long grass that resembles ripe wheat.

OSA'S LIVING ROOM AND ROCK GARDEN

With Spanish moss festooning the trees overhead, Osa has laid out a rock garden, surrounded by a wall of stones and brush for protection.

LAKE PARADISE FROM ABOVE

Across the lake is the elephant trail making the "entrance" to the crater, and above it on the right, the Johnsons' camp.

reached the cave, she lay down wearily to recover her strength. Her babies were immediately all over her again, and she looked very proud as she licked their faces and coats, one after the other. They toddled over to smell the impala, but recoiled at the strange object and didn't seem to like it. On the following day she would probably show them how she tore the flesh and ate, as a first lesson in how they must later support themselves. We went back to camp that night with some fine pictures and a great deal of personal satisfaction.

Later, in the same area, we saw another mother teach her cubs to make a kill.

This mother was also very skinny and hungry and had apparently not had anything to eat for several days. With her was her young son, about nine months old. He, too, looked half starved.

But shortly a large herd of zebra appeared and began grazing toward us. The mother immediately rose stealthily, her son standing beside her, and both watching this tempting dinner. She turned finally and licked the cub, and nudged him encouragingly. He set out in a long detour to the rear of the herd, while she stole forward and hid in the tall grass. Ultimately the cub rose and gave an imitation roar, which was little more than a slightly falsetto growl and started for the zebra, which promptly stampeded toward the mother and us. As they passed her, she made a running spring and downed one of the animals. In a flash the cub was helping her despatch it.

We crept close, and stood behind trees to watch them. She ripped open the zebra's belly and began to tear out the entrails, urging the cub, the while, to do his part. Soon the cub's head was inside the zebra, and then more and more of him disappeared inside. Finally the mother stopped eating and sat watching him with what seemed to be both pride and amusement, as he ripped and tore at the food. When the little fellow finally emerged, he was covered with blood from head to foot; but, gruesome as it was, we couldn't help laughing.

But the lesson was not yet over. Her son must learn to be "tough" and demand his part of a kill, standing his ground against all other lions. So she pounced on the carcass with a terrific growl, leaped back, pushed him forward and jumped forward again with a growl. Keeping him at the carcass, she urged him to eat and kept growling at him as though she were going to fight him. Finally the idea penetrated, and now he began to tear viciously at the meat and growl in real earnest. As he did so, the mother again looked on approvingly as if to say, "I guess he has learned how to take care of himself now."

Before we left this lion retreat, we spent a night in a tree blind to get flashlight pictures of the waterhole life. The moon was bright and we had to be extremely cautious, although it gave us a very clear view of everything about us.

About eleven o'clock a herd of zebra came down to drink at the opposite side of the pool. Suddenly they were startled and ran away in great alarm. I saw something, a large body, swimming across the pool. It had evidently been concealed in the reeds. The animal crawled out on the opposite bank and shook itself.

"It's a lion!" whispered Martin. "And everybody says a lion can't swim!"

The commonest food of the lion is, of course, nice juicy zebra steak. And since the zebra can be seen at a long distance, especially in moonlight, and lacks the protective coloring of other animals, he has no chance against the lion, except by using his quick feet. With forty million zebra in Africa, the lion doesn't have far to go to find his meal.

On the Northern Frontier we had the small-striped and large-eared Grevy zebra, which brays like a mule, as well as the common zebra, which barks like a dog.

"George Eastman says you're photographing every zebra in Africa," I remarked one day as Martin ground on and on at a waterhole.

"Well, why shouldn't I? They were *made* to be photographed," he snapped. "And you just watch him rave when he sees these pictures back in New York."

At this waterhole, late in the afternoon, two little baby zebra came slowly toward the pool. I had seen them standing some distance away for nearly two hours. Evidently they were afraid of what might be lurking in the reeds or were too timid to push in ahead of the other animals, and were trying to work up enough courage.

They were so underfed that their little ribs made shadows on their sides, and they seemed very wobbly on their spindly legs. No doubt their mother had been killed by lions and the impression it left with them was still too clear in their minds to give them any confidence.

Finally one youngster made the start toward the pool, and the other followed, both coming very cautiously, as though feeling their way. They would pause now and again and look longingly at the water, then scan the plain before moving a few feet nearer. Finally, when all the other animals had gone with the exception of a few tommies Grant's gazelles—not any of which was bigger than the two baby zebra—they made a rush for the pool, plunged in and drank and drank.

I hoped that some good zebra mother would adopt them and give them the protection they needed until they could care for themselves.

On the way back to Lake Paradise from a plains trip, we stopped at a stream and pitched camp. I was fishing for catfish and hooking plenty, when Martin said:

"Osa, I think I'll walk down the river for a stretch."

Off he went, accompanied by his gunbearer. Suddenly, I heard his big elephant gun and thought he must have bumped into a rhino. When he came back to where I was fishing, he said that he had seen and startled a large black-maned lion, and that it had looked like a sure charge. The lion circled some brush and Martin, fully realizing how clever these animals were and how often they had mauled the best hunters, prepared for a charge. Sure enough, the lion rushed at him. He had the elephant gun in his hand and fired, but had forgotten to remove the safety sight and consequently missed. However, the shot frightened the lion off.

"I almost had a fine trophy—or else, the lion almost had one," was his comment.

For a flashlight picture, we made a kill of zebra one day, and I camped alone to make the exposures. While it was still daylight (6:30 P.M.), a lioness came and greedily began to devour the food. She was very hungry and ate for a long time. I heard other lions near by. One of these finally came up, a fine male and evidently her mate. He seemed starved and so enraged that she had eaten without roaring an invitation to him that he pounced upon her, cuffing and biting and clawing her, and finally snapped off a piece of her tail.

I was heartbroken that the light was too hazy to get a good picture. But that was one of the hazards of the job. Priceless incidents and actions would materialize, sometimes right under our noses, and the light would be too poor or something would go wrong with the camera—and we would lose the picture.

Martin was often so upset over losing a good shot that he picked up the nearest object and threw it as far as he could. One day he completely lost his temper when a lens jammed at a crucial moment. He tore off the lens and threw it for all he was worth. With a sinking feeling in my stomach, I watched it whirl in a wide arc through the air; it was one of the most expensive and most useful of our lenses, made especially for us by Bausch and Lomb. It crashed against a tree and broke to smithereens, and I was so angry that I drove the car home in pointed silence and wouldn't speak to Martin all that night.

Watching a lion devour his zebra·kill one morning, we saw a dozen wild dogs steal up through the grass. They were evidently starved, for they crept very near the lion, much nearer than they had any business doing. He made for them and they scattered, but they came right back again, sat on their haunches all around him and licked their chops.

He became so furious that he growled and ran about, and finally began clawing the zebra hide, to work off steam and probably to show the dogs how he would tear them to ribbons if they didn't keep their distance.

He ate until he was full. Then, obviously drowsy, he went over to the shade of a small tree and lay down. As soon as he was quiet, the dogs stole up to the zebra, and one was actually tearing away a piece of meat when the lion awoke, and with a roar and a bound was again on the kill. There he stood, growling and lashing his tail, as much as to say, "I worked all night for this food, and it's mine. I'm not making kills for you lazy louts. If you want to eat, go and get your own meat!"

Then he sought the shade to resume his nap, and back came the wild dogs. Again the fracas was repeated; and so it continued over and over again all morning.

At noon we went back to camp for lunch and to scout for pictures elsewhere, but at evening we came back to see what was happening to the old lion.

There he was, still master of the situation, but now he was surrounded by scores of vultures as well as wild dogs. On the ground near the zebra was a dead hyena, which told its own story. The poor lion looked almost exhausted with the heat and constant battle.

As we stood there, a small figure trotted up to the lion as confidently as though he had a message to deliver. It was a jackal.

The lion eyed him critically but did nothing, and the jackal walked right in and began feeding. The lion probably said to himself, "Well, he's so little he can't eat much anyway. Besides, he scouts for me and this will be his pay in advance for his next job."

On our way back to camp, we spotted two hyenas going in our direction. They ambled along, laughing away as though they were enjoying a huge joke. Possibly it was the predicament of the lion, their worst enemy, that amused them.

Nothing revolts me more than the hyena. Probably this is because I have seen him do so many contemptible things—hamstringing young animals which cannot get away or defend themselves; killing sheep and goats just for the lust of torturing them; feeding on rotted and putrid flesh on the plains, his hideous mouth leering and drooling saliva. The hyena is a born murderer, coward and sneak.

That night we were standing at the campfire when we saw a hyena making off with a leather camp chair.

"Damn that thief!" yelled Martin, and threw his shoe, hitting the beast in the hip.

The hyena dropped the chair, picked up the shoe and disappeared, much to Martin's chagrin.

At night we would see from twenty to fifty pairs of yellow-green eyes of hyenas in a circle about camp. They would steal anything made of leather—carrying cases, binoculars, belts, coats —or anything with animal fat on it, such as cooking utensils. I often caught them getting into my food boxes.

One night a hyena came right in among the sleeping camel boys and pulled a cow-skin blanket off one of them. The boy yelled and started after the thief, the camels stampeded, and we woke up to find the camp in an uproar.

We learned to fear leopards even more than lions. They have

none of the lions' majesty and grand manner, but operate like deadly gunmen, stealthily and alone, without friends or companions, and without the trust of any other animal in the jungle.

We were making a movie of baboons at a waterhole when a leopard—who regards baboons as the choicest of food—stole up from the forest. He flattened against the earth and moved forward to the cover of some grass, so smoothly that we were fascinated. We swung the camera to catch this superb action and opened wide the window of the blind.

The baboons heard the window and panicked into the trees. But the leopard, probably enraged at our robbing him of his dinner, came for us like a streak, and before we could close the window, he bounded for it.

I shot him as he leaped, and he fell on top of the camera. It was a close call. Martin ducked, but the leopard's paw had knocked off his helmet, just missing his eyes and face.

I picked up the blood-stained helmet and almost fainted as it came over me what it might have signified. Immediately I thought of Rattray with his mangled arm.

"Good girl, Osa. He certainly was after us," I heard Martin saying.

I seldom cry, but now my nerves went completely to pieces.

"I never want to see another leopard as long as I live," I sobbed, as Martin took me in his arms.

22

". . . Much of Boculy's skill could no doubt be cultivated by the white man if he gave years of time and concentration, but never the fine points. Boculy was an exception, even among the Africans . . ."
—MARTIN JOHNSON

"MARTIN, LOOK!" I handed him the binoculars. "Isn't that the cutest baby elephant you ever saw?"

"Looks more like a mouse than an elephant, all but the ears."

"I'll bet his trunk isn't a foot long. He isn't over a few days old. I'd love to have him for a pet."

Down in the donga below us, an elephant family was browsing, but the little fellow was getting all the attention. His mother stood there proudly watching him as he floundered around on his wobbly legs. And his two young "nursemaids" stood by, ready to take charge of him when the mother tired.

He was trying to go everywhere at once, and to discover everything about his new world. But the excitement was too much and he would weaken and fall on his side; he would lie there and blow little blasts on his tin-whistle trumpet. Then he would come alive again and stagger to his feet, and stand up against his mother's leg while she rubbed him gently with her trunk. He was so tiny that his mother had to kneel to give him his dinner.

Martin thought they were too far off to photograph, but I asked him to let me try it with a twelve-inch lens and we got a splendid picture of maternal love in the jungle.

The elephants moved slowly away, the baby constantly getting under his mother's feet, so that she had to step very carefully. Now and then she would give him a gentle smack with her trunk to keep him on the trail. When he tired the entire family would stop and wait, or graze while he rested, until his mother prodded him to his feet again and pushed him on.

Finally he caught with his trunk the end of the tail of one of the nursemaids and she pulled him along towards the waterhole. We followed, and when we saw them again his mother was dousing him in the water while he squealed with fright.

I have always observed that animals in the jungle are entirely different than they are in captivity. In cages all animals are bound to be restless and nervous, and usually bad-tempered. But out in the open, where they belong, they seem entirely normal and even peaceful, and they live their lives with the same family sense that human beings display.

Whenever we went into the forest or out on the plain we always took with us, in addition to our guide Boculy, our gunbearer Bukhari and our personal boys, at least fifteen trained boys to carry our important movie and still cameras. Each and every boy knew his duty and was always on the alert to fetch equipment or supplies when we called.

This made too large a company for stalking game, so we kept only our gunbearers close at hand. As soon as the cameras were set up, we had the porters retire to a little distance, where they could keep an eye on us but not be in the way.

Some of the bush was so thick and high that I could not see out of it unless I climbed up on a rock or into a tree. Here Martin's six feet two was a great help. He could not only see over the bush but could boost me up when something important came along, and I often sat on his shoulders and scanned the country with my glasses. Sometimes, without warning, he would hoist me up, saying, "Here, you little pygmy, have a look at the scenery." Or, "You've got eyes like a hawk: are there any elephants over there?"

There usually were elephants. But when we found a single elephant or a pair, we were always happier than if there was a herd. A herd always kept us busy keeping out of its wind or its way, and because it moved about a great deal it was easy to get action but not easy to record the elephants' personalities and characteristics. We now wanted more than anything else to study single elephants closely and in detail.

We happened upon an elephant one noonday, apparently sleeping under a thorntree. I climbed up into the crotch of a tree with my binoculars and looked. It turned out to be a mother and her baby. The toto stood beneath his mother, drowsing. She was sheltering him from the sun.

The baby waked and began to frisk around and the mother patiently followed, with slow, stately dignity, evidently willing to let it have all the fun it wanted, but unwilling to let it stray more than a few feet away from her, for there was no telling what might be hiding in the grass to do her baby harm.

They moved towards us, but when they were a few yards away the mother stopped suddenly, reached out and caught the youngster with her trunk, and pushed it, squealing, back under her.

Out came her great ears and up went her trunk to feel the wind. The baby now stood there bravely and held out his ears too. Then they hurried off, and after they disappeared we could hear the mother trumpeting and the baby answering with its squeaky little tin horn.

One morning Boculy rushed in as we were having breakfast to tell us he had just found a fine bull elephant near by. Whenever he found something he knew we wanted badly, he would come up rubbing or "washing" his hands, almost speechless with satisfaction and excitement. Another trick he had was to wipe his hands,

palms and backs, up and down his trousers, and then rub his head
as though warming up his thoughts.

He now led us to a donga about a mile away where we found
the big bull wandering about by himself, feeding among young
trees. From the way the trees were broken and torn, we judged
that he must have been feasting there for several days. He was a
huge fellow, with tusks that must have weighed two hundred
pounds each.

"N'guvu sana" (very strong), whispered Bukhari.

Whereupon the elephant, eyeing some fine branches out of his
reach, put his head against the tree, straddled it with his tusks,
tried the ground with his feet, and started pushing.

He would push forward, then yield, then push, then yield, with
a steady rhythmic movement of his entire bulk. Gradually the tree
began to sway gently. A root snapped. The tree gave more and
more, as more root stubs appeared, and finally crashed as the
elephant bore forward.

The big fellow was so petered out that he had lost his appetite.
He stood there for a few minutes, then went over to a supporting
branch, rested his tusks and fell asleep.

Meantime, Martin had been getting priceless films and as we
left for camp he was extremely happy.

"Boculy, Missouri sana!" (very good) he said. And Boculy,
always relishing a compliment, especially before the other boys,
stepped out with his gun on his shoulder as proudly as though he
had just received a medal.

An elephant is known to have very poor eyesight, not being able
to see well beyond forty yards. But he could always see me well
enough and certainly much better than a rhino.

Whenever he retreated, I felt it was from my gun more than
from me, however, for an elephant knows that he has nothing to
fear from anything but a gun or a spear.

Even when he ran, the elephant showed his intelligence and

superiority. Faced with danger, a member of the cat family would stand and lash himself into a fury and charge, whatever the odds. A rhino would snort and paw the earth and kick up a huge cloud of dust to show his importance, but he never used his head whether he charged or ran away. A zebra or giraffe would never be able to decide what to do, and would finally panic away from, or right into, the danger. But an elephant was always wide awake and using his brain, and he was usually prudent enough to get into some cover without any loss of time.

I went alone to a waterhole one day, hoping to get pictures of a big bull elephant that I had seen in that neighborhood. Boculy was sure he would come back. The day was cool and bright and I felt ever so peppy and confident as I set out.

Arrived at the waterhole, Boculy and I scouted and then determined to wait. We walked down the muddy elephant trail to the water and surveyed the place, then selected a cliff opposite the waterhole for a good spot and set up the cameras in camouflage.

We had scarcely settled down when I heard the rocking tread of elephants and the breaking of trees and trumpeting. I knew it was a sizable herd and my heart pounded, for I was sure that this day I was going to get one of the *best* of pictures. Everything was right for it.

Thirty elephants came out of the forest. The leader came ahead cautiously, while the others waited for his "advice." He seemed assured and came down, swaying majestically from side to side, the others following. I waited for them to come into range of the cameras and—they stopped dead in their tracks! The leader was "feeling" about the ground. Up went the trunk, out came a terrific trumpet blast and off they all went pell-mell. He had got the scent from my tracks.

They probably had to go miles for another drink of water, but nothing would have coaxed them back to that place that day, and I had missed one of the very best pictures of our career. My gunbearer, in tears, said, "Why did they come so close and run away?" Boculy shrugged his shoulders as much as to say, "Tough luck" or "Bad business," and looked extremely disgusted. "Missus," he grinned wryly, "why didn't you give them a shilling?"

Later that day we spotted two elephants under a tree, evidently asleep. We were in heavy bush and were able to creep up very close to them. There, leaning against the tree, was a female elephant sound asleep. Behind her stood her mate, a huge fellow with two of the biggest tusks we had ever seen.

He was fidgety, and seemed just too tired to hold up those heavy tusks. He rested them against the tree trunk but that wasn't comfortable. Then he put them in the crotch of the tree, but that screwed up his neck too much. Finally he hit on a fine idea. The female's rump was just the right height, so there he carefully laid his tusks.

She went on dozing for a moment, then woke and shook off his tusks with a muffled trumpet. The old fellow waited for a bit and then carefully lifted his tusks up on her back once more. Again she shook him off.

When he repeated this performance a third time she was completely out of patience. She shook him off, let out a terrific trumpeting blast, whirled and jabbed her tusks into his side. He took this punishment as though terribly hurt, and eyed her while she settled herself against the tree trunk. Then, thoroughly discouraged, he plodded off until he found a tree with a low branch to hold his ivory and there he fell asleep.

One fact that we often noted about elephants was what seemed to be a form of mental telepathy between them. We saw this sort of thing so many times that we wondered if they could use some kind of wireless system. The elephants have very stiff hairs in their ears, and in their nostrils. These might be used as antennae to catch vibrations of which a human being is quite unconscious.

On many occasions we saw an elephant, separated by several

hundred yards from the rest of the herd, seemingly warn his comrades of a danger he and he alone had discovered. It was almost as though he sent some radio signal to the other elephants, for they would suddenly become alarmed, even though I am certain they could not have seen the lone elephant nor could they have discovered the danger for themselves.

Just as perplexing to us was how they could carry those huge hulks over the trails and through the brush with such silence. They were so quiet we had to depend on our eyes and watch for them, for oftentimes we could not hear them, though they were only a few yards away. Even when alarmed they would sometimes simply vanish out of sight and hearing in an instant, and this was especially true of a single elephant.

They frequently came right up to our camp in the night, and although we found their great tracks in the morning none of us, not even Boculy, would hear them at the time.

The picture we always wanted to make was of elephants squatting and sliding down an embankment, but we never got a good one except of a toto. These great slides make fine toboggans and I think the elephants get more fun than use out of them. However, I have often used their slides for short-cuts, disregarding the mud, sitting right down on my breeches and scooting downhill.

Our best experiences and opportunities were often the ones we missed photographing. This would leave us very discouraged for the moment, but we were stubborn and, since chance had come that close once, we knew it would come again. So we persisted. Also, we often saw our finest specimens when we were merely moving camp or shifting from one waterhole to another, and before we could get the equipment set up, the game was gone.

One day Boculy came running into camp. I could tell he was excited because of the way his hands moved around. He kept lifting them and letting them fall, and then gripping his fingers. He was talking in short, inarticulate phrases.

"Bwana! Very good herd of elephants!" He pointed over his shoulder with his thumb and added, "All feeding and moving very little."

Martin called his camera boys, I grabbed my rifle, and, with Boculy leading, we started at once, for this sounded like something worth while.

We came to a fine small herd about a mile away, but no sooner had Martin started his camera than the elephants startled and hurried away.

Boculy thought they would pause to drink and feed at a small waterhole, so we followed them. Coming over the rim of the donga, we saw them drinking just as he had predicted. Martin swung his tripod into place, clamped on a lens, and in a flash the elephants were gone again.

It was boiling hot. Martin was now quite out of sorts and started to bawl out everybody. Boculy was very impatient, as though he were thinking, "What's the use? I lead them up to chances like this and then they get nothing."

But Martin was stubborn and would not give up. The light was now perfect and there were tracks of elephants everywhere, so Boculy climbed a high tree to scout and soon reported elephants moving about two miles away, towards an open waterhole.

We bundled off after him, and did the last half mile almost on the run.

There, at the waterhole, was a magnificent herd. Some were splashing about in the water, trumpeting and having a good time; others were drinking, and the rest were feeding in the grass and among the trees.

While Martin was setting up his cameras, I spotted another herd a half mile off and could see even more elephants several miles away.

Boculy was shifting from one foot to another, the boys were very excited and Martin was red with heat and exertion. He handled the cameras very quietly now, carefully fitted his lenses, and started turning the crank.

There was a crunching sound and the camera stopped. The film had buckled.

Martin tried to straighten it out, but it was so firmly wedged in the magazine roller that he had to pry it loose and load another magazine.

By the time he was ready, clouds came up and ruined the light. The elephants began to drift away. When the light returned, the elephants were too scattered for any use. And before long it was dark.

I glanced around and there was Boculy, sitting on a rock dangling his feet and looking very disgusted.

When it came to photographing elephants Martin never showed discretion, partly because of his eagerness to record everything they did in full detail and partly because he knew that the public always wanted the daring and the unusual in its films.

"I don't like this at all," I said as he shouldered his camera and started to move closer to a large herd of elephants we were photographing. "It's too risky and it isn't necessary."

"But the wind is right, darling, and they're beauties."

"What if the wind shifts?"

"Well, then it will be just too bad. I've got a three-inch lens on the camera and this is going to be a peach."

"M'baya sana," (bad business) mumbled Bukhari as he shook his head quietly.

But we all moved forward; Martin planked his camera and ground out film. A big female had started toward us and now she had stopped and was "rocking" her whole body, her ears out and her trunk waving. She was undecided and turned broadside to us. The others gathered behind her. I raised my gun and Bukhari stepped close to me with my extra rifle.

A MAGNIFICENT BULL ELEPHANT AT PARADISE

From behind a bush Osa photographs him emerging from the forest.

THE HABASH OF ABYSSINIA AND HIS BODYGUARD

Africa's most hunted ivory poacher poses for Osa's camera on the Northern Frontier.

Slowly she turned as if to run away, but then swung back to face us, laid back her ears in a "streamline," and charged toward us. Halfway, she stopped and "rocked" again.

Martin continued to grind away. I am sure it was that maddening and unfamiliar sound that caused her decision. She came for us, headlong.

At fifty feet I took aim and heard an explosion which nearly cracked my eardrums. Bukhari and Boculy had both fired. Boculy fired again. Martin yelled to them both to stop shooting. The elephant ran away with the herd.

"Who told you to shoot, you fools?" shouted Martin, and he lit into them. It is one of the first rules of safari that no black boy is allowed to shoot without orders unless the master is being gored, for they are bad shots and invariably only wound the animals. Fortunately our elephant was not badly wounded.

"She's only got a flesh wound in her trunk," Martin said. "I think she'll be all right."

Boculy was a great pal of the porters and they all loved him. His manners and wisdom were those of a sage. He would sit by the hour at the campfires at night, entertaining the boys with his exploits. He must have added lots of comedy for they often rolled with laughter.

He was always trying to please us when we were out on safari and if he came upon a beautiful girl or child he would bring her in for a picture, which we would solemnly take just to avoid making him lose face. Most of his jungle belles were hopelessly fat or otherwise poor camera subjects, and to economize without discouraging him we often took the picture with an empty magazine.

Sometimes he would bring in natives who had heard we were near by and had traveled miles to see us and say "hello." Sometimes they asked for work. but when we said we had none they

never seemed unhappy about it, and I concluded from their ex-
pressions of wonderment that they were just curious to look us
over and they felt that the experience was worth the long safari.
They were almost always easy-going and friendly.

But Boculy took his responsibilities very seriously. If he found
too big a herd of elephants, he would try to lead us away, knowing
the danger, and would become extremely nervous if we remained.
Although at first he looked upon us as hunters and took chances
that were not warranted, he finally caught on. It took him a considerable time to find out that we did not want to kill the animals,
but when he fully understood the situation he went to the other
extreme of caution.

His cunning had its domestic twists and, though his wants were
few, he usually got what he wanted very smoothly. If natives came
up with ghee, he would bring it to me and ask if I wanted to buy
it, knowing full well that I did not, but the look of hope on his
face and the sly twinkle in his eye always led me to buy it, for
him, as he intended I should. Martin was always extremely generous with him too, and often said he could not show too much
appreciation for Boculy.

If Boculy disliked a porter, especially a smart-aleck or bounder
or bully, he never abused the fellow. He patiently endured him.
But he kept that boy in his place like a fly in a spiderweb, and
saw that he got the hardest and most disagreeable assignments
and the fewest luxuries.

If natives brought in bad goats or sheep, he would harangue
them like a straw boss: "This is wood, not meat! Look at his ribs!
I am an old man; I can't eat wood. Why don't you feed your animals; are you so stingy? The master must have the best! You
want shillings for nothing, do you?"

He would often buy sheep on his own salary, and when he
did he would always bring in the cook and have him offer Martin
and me the leg with a grand gesture, saying, "Would you like

meat, M'sahib: it is delicious. The chief wishes to give you a present." All this was done with the haughty air of a man of great importance. And whatever his mysterious past, there was no doubt about it, Boculy was a man among men.

He never wanted shoes, as all the other boys did. The boys were always begging for shoes, but if I gave them good ones these were carefully preserved to be shown at home, and they went on wearing tattered sandals or nothing at all. Boculy took our old tires. One of these would make him several pairs of sandals, and these he regarded as the most comfortable thing a man could wear.

He loved snuff, and obtained it from the Somalis who came down with herds from Somaliland. He carried this in a little gourd or horn.

He was never without his fly swatter, made from the tail of a colobus monkey. Otherwise, he wore a tattered blue KAR shirt, khaki breeches and puttees, and as he stood with one foot crossed over the other and resting on the opposite knee, he looked something like a stork but like no one else in the world.

I tried to get the story of how his jaw had been crushed by an elephant. I could hear him telling it with many flourishes and embellishments at the campfires, but he was always reticent about himself with Martin and me. According to the boys, he said that an elephant had picked up a tree and hit him with it. Actually, he was probably charged, struck by the elephant's trunk, and when he fell down, the elephant thought he was dead and ran away. He probably never knew what hit him.

If Boculy failed to find elephants, he always became very nonchalant and had a plausible excuse. His usual explanation was that the elephants he had seen today were not very good and we would catch better ones tomorrow.

Sometimes, when Boculy called me at five o'clock in the morning and I was very sleepy, I would call back to him: "All right, uzee (old man); the elephants will be there tomorrow."

The boys began to tease him about this, and as we safaried along from place to place they would chant:

> "Catch tomorrow,
> Old man.
> Yo-ee-yah.
> Old Boculy
> Catch tomorrow,
> Yo-ee-yah."

Boculy would walk along stiffly and haughtily, his jaw set, completely ignoring them. But next day he would be up long before dawn and quietly he would take us up to some fine elephants. Then he would stand on one foot and grin, while the boys' eyes popped.

23

"... If any man deserved to be a great leader in industry and public affairs, it was George Eastman. We found him to be not only a brilliant mind but a splendid sportsman, extremely considerate, hating fraud and front, and possessed of one of the sweetest dispositions we have ever known ..."

— MARTIN JOHNSON

ONE MORNING, A runner came up to our house at Lake Paradise with a cable. Martin tore it open.

"Mr. Eastman is coming, Osa! He will be in Nairobi in a few days."

"Let me see!" I snatched the yellow piece of paper and read it.

The message informed us that George Eastman, Mr. Daniel Pomeroy and Dr. Audley Stewart were arriving in Nairobi for their long-promised visit to us. Also that Carl Akeley, with his party of artists and taxidermists, was in Nairobi.

"Well, what are we waiting for? Call Bukhari. Let's get going!" Martin shouted.

We hastily packed our chop boxes and set out to meet our friends.

We had spent six months building a strong log cabin right on the elephant trail so that Mr. Eastman would have the thrill of hearing the big beasts pass his house at night. It was our largest and strongest and best-equipped building.

When we returned with him from Nairobi and showed him where he was to live, he was completely undaunted by the thought of elephants brushing right past his cabin.

291

Here, taken from his published letters to his secretary,* is his own account of that arrival in camp, which will tell better than I can the things that impressed him most about Lake Paradise.

Paradise Lake
Sunday, June 20, 1926

Dear Miss Whitney:

We arrived here just a week ago today—our farthest north objective, and the one we have looked forward to with the greatest interest. We found it fully up to our expectations. The lake is a circular body of water, occupying the crater of an old volcano, and is perhaps a third to half a mile across. The side of the crater is blown away on the southeast and rises to a couple of hundred feet on the north. The Johnsons' houses are on the ridge overlooking the lake to the east. The various houses which are all made of wattles, plastered with mud and thatched with straw, except the one Audley and I are quartered in, are on various levels following the undulations of the ridge, and consist of a living and dining room with fireplace and dirt floor, a kitchen, a sleeping house for the Johnsons, a guest house, a bath house, a workshop where the Delco electric generator is, the laboratory and a storehouse where the supplies are kept. The ground slopes from this string of houses away from the lake to the shamba or garden, and below that is the native village of huts where the men (or "boys," as they are called) live who are employed on the place.

The houses are all picturesque and rough, and serve their various purposes excellently, and the living rooms are very comfortable. The log house where Audley and I are is new, having been built for our occupancy, Dan having the guest house and the two white hunters living in tents. Our house is about 20 x 25 ft. with a big alcove for the fireplace, and is all open on one side, there being no windows on three sides. It has a dirt floor (covered with a canvas tent fly), a 2-ft. base of cut lava, then log walls up to about 7½ ft. of 5-in. logs, then a steep roof thatched with straw on small poles held in place by rawhide thongs. There are pegs on the walls upon which to hang our things and around the top is a string of Osa's hunting trophies. With a fire in the deep fireplace the house is most attractive. The surrounding forest extends for miles. Only hard wood grows in this country. It is surprisingly heavy, and makes wonderful firewood and burns with little smoke and no soot. All the cooking is done on the open

*"Chronicles of an African Trip," by George Eastman.

fire, both at the house and in camp, and the utensils (mostly aluminum) are easily kept bright and clean.

They have a very effective "stove" in the kitchen. In the middle of the room (all open on one side) is a raised bench about 3 ft. wide with a trench in the top about a foot square. One end butts against the chimney. The top of this trench is covered next the wall with a hot-water tank, then about 5 ft. is covered with a sheet of iron with holes and covers. The end, away from the chimney for about 2 ft., is open. The bottom of the trench is about 3 ft. from the floor, making it convenient to work at the fire. The fire is made in the trench with long slender sticks of wood. The bread-making is done in the rectangular sheet-iron Dutch ovens set on top of the stove, the bottom heat coming from the stove and the top heat from coals shoveled on top of the oven. Any person with a little practice can do perfect baking in this way. It is especially good for baking pies, as the bottom heat can be regulated so accurately in reference to the top. I think I will build one at Oak Lodge.

The weather here is simply delightful, the range of temperature from 61 degrees at night to 75 degrees in the daytime in the shade. In the direct sun it is hot, but I have not been oppressed by it at any time. I have, when out on the desert on the way here, felt the heat of the ground through the crepe rubber soles of my shoes, a $\frac{1}{4}$ in. cork insole and two pairs of heavy wool socks, and still been quite comfortable. When hunting we usually come in for a siesta from ten to four, but the middle of the day in the field so far has not been unbearable.

After we left the beautiful camp at Guasamana, where Audley and I both got our lions, we moved seventeen miles across the Eauso Nyiro River to a place called Kissimani (the Wells), where we stayed from May 31st to June 6th. The crossing of the river was interesting because we had to be pulled over by a rope. The day previous two of our trucks had been towed across by mules and they in turn pulled us across. The rope broke several times but we finally made it with the help of fifteen or twenty of our "boys" pushing and pulling. Audley and I went over ahead on mules so we could make some photographs. We had pretty good shooting at the "Wells" and all got some good specimens.

On the 6th we moved again about twenty-three miles to Karo, a place where we had to get water out of holes dug in the sand of a dry river. By this time our still proved its value as the water was not fit to drink. At a waterhole, two hours from Karo, Martin had a blind built and he and I sat in it all day hoping to get some pictures of animals but nothing came. The next morning we started at daylight for the same place, but as there were no fresh tracks we were advised by our native guide to try another one two hours further on. After we had been marching an hour (on foot and mules), we ran across a rhino. As his horns were not good specimens I thought to try making a Cine-Kodak of him. After stalking him a little way I got within 20 yards of him when he saw me and charged. Phil and Martin had their big guns, of course, and when he got within 10 yards Phil opened on him, Martin following. He began to crumple at once and fell 5½ paces from where I stood. I kept the camera trained on him all right but the film, we found on Martin's developing it, appeared hopelessly over-exposed for a good picture, but it records what happened. The affair could not have been more perfect if it had been staged and was the opportunity of a lifetime. I am much disappointed not to have got a good picture.*

I forgot to say that at the "Wells" one night a lion tried to take one of our mules. Three mules were tethered right in the middle of the camp between our tents and the boys. He got his claws into both jaws from behind and why he did not hang on is a mystery. Phil thinks he did not realize when he tackled the job what a nest of men he was getting into, and let go when he saw what a big camp was there. The mule broke away and we did not get him until the next afternoon. He had run back to the river and was caught by a native. His jaws had swollen and they began to suppurate right away. We nicknamed him "laudable pus," he ran so much of it, but he was getting well at last accounts. We left him at our last camp and expect to pick him up again when we go back tomorrow. The next night a leopard came into camp and was seen by one of the chauffeurs with a flash lamp. He did no harm. Martin got a fine flashlight picture of him on a zebra kill the night following.

Our last camp before we reached here was at Lasamis, a waterhole in a desolate country where Paul Rainey made some of his best pictures. There is little game at any of these waterholes now because there is some water nearly everywhere and the game has spread all about. We are anxious to get elephant and buffalo, as well as rhino, and are shortening our stay here a week in order to go on a camel safari to a place where it is just possible we may get elephant and buffalo. It is only a chance, but we are going to take it. In any case the camel safari will be an experience. As the country is too rough for motors, we shall ride on donkeys and the boys will walk. The camels will carry the outfit and food. There are not enough boys.

* When printed at Rochester this picture turned out all right.

Have had no mail since leaving Nairobi, May 21st. Hope there will be a lot at Meru when we get there in about two weeks.

Everybody is feeling fine in the party, except one of the chauffeurs and two or three boys, who have fever off and on.

Yours,

GEORGE EASTMAN.

Mr. Eastman was very keen about "barbecued" meats and liked to watch me doing guinea fowl or bustard in the deep pit. But he was impatient to take them out and look at them, fearing that they would be ruined, and I had to restrain him.

He had brought with him a ready-mixed flour, which he invented long before it was available commercially, and we whipped up many a pan of hot biscuits in no time at all.

Returning from the field, he would begin planning dinner and always had a pie or fine dessert. He and Martin both shared this dessert-affection. He was especially fond of lemon meringue pie and made good ones.

His fish chowder was excellent. He brought this and other recipes, or made them up on the spot and gave them to me. But he swore that my Kansas fried chicken was the best thing he had ever tasted, and so liked it that he made me do guinea fowl that way. With fresh wild asparagus, this was his favorite dish.

One day he shot a guinea fowl and wanted to bake it in clay. He got the clay all over himself and we had to clean him up with Supersuds.

Watching me strain and sterilize my milk from the hump-backed cattle, and churn the butter, he said that he thought it better than from his prize Jerseys in Rochester.

"Wait till I get back and tell Lovejoy that his Holsteins aren't in it with your razor-backs. Ha, he'll be wanting you to bring him some!"

When we arrived from Nairobi, the cooks had twenty-five pounds of fine, washed and salted-down butter waiting for us, and George

Eastman was astounded. He was delighted with the old-fashioned rose-bud wooden butter mould I used; he liked this touch out in the rough jungle.

He was also enthusiastic about my garden and used to spend hours in it. He marveled at the variety and size and rapidity of growth of the vegetables, and got a great thrill out of these luxuries right in the midst of the wilderness.

I think it was our common interest in cooking that brought us closest together. He not only liked cooking as a hobby, but good food was an actual necessity to his happiness and peace of mind.

"You and Martin have the right idea," he said. "Good food is absolutely necessary to health, and working as hard as you do, you owe it to yourselves to have the best."

We tried everything in our cooking experiments, but these are the recipes that George Eastman and I had the most success with at Paradise—or at least the ones which everyone seemed to enjoy:

SAUCE FOR FRIED CHICKEN

Put one cup of milk and one cup of cream into the pan in which the chicken was cooked, place over the fire and stir constantly until mixture boils. The crumbs in the pan left from the fried chicken will thicken the sauce, but if they do not, add a little flour. Season with salt and pepper, add one teaspoon chopped parsley, a little onion juice and diced button mushrooms and it is ready to serve. Use same sauce for any fowl.

ONIONS AU GRATIN

Peel and slice thinly 3 good-sized Spanish onions. Butter a baking dish, arrange in it a layer of the sliced onions, dust with salt and pepper, sprinkle over 1 tsp. melted butter. Continue in this order until the pan is filled. Bake in moderate oven until onions are tender; this will take about ¾ of an hour. Over the top sprinkle a thick layer of grated cheese and return to the oven until it is melted and browned.

HASHED BROWN POTATOES

Chop cold boiled potatoes rather thin. To each pint, add 3 tbs. cream, ½ tsp. salt and a dash of pepper. Mix. Put a tablespoon of butter into a shallow frying pan, put in the potatoes, flatten them in a perfectly smooth layer. Cook slowly until a golden brown, fold one-half over the other and turn out on a heated dish.

MRS. KELLY'S LEMON MERINGUE PIE

2 cups hot water
2 cups sugar
6 egg yolks
Grated rind and juice of 1½ lemons (moderate size)
5 heaping teaspoons flour (all that can be heaped on the spoon)
Salt to taste

Beat egg yolks well. Add sugar. Mix flour with enough cold water to make a paste. Then add to it the mixed egg and sugar and beat until creamy. Stir into the boiling water and when partly cooled add grated lemon and juice and stir until perfectly smooth.

For the meringue: Beat whites of eggs until perfectly stiff, then fold in ½ cup of powdered sugar.

ELIZA'S FOAMING SAUCE

½ cup butter
1 cup sugar
1 egg

Cream butter and sugar. Add yolk and stand over boiling water. When melted, add 1 tbs. boiling water and 2 tbs. sherry wine. When ready to serve add beaten white of egg.

COOKING IN CLAY

An excellent way to cook birds and fish, where clay can be had, is to cover the bird, unplucked and undrawn, with a coating of clay two inches or more thick. Place in hot coals. In about an hour, when the clay is baked hard, crack it open lengthwise and take out the meat; the skin and feathers will remain, adhering to the clay. Open the bird and drop out the entrails. Fish may be done in the same way. If desired, the birds and fish can be cleaned before baking.

"I have two cooks at home, and *they* can't make as good bread as this, and you have to make it in those tins in a heap of ashes," Mr. Eastman would exclaim.

And he did relish that bread. He would go and peek into the tins as it was baking and watch lest it overbake. When it rained and we still got bread out of the open fires, he was almost incredulous.

One night I had guinea fowl ready to broil. George Eastman came in and said:

"Osa, don't you think it would be a good idea to have corned beef hash and poached eggs tonight? I have a craving for hash." I at once agreed that I wanted nothing more, and it was a pleasure to see him enjoy it.

Or he would say:

"Osa, let's have one of those English Plum Puddings out of a tin; you know how to make that foaming sauce the way I like it." He called that sauce the "George Eastman—Osa Johnson Famous Foaming Sauce."

After a satisfying dinner and a smoke, George Eastman would kiss me on both cheeks and bid everyone goodnight, then turn and say:

"What do you say to some of those famous hot cakes for tomorrow's breakfast?" Or it might be "chipped beef and cream, country style." So up I would get at four a.m., rout out the cooks, dress for the field, have breakfast at six, and then prepare lunches for nine men, and off we would start promptly at seven.

Mr. Eastman would usually shuffle into the kitchen, say "Good morning," look over everything on the stove, ask me if I thought it was going to be good, ask me to slice the bread thinner or make the poached eggs softer, then take me by the arm and march me to the dining room, singing "Roamin' in the Gloamin'," or some of the other songs he loved. I knew he was really enjoying Paradise to the full.

George Eastman had bought a white mule on the way up to camp. I had protested at this and said, "The lions will spot him. They can see him at night. They will spot him and maybe get you both." But he had joked about it and said he thought the mule looked faster than that.

One night lions came into our camp at Longai and mauled the little white mule so badly that he was permanently maimed. They touched no other mule.

All this occurred as we were sitting at the campfire after a delightful and quiet dinner, and singing old-time songs—at that moment, "Oh, How I Miss You Tonight," a favorite of George Eastman's.

Mr. Eastman was crazy about my primitive outdoor stove and often examined it and said he was going to build one for himself at Rochester for outdoor grills. But he spoke of it mostly when we were having feasts beside it, so I was never sure he was not influenced by the food which he, himself, took such pleasure in preparing.

He respected work and often spoke scornfully of "goldspoon" babies, and remarked that he liked us because we had had to work our way and had to earn the pleasures and happiness we had. He often reflected on his struggles and of his admiration for people who had started with nothing, and he said that people were happier if they had no burdens of wealth at any time. He told me of his mother and how she and he had scraped along.

"She scrubbed floors and did all the work, and nursed me through to success. I loved her, almost worshipped her, and I have never seen her equal. Her advice was 'George, always do the right as you see it, and have Faith.' "

When he did become wealthy, he gave her everything he could think of for her comfort and happiness. As he said:

"She gave her last pennies to carry me through. I could never forget her. Without her I would have been nothing."

George Eastman had an intense curiosity about everything. He asked me how we made our bricks and got them hard. He inquired how we built our ovens and fireplaces and how the houses were put together, and thatched, and plastered. He was amazed at the ingenuity of Martin's laboratory, and curious about the Eastman film and how the chemicals were standing up, and about how Tom Craig was packing our shipments. He was equally curious about all the animals and plied me with a thousand questions about what they were and how they behaved.

When his active mind was not prying into new information, he was inventing something. His proudest achievement was to build a shower bath.

This shower consisted of a regular collapsible automobile canvas pail, to the bottom of which was attached a hose connection. From this led a four-foot length of soft rubber tube, near the end of which was a common everyday clothespin which regulated the flow of the water. Every night after the day's work, Mr. Eastman's tent boy, Abdulla, hung this pail on the front tent pole about head high, put the zinc bathtub underneath, filled the bucket with warm water, and the shower was ready.

In the Kedong Valley a terrible encounter with rhino had been reported at this time. We read about it in the Nairobi papers. Mr. Eastman sat by the fireplace in the late afternoon and read the account aloud from the paper:

WHITE WOMAN CHARGED BY TWO RHINO

Mrs. Bailey, wife of Mr. G. Bailey, of "Sterndale," Naivasha, is an inmate of Nairobi European Hospital after being the victim of an experience which comes within the lives of few women. She owes the fact that she is alive to some miraculous intervention or accident of which she is quite unaware.

Mr. and Mrs. Bailey were on safari and had established their camp near Suswa for a week. On the night before the accident they had been sitting up for lions, and Mrs. Bailey caught a chill. On the following day she decided that she would not go far and intended to spend an uneventful day hunting around the camp for reedbuck with a small rifle. Mr. Bailey departed with a gunbearer to seek game on the plains and Mrs. Bailey, with another bearer and a second native, decided to climb Suswa. She found no sign of reedbuck and set out to return to camp.

On the way home she discovered fresh tracks of rhino and suddenly came upon two of the animals lying down under a tree in more or less open ground. She hurried to camp and brought her husband's double .470 rifle and the natives back to the spot. When she arrived she found that the two animals had changed their position and were resting under a thick bush.

Mrs. Bailey crept slowly forward until she was well within forty yards. The rhino were in such a position that one was practically covering the outline of its companion, and she supposed they were an old rhino and a full-grown youngster. The latter was nearest to her and she fired at the rhino on the farther side, choosing as a mark an exposed shoulder to get a good heart shot.

The next thing she knew they both rose to their feet and rushed through the bush at her, charging side by side. She had no time to turn about or fire a second time.

One of the animals caught her with its horn on her side; the horn traveled right up her body and tore away the whole of her scalp on that side. She was thrown high in the air among the trees, and when she came down the rhino trod upon her as she lay on the ground.

Both native gunbearers stood the strain well. They were experienced men, and they kept their ground. As soon as opportunity offered they lifted the injured woman up—her face was streaming blood—and when she regained her feet, she discovered that one of the rhinos was rapidly returning. The natives dragged Mrs. Bailey into a dry water gully and the gunbearer drove the animal off with rifle fire. Then they set out to carry Mrs. Bailey four miles to camp and luckily met another party of the camp porters who had been in the same locality for the camp water supply. Among them they brought her down, quite unconscious, and one native hurried on ahead to inform Mr. Bailey who met the party bringing his injured wife about a mile from camp.

Mr. Eastman put down the paper. It was an introduction to Africa. He smiled, as much as to say, "Well, that is Africa, I suppose." He merely announced quietly that he was going to take a shower.

To obtain animal groups for the new African Hall of the American Museum of Natural History, which was one of the chief objectives of Mr. Eastman and Mr. Pomeroy, we had made safaris all about Paradise and the desert below, and we now determined to follow Carl Akeley's suggestion and join him in Tanganyika for a study there of the Serengeti lions.

But three years had elapsed since we had begun our expedition and we had so much work still undone that we were impatient to return to make the most of our limited time and finances. So, after a few weeks of this pleasant safari, we hurried back to Lake Paradise.

24

"... Of course there are hardships, but with our years of experience to help us we have found ways around the hardships, and we manage to keep just as healthy and happy as though we had all the comforts of home . . ."

—Martin Johnson

"I think Mr. Eastman understands what we are doing."

Martin and I sat on the cliffs at Paradise and talked about our recent visitors. We felt sure that George Eastman had not regretted his decision to finance us.

Almost every clear evening Martin and I would sit on the cliffs until late into the night and reminisce. Martin would have been the last person in the world to admit it, but he had a sentimental streak in him, just as I had.

Sitting there under the moon, my husband would suggest that I sing, and tease me by saying that my singing was why he married me. He loved to have me sing to him "Mighty Lak a Rose," "My Wild Irish Rose," "After the Ball Is Over," "Cheyenne," "In the Shade of the Old Apple Tree," and "Put On Your Old Gray Bonnet." I had quite a repertory of songs left over from the days when we barnstormed through the West and Canada, showing Martin's pictures of the Jack London voyage, and I had had to burst into the performance with what passed for vocal interludes.

Martin and I both loved the old-time melodies because of their sentimental attachments. Each melody had a particular association. "After the Ball Is Over" commemorated the day I had worn my prettiest blue dress to a school dance in Chanute. "In the Good Old Summer Time" was the first song I ever sang on a stage before an audience. They were all bundled up with happy memories. "Put On Your Old Gray Bonnet" held memories of Kansas when Martin and I first met.

"Give me a Chanute Kansas and Independence Kansas kiss," he used to say in his old joking way.

On safari, as we walked along the monotonous miles, nothing much happening, I would sing at the top of my voice. Every so often I would strike a marching military rhythm when I wanted to make my tired feet go faster. If we were out in animal country, and I persisted in singing, Martin would often remark that it was a wonderful way to develop my lungs and chest power, but he didn't know how I expected to find any animals when I deliberately frightened them away.

And so we had spent our four years in Paradise with plenty of singing. Often on a cold or stormy night, I would curl up in my cot and draw Granny's crazy patchwork quilt close around my neck and hum to myself. My thoughts somersaulted over one another. Why, we had things pretty easy! Compared to the trials and tribulations of the pioneering days of the Great West, ours was a mild adventure.

Bundled in the quilt, I could see each design on the cover. This little red patch must have been a piece of an old thread-bare dress from an ancient trunk. Perhaps Granny had worn that dress when she crossed the Alleghenies from Pennsylvania into Missouri in a covered wagon as a very little girl. That blue calico patch might have been from a dress she wore when they were fighting hostile Indians to gain a foothold in a wild, barren country known as Kansas. I realized just how much the pioneer women meant to their men in those days of the opening of the West. Little could have been accomplished without them.

As a change from Lake Paradise, and to celebrate my birthday, we decided to make a safari to a lovely spot on the Gura River. Secretly, I hoped that the fishing there might be good. So we loaded our belongings into a truck and off we went.

Arriving at a bridge, I got out and walked across and decided that it was all right, and motioned for Martin to cross. He did, but half way over the bridge gave way and down he and the truck went, with a crash. I was terrified. Fortunately for Martin, there was a huge tree jutting out from the bank beside the bridge. The body of the truck miraculously caught on the tree and Martin scrambled out unharmed, though the truck hung there perilously. I spied some natives not far away and ran over to them and they came to our rescue, and with all of us tugging and shoving for something over an hour, we managed to extricate the machine and found the motor and the chassis in good order, and so moved on our way.

The air was deliciously sweet and mellow, and we found a heavenly place to camp beside the tumbling stream. We were too tired to enjoy it awake, however, and were soon fast asleep with the Gura doing its softest lullaby.

At dawn, I awoke and was off to try my luck at fishing. Martin was still asleep when I returned to camp with a two-and-a-half-pound brown trout. I was very proud and excited over the surprise which I would give him for breakfast.

But I was dripping wet, for I had fallen into a pool in trying to jump across, and it was so refreshing and cool that I had just lain there and soaked. I had slid down elephant trails and was covered with mud. My hair was moist and unkempt. My nails were dirty. And my boots were soaked and smeared with goo. I was so wet that I just stood on my head and let the water run out of my boots. The fish was the only clean thing in the picture.

But what a breakfast we had, with the delicious fish, good coffee, sweet butter and baking powder biscuits and jam, to say nothing of our favorite tinned grapefruit.

"Fit for any king," said Martin, rubbing his hands and smacking his lips. And I was pleased as punch.

I went into my tent, and lo and behold! there was an array of presents on my camp cot, and they were too beautiful to believe. Martin had ordered me the most luxurious silk and lace lingerie that I had ever possessed.

"Isn't Mother a dear to send these!" I said, still fishing.

"Mother, my eye!" said he, rising to the bait. "I had them made and sent from Paris."

After breakfast and the gift-giving, Martin was so exuberant that he had to get out his cameras, and he sent off the boys to bring in some natives.

"I feel a picture coming on," he said.

The natives arrived—the warriors well painted and the belles loaded down with their best brass wire trinkets, and for hours Martin posed them, got excellent studies of "types," and then paid them off with three times what they were worth. When I reasoned with him, he swept past me with "Oh, but you forget that it's a holiday and we'll never miss it a hundred years from now."

But soon I found him "paying off" the children with precious bread that I had slaved to bake, and with my jars of almost priceless stuffed dates and figs, and, to top it all, my expensive jams, brought all the way from New York.

But there was a bright rebound to all this, for soon the natives came trooping back from their villages with gifts for us: pineapples, sweet potatoes and luscious papayas. "Just what I want," I shouted, "to make the stuffing for those partridges." And what a stuffing they made!

One old woman brought almost a bushel of dried corn. But it was so hard that it was hopeless to use. However, I thanked her as though it had been a bushel of diamonds and tossed it into the car, for my chickens at Paradise would relish this.

Our villagers pressed in and we soon had a thriving, noisy

campful. I went on preparing dinner, and by the time it was ready to serve the natives were singing and some were dancing.

On our return to Paradise, one distressing incident occurred. It was an accident to Martin, and the greatest shock in the entire four years.

I was returning from the forest one evening when I heard, from the direction of the Lake, a terrific report, like Martin's .470 elephant gun.

"He has been charged by an elephant," I thought, and I jumped off Lazy Bones and ran toward camp for all I was worth.

As I reached the kitchen I met Suku. He could scarcely speak.

"Very bad. The Bwana is dying," he stammered.

"Where is he?" I cried.

"Inside." He pointed to the bedroom.

There was Martin on the bed, moaning terribly. His face was charred, part of his hair burned away, and his eyes swollen shut. His face was covered with a mass of salve.

"My God, what has happened, Martin?" I threw my arms around him.

"I was making a flashlight at the Lake, a big one. One of the boys blundered into the wire and it got me."

I looked at his closed eyes. "Blind!" flashed into my mind. I held up two fingers.

"Martin, what am I doing?"

"Holding up two fingers," he replied weakly. At least he could see! I hurried to the kitchen.

We had plenty of disinfectants, so I ordered M'pishi at once to put on lots of hot water. I ran to the storehouse and took down a large roll of gauze, absorbent cotton and Lysol.

I had had no experience with this kind of injury, but had learned enough about treating minor burns. I quickly dumped our instruments into boiling water and sterilized a Turkish towel. Then I began sponging Martin's face with cotton and disinfectants to remove the burned flesh and powder.

Three times a day I dressed his face with Unguentine and fresh bandages. The skin came off and for ten days he was in terrible pain.

His recuperation was slow. In three days he could see better and the swelling began to go down. I nursed him day and night and read him magazine stories to keep his mind off the pain, until I fell asleep myself.

He talked constantly about the delay and how much work there was to be done. "Those still prints, for instance. I promised Mr. Pomeroy and Mr. Eastman that I would get them right off."

"Never you mind about the prints. I'll do them."

I went on with the laboratory work and the correspondence with home. A great deal of developing and printing had accumulated.

"Be careful with your timing on those prints, Osa, or you'll burn them up. Glossy velox is tough and these have to be good. And don't get them too light and wishy-washy, either."

I burned up plenty of paper and had a stack of wishy-washy ones, but I never told him.

When I finally showed him two hundred and fifty good prints, he was delighted. "Doggone!" he exclaimed. "That's fine. Now you go right ahead and I'll just stay here and have my breakfasts in bed!"

The camp and the boys had to be watched more closely than ever. With the Master out of the field the boys were inclined to oversleep and to let the garden go, to neglect the water and other chores. And they loved to sit around and talk about the accident and all the woes that might befall.

Calves were born. I took one in my arms, a little speckled, gold and white fellow that I promptly named Spotty, and took him in to show to Martin. And I noticed that always thereafter Martin was very fond of that little calf.

Marauding animals gave us trouble, boys became ill, our pump got out of order, mice got into the posho and it seemed to me everything decided to happen at that particular time.

Martin was miserable for three weeks and I made him stay in bed. After his long months of intense work this was just what he needed and the rest did him good. Moreover, he came off without a single scar for the experience, except for one small mark on his neck. For this I was thankful.

We celebrated, the first day he was up again, with a fine dinner of the things he most liked.

"Let's go down to the cliff tonight," he said, his eyes brightening. "You know I haven't seen the Great Parade for a long time and I've missed it."

As we sat there under the moon, watching the animals come and go, he said slowly:

"Osa, do you know what worried me most? I suppose it's crazy, but when I lay there those first few days I couldn't help thinking of our boy who got lockjaw. I think seeing that poor boy die was the most awful experience I've ever had."

25

"Martin, I'm going after him!"

I had just seen an eagle swoop down into a flock of ostrich, seize something in its talons and carry it to a palm tree. The ostrich fled. It was evident what had happened.

Off I drove in my car, as fast as I could go over the bumpy plain, to the palm tree roost. Seeing me, the eagle dropped his prey and flew away. Sure enough, there on the ground lay a baby ostrich, stunned and bleeding, with his side completely ripped open! As I handed it to the boys, I heard some squeaky sounds in the grass. I looked, and there were two more abandoned babies.

We took all three of the scrawny little birds back to camp. Martin helped me give the wounded one first aid and I at once adopted them all. We had the boys build a small corral to hold them.

I thought how careless their parents were, for if they had chosen to they could not only have fought an eagle but almost anything in the jungle, with those ripping two-toed feet of theirs. I had seen ostrich fight desperately for their young. But they are such silly and unpredictable birds that one never knows just what to expect of them.

My ostrich pets were a great novelty. They were different from anything I had ever had. I fed them well on meat and tidbits, and when I released them from the cage, they made no attempt to run away. They hung about my tent, as though always expecting me to give them something to eat.

They ate pebbles galore, and would gobble up anything that shone brightly. I began to miss all kinds of things—buttons, my thimble, spools of thread, anything within their reach that they could swallow.

Back at Paradise, they grew rapidly and Martin began to be alarmed.

"Do you know what you have on your hands, young lady? Those birds will soon weigh two hundred pounds and stand nine feet high. They will be the worst nuisance we have around here."

So I consented to letting him send them to a farmer friend of ours at Nanyuki, the next time we sent to Isiolo for supplies.

Out on the plains we were always encountering ostrich, occasionally stumbling on one of their nests which they build right out in the open. These would contain from twenty to a hundred eggs, and off on those safaris any egg tasted good.

Each ostrich egg weighed about three and a half pounds and they were especially good when scrambled. Once I tried to hard-boil an ostrich egg and after four and a half hours I opened it and it was only soft-boiled. One egg equalled about two dozen chicken eggs. It took a hatchet to open an ostrich egg.

I wondered if an ostrich really did bury his head in the sand. One day I thought I had caught one doing it, but when I was near enough to see him distinctly, I found that he was only feeding. He was taking on his morning roughage and shoveling up sand and pebbles with that low, forward push of the beak which I had seen him use when he drank at the waterholes.

One day we came upon a female ostrich setting on her nest, and moved up to her cautiously to see what would happen. I think she was getting ready to lay or else her chicks were nearly hatched, for she remained much longer than we expected. If an ostrich makes up her mind to defend her nest, she can give you a bad time, so we were on the alert.

When we were fifteen yards away, she rose and started off. She trailed one wing as though it were broken and limped in an exaggerated way from left to right, seeming to support herself with her fluttering wings as though she were terribly wounded or crippled.

"Yes," said Blaney when we later told him of the incident, "that was a trick of hers to decoy you away from her nest or to arouse your sympathy. Ostriches look and act foolish most of the time, but even if they have no brains, they do have their instincts."

Often, while out on the plains, we saw a giraffe mother with twin babies, hobbling along like cute little toys out of a toy shop. They were all neck and feet, and each had a little spit curl where its horns should be. Never was a mother more attentive, but she had to eat occasionally and then, taking a cue from the elephants, she would turn the youngsters over to a nursemaid, a half-grown female who took her duties very seriously.

Following a pair of newly born twins to a waterhole one day, we saw them boldly lead their timid mother and the distracted nurse down to the water. Like all children, they did not know the meaning of danger and were consumed with curiosity. While the elders looked everywhere for lurking lions and other enemies, the youngsters had a great time trying to get a drink. They tried first to reach the water standing straight up, but found that their necks weren't quite long enough. So they spread their feet and made another try, but still couldn't get to the water with their mouths. They spread their feet very wide and with a long sweeping flourish dipped their noses into the water. They seemed more surprised at accomplishing this feat than thirsty, but finally got down to drinking like old professionals. As they sucked in the water, we could see the ripples down their satiny brown throats.

Again, we saw mothers with their own twins or two or three other babies. The latter were no doubt adopted from mothers who had been slain by lions. Watching giraffe on the plains day after day, I began to feel that their gentleness and good manners were true to their character, for the herds always seemed to be thoroughly considerate of each other and the families lived in harmony. I never saw a giraffe harm another animal nor fight with one of its own kind.

We respected the giraffe, too, because they were so hard to photograph. They were easily frightened and very difficult to bring or keep within camera range, and their eyes were extremely sharp. Furthermore, their height enabled them to look right into our blind if we had no roof and also to detect blinds which other animals could not see.

One afternoon at about three, just as the game was coming down to our waterhole in goodly numbers and Martin was limbering up his cameras in anticipation of some fine shooting, we spied fifteen giraffe walking slowly but confidently toward the water. Martin swung his camera to get them. Immediately they started and ran just as though they had seen him. But they couldn't have done so, for we were well concealed. I peeked out the back of the blind to see what might have scared them from that side, and there I saw our three boys, whom we had instructed to lie down and hide and wait for us, climbing a tree. Martin looked at them and was furious. He opened up the blind and climbed out and raced over to them to give them a piece of his mind for playing pranks and scaring away the game. Halfway to them he stopped. A rhino popped out of a bush and looked at him. Martin came back to the blind on the run. He picked up his gun, but the rhino was already running away, leaving a trail of dust.

When we questioned the boys, they told us that the rhino had come down to our blind and had given us a good inspection, but had decided to go off and have a mud bath in a near-by puddle. Then the rhino meandered right past the boys and made for them. They had saved their necks, but the game would not come back after all that commotion, and our afternoon was ruined.

Frequently we photographed herds of a hundred and more giraffe and followed them for days, as they browsed and meandered from one waterhole to another. Their color and their patterns gave them an eye appeal that many of the animals lacked. Here on the Northern Frontier all the giraffe had the reticulated or fishnet pattern, distinguishing them from their cousins farther south which were marked with an "autumn leaf" design. The cows and babies were a light orange, with ivory-white lines between the patches of color, their manes, tails and "horns" being jet black. The old bulls were so dark a brown that they looked black at a distance.

In spite of their disjointed gait, they walked and loped with a rhythm that was truly beautiful. Of course, Martin's artist-eye caught it at once and he not only squandered film on them, but finally succeeded in getting at close distance some beautiful slow-motion film which he regarded as representative of his very best work. One day he caught a lively stampede in slow motion and was almost hilarious when it came out of the developer perfect in every detail. These little successes were worth a world of pain and discomfort and made up for months of irritations and disappointments.

Whenever we came upon bush-pig we had a good dinner, for they were just like our razor-backs at home and were even more delicious. I would never eat a wart-hog—they were too ugly and disgusting—but a little red bush-pig seemed to have been put there for our very use and they were mighty welcome on a long safari when we were reduced to a lot of uninviting bully beef.

The hippopotamus is not far removed from plain pig, though he is so huge that most of us miss the resemblance. A grown hippo weighs from six to eight thousand pounds. Boers and natives eat them, and I am told that the lard makes excellent pastry.

Blaney told me that he had once been given a hippo tongue to eat and found it delicious, but that it lasted him and a companion for an entire week. The hippo always seemed so comically helpless and harmless that I never shot one, although a female hippo did once charge me.

Natives are often killed by hippo, and our boys were always very frightened of them. For no reason at all, a hippo may make for a canoe, come up under it unexpectedly and capsize it and kill the occupants. We pitched camp at one spot where we learned a native had been killed by a hippo only a few nights before.

I never worried much about the hippo, but always gave a mother with a baby a wide berth. Being in a canoe with hippo and crocodiles around always frightened me, for one can never tell what those excitable submarines may do.

Hippo mothers have a bad time keeping their babies out of the jaws of the crocodiles, and guard them jealously. At the Eauso Nyiro River one day, I was walking down the bank when a cute baby hippo popped right out of the water in front of me, eyed me and blew a few frightened bubbles. He was so ludicrous I howled. Then his mother's head appeared; he was clinging to her back. At once they both ducked, but since hippo can remain under water only about two minutes, she soon came up for air and both of them blew more bubbles at me and ducked again. I saw their wake as she bore her precious little pop-eye away under the surface.

In the jungle the hippo is pink in color. When he is excited, he perspires a red oil that looks like blood and he then looks even pinker. He is very shy, and is particularly jittery out of water. All day long he wallows in the river, preferably a backwater or a quiet pool, except when he comes out at noontime to find a nice mud puddle and take a mud bath, wrapped in which he promptly falls asleep.

He is one of the cleanest animals in the jungle. His food is grass and water vines, and he lives an altogether exemplary life.

Martin and I were walking down the Eauso Nyiro on a fishing jaunt one pleasant afternoon, and as we came to a reed bed, Martin started to step across it on some rocks. He exclaimed and tried to step back but was off balance and I just managed to catch him as he fell. The stone was a hippo's back!

Wherever we were during the rains or immediately thereafter we had insects to contend with, for the moisture hatched them in billions. They became so annoying that ultimately we had to have a tent made of mosquito netting in which to have our meals, and sometimes we went into it at other hours just for comfort and protection. At night we had to have lanterns, which attracted the flying ants, moths, mosquitos and beetles and, even if we were not dead-tired, as we usually were, we would climb into bed early in the evening and tuck in our mosquito nets—the only escape we knew. We used gallons of Flit and citronella and ammonia, but there are limits to these protections when one is as busy as we were.

Fortunately, we were spared the tsetse fly at Lake Paradise. They did not trouble us much on this expedition, for the Northern Frontier District seems to be free from them, except for isolated belts, but we lost enough mules and domestic animals in certain areas to know that we had them to fear. Tens of thousands of them must have bitten me in Africa, and every one raised a hard, white welt on my flesh like a small bird's egg, but I have always been fortunate enough to avoid the dreaded sleeping sickness which they carry. Only about one in ten thousand of the insects is said to be infected with the disease, and the government clinics have done a great deal in recent years to check the malady, but the natives are very subject to it and entire areas have had to be closed and all human population moved away, in order to bring matters under control. With all that the government has now done, the tsetse fly danger is minimized.

On one occasion we were at Issedan waterhole, on one of our plains safaris after elephants during the rainy season. It is a desolate spot in the midst of nowhere—a small sand river with rocky banks and scattered boulders with a fringe of dom-palms, and semi-desert for miles in every direction. The waterhole was full of rainwater and the place was covered with elephant spoor, so we decided to camp.

During dinner the insects began to descend upon us in swarms, got into our food and littered the ground. The flying ants would drop their wings upon touching anything, and I didn't share our porters' idea that these insects were a table delicacy. Suku took our table lantern away, hoping to relieve matters, and we tried to eat in the dark.

M'pishi was distracted, and when Martin grumbled that we were eating cooked insects and that the dishes probably contained more ants' wings than food, he burst into tears, thinking that we were blaming him. So we gave up dinner as a bad job and crawled into bed. I was not sleepy, so I had Suku hang an extra mosquito net over each end of the tent and began to read.

I heard a buzzing, like a bumblebee, at the Coleman lantern and looked up to see two large rhinoceros beetles flying around the light. They were big black things, and their hard shells could easily put one's eye out if one were not careful. Before long, others came, and soon they were burning themselves on top of the lantern and falling dead to the ground sheet. Flying ants had now also found their way in and were joining the heap on the floor.

While I watched this in drowsy disgust, a toad crawled in and began devouring the dead insects, and then came two more. I don't mind toads so much, but when a scorpion sidled in to the feast, I screamed. Martin woke with a start and I yelled to him to stay in bed. There we lay and watched the picture of our Africa in action, with everything seeming to eat everything else.

Suddenly I saw what looked like a stream of black oil slowly entering the tent under the front flap. I knew it could not be oil, but safari ants. We didn't dare now to get out of bed, for I had been bitten enough by safari ants not to want even one of them on me. I hoped they wouldn't get into our beds. The advance guard was already working at the dead insects and soon the whole column loaded itself down with wings and carcasses and marched away with the booty.

Meanwhile more scorpions had moved in, some gold and others black, with red nippers like a lobster's, and the toads and other pests kept out of the way of their sharp and deadly tails. Sausage flies, dragon flies, hunting spiders, tiger beetles, crickets, praying mantis, spiders and ground-beetles of many colors were arriving; centipedes and six-inch worms, with as many legs as a centipede, one variety a light sand color and the other variety black; tarantulas, and finally a night adder about a foot long. The adder swallowed one of the toads, and I shut my eyes as I felt my stomach turn over.

I called Suku and Bukhari, and several boys came running. They killed the adder and I had them get brooms and sweep the whole place out. Martin got up and went out in the air, but I didn't want to step on that floor sheet, for it seemed to me still to be crawling; so I had the boys get the Flit guns and give the whole tent a good dousing.

When I finally fell asleep, I had one long, continuous nightmare. I felt like Alice in Wonderland, with scorpions the size of elephants and toads with rhino bodies and safari ants as big as aeroplanes pushing me around. I shot them with my .470, but more came on for every one I dropped, and I woke up before dawn, wet as a rag and utterly exhausted.

When morning broke, we found the ground littered with dead

CAMERAS SET FOR A NIGHT'S FLASHLIGHT PICTURES

Under a tree in which the Johnsons have built a blind, cameras are set for close-ups. The zebra has been dragged for miles across the plain to attract the cats to this spot.

LEAVING LAKE PARADISE FOR THE PLAINS

Osa organizes the camera boys and special porters for a three-months' safari for rhino and other game. Lake Paradise in the background.

insects, for what we had seen inside the tent was apparently only a small and concentrated part of the plague.

"Thank God, that doesn't happen every night, or I wouldn't stay in Africa even for you," I said to my husband.

"That's the worst we've ever had, isn't it, honey? And I'll bet you dollars to doughnuts you never see that again."

And although we saw plenty of insects, we never did have to repeat that experience.

During one of our rainy safaris from Lake Paradise to the plains, we arrived at the beautiful Kampiatoonia waterhole in the N'groon Mountains, a favorite of ours. Here there was enough grassy plain to vary the monotony of the desert, although there was still sand enough. The dry river bed had ample waterholes and was surrounded with a fine growth of palm and umbrella-like acacia trees. Even beyond the line of the river bed was a great area of thornbush and scrub growth that gave the place something of the air of a vast park, and the game liked especially to come here.

Now we found herds of elephant and many rhino, buffalo, lions, leopards, giraffe, and all the plains game, with even some of the shy lesser kudu putting in an occasional appearance. We promptly set up camp and prepared to stay several days at least. Martin was more excited than I had seen him in a long time.

While the boys were setting up the tents, I strolled off under the trees and spied several in bloom. They were gorgeous, but I said to myself, "That's odd. They look like thorn trees," and took out my glasses for a closer view. The blossoms suddenly flew up and off to another tree—a great flock of parakeets. Half again as large as those we see at home, they were a mixture of vivid greens, with blue down beneath their wings. Against all the drab color of the thorn, they were as striking as flowers on cactus.

The trip had been very dusty and Martin and Ouranga began at once to clean and oil the cameras. But no sooner had they fin-

ished than the breeze blew up a fine alkali dust that got into everything, including our eyes and teeth and bedding and clothes boxes.
The cameras had to be cleaned all over again.

Late that afternoon the wind died down. As we sat waiting for
dinner, Martin pointed to the ground a few feet away. I looked
and saw what seemed to be a miniature volcano. Fine dust came
flying out of a small hole and piled up around the aperture in a
little mound which grew and grew as the invisible something
spewed it forth. Then we noticed that there were many of these
mounds near by, some as high as ten inches and growing higher.
Fascinated, we called Boculy who told us that a little beetle had
dug these holes, probably for ants.

After dinner we saw wind clouds coming over the mountains.
Martin warned the boys to peg everything down well and to get to
bed early. The clouds swept down at us and in what seemed to be
no time at all, sand was flying and leaves and twigs were blowing,
and we knew we were in for a good storm. Lightning began to flash
over the mountains, and the thunder rolled and echoed. Lightning
always terrifies me; I would almost rather deal with snakes.

For a long time it did not rain, but the sand whipped at our
tents and whistled through the trees and I could hear the boys yelling and things falling. I looked out and saw our kitchen go over
and pots and pans roll away. The boys' tents were blowing away
and Bukhari came running to us with a group of boys.

"We must hold down the tents, Missus," he shouted. "Today is
very big storm. Pretty soon, plenty rain!"

And he was right. They had no sooner driven fresh stakes for
our tent stays than the water came in a torrent. For three hours
it rained without stopping, while the lightning continued. Water
ran in rivers through our tent, and although we had the cameras
on logs, we had to pile everything else of value on our beds. When
we finally tried to sleep, we had to curl ourselves around this array
of boxes, and I marveled that the beds held the weight.

In the morning the dry river bed was a wide stream in full flood, at least ten feet deep, with huge logs and dom-palms fifty feet long floating on its surface. It seemed incredible that so much water could have fallen, and equally incredible that in twelve hours the river would be almost dry again. Several little gazelle, caught in the torrent, were drowned, and we found their bodies when the water receded.

The rains were extending beyond their usual season, which often happens, and since the sky threatened another downpour, we decided to go back to Lake Paradise and wait a few weeks for the rains to end.

We came out of the mountains at about one o'clock in the afternoon, and determined to pitch camp there on the plains and rest until the following day. Just as the boys were unloading the camels, up came a Turkana runner with a note from the officer in charge of the post at Barsaloi. He had been four days out with this message and had covered at least two hundred miles. But most amazing of all, he was traveling blind and had no idea where he would find us. He had happened on our trail and had followed it for a day, hoping it might lead to us. A miracle of desert communication.

The note warned us that Abyssinian poachers were raiding the area, and to be ready for any emergency. The officer in charge was going after them with askari. The note also stated that Samburu natives we had met two weeks before had reported that we were on safari outside Lake Paradise, and that he had other reports from Wanderobos who had seen us, although we had seen no Wanderobos.

The poor runner seemed nearly done in. His food and water were gone. So, while Martin wrote a reply to the officer in charge's note, I had Bukhari and M'pishi prepare dinner for him, as well as give him water and posho for the return trip.

A few minutes later, M'pishi came over and asked me where

the runner was. The boy had eaten his food but had not taken a single thing we had got ready for him. We looked throughout the camp but could find him nowhere. He had gone! I have never seen a better show of endurance.

Back at Paradise, Martin plunged into developing the film taken on the trip, and I to tidying up the household. We were very short of meat, for we had seen little game on the way back, and I decided to make a short safari back to the plains to take some antelope or a buffalo. Martin was very reluctant to let me go, but finally consented and gave the boys a good lecture about taking care of me and repeated his threat that if anything ever happened to me, he would "skin them alive!"

"Nonsense. I can take care of myself," I assured him as I kissed him goodbye.

The rains had made the going very slow and had so scattered the game that we saw very little. On our second day out, we were scouting along the edge of the forest when in the distance we saw a camel safari coming in our direction. Could we be having visitors, I wondered? Would it be the officer in charge from Barsaloi? We turned toward them and as we approached each other, I looked through my binoculars and saw that the caravan was very pretentious and that ahead of the camels there were blacks riding horses. Abyssinians!

"Hmm. M'baya sana" (very bad), Bukhari mumbled.

"Give me my gun," I said to him. "We will go and talk to them."

"What will the master say?" he said, acting as though he was sure I had gone out of my mind.

When we came up to the column, it had stopped; the camels were being unloaded, and tents were going up. Abyssinians they surely were. A young man was walking toward us, a gun over his shoulder. His hair was heavy and bushy. He wore a khaki uniform, woolen puttees and leather sandals.

"How do you do, madam." He addressed me in perfect English. "What on earth are you doing out here?"

"I am looking for meat," I replied. "My husband and I have a large camp just back there and our boys need meat. May I ask who you are?"

Six khaki-clad, fuzzy-headed natives, with guns over their shoulders, had now moved up behind him. They were a tough-looking lot.

"This is the safari of the Habash of Abyssinia," he replied noncommittally. "Are you American?"

Assured that I was not British, he ushered me to a man, dressed in a heavy, white silk robe, seated in a camp chair. He was hatless and his hair was also heavy, black, and very bushy, and he wore a full beard. Beneath his chair was a large Persian rug. He likewise wore woolen puttees and hide sandals. His face was strong and heavily furrowed, and he rose to a full six feet as he first saluted and then held out his hand. He smiled broadly and turned to speak to his interpreter.

"The Habash gives you his greeting and apologizes for not having tea; we have just arrived. But he begs you to stay and tea will soon be made."

A servant brought a small but beautiful Persian rug, which he spread for me, and another brought a small leather hassock on which I sat as I lay my gun carefully at my feet. Still another servant removed the Habash's sandals and placed on his feet a pair of beautiful soft leather slippers, blood-red in color and turned up at the points.

Martin had always kidded me about wanting to see a "Sheik," and here he was. He was nothing like the movie version, of course, and was about as dirty and greasy as his natives. But I could see that he was no mean personage, and in his present mood he was quite a nice old fellow.

"Aren't you afraid to be out here alone, like this?" he asked through his interpreter. "It is not usual to find a woman on safari by herself."

When I assured him that I had no fears, he plied me with questions about who we were, and what we were doing, and whether we had seen any elephants recently, and whether they were good tuskers, and whether I had ever shot an elephant.

"No, we do not shoot for ivory; we are making pictures and we never shoot at all if we can help it."

He smiled as though he only half believed me, and asked about our pictures.

"May I take your picture?" I asked him, as I rose and called the camera boys and confidently took out a Graflex.

The Habash not only posed for me, but posed his interpreter and bodyguard as well.

"Where shall I send you these pictures?" I asked.

The Habash laughed. "I am afraid that will be a little difficult. We are moving around a great deal. But perhaps we shall meet again out here and I shall be happy to have the pictures."

As we drank tea and nibbled at hard biscuits out of a tin labelled "Carr's Tea Biscuits," I admired the beautiful Arabian horse tethered near and which I knew to be the Habash's.

"I would gladly give him to you," said the Habash gallantly, "but we are traveling hard just now and I shall probably need him. We must be in Abyssinia tomorrow."

He admired my white fly swatter of colobus monkey fur with braided leather handle, and when I told him it had come from a Somali chief, he wanted to know his name. He asked all about the cameras and looked over all my guns and was extremely inquisitive, asking a thousand questions, even to my age.

I rose to go, and he rose politely, shook hands, saluted, and said, "Good luck, young lady. I hope you get your buffalo," and waved me off.

I returned to Lake Paradise two days later with a load of buffalo meat for the boys and fowl for our table. I beamed as I told Martin I had got a picture of an Abyssinian poacher.

"Stop kidding me!" said Martin, as he took my plates into the laboratory.

When he saw the developed negative, he sat down and scratched his head. "Well, now you won't *ever* go out alone again! Thank God, you're back here safe."

We reported the matter to the officials; and when we later made a trip to Nairobi, I told the story to Archie Richie, the Game Warden, and gave him the pictures of the Habash and his interpreter.

"Why, Osa," he said on examining the photos, "that is one of the worst old Habashes in Abyssinia. We have been trailing him for years."

"I thought he was very nice and polite. He didn't look to me like such a bad man."

"No? Well, just for your information, young lady, he raided a native village last year. He killed off all the men, seized all the cattle, and took the women and children over the border as slaves. He keeps us busier on the Northern Frontier than all the other poachers put together."

Archie shook his head and added, "You American women!" Then he looked at me as though trying to think up some appropriate reprimand, but all he said was:

"You're a pretty lucky girl, Osa!"

26

*". . . Osa said the lions were like
human beings . . . when they were
young they wanted to roam and see
the world, but when they got old they
wanted a nice quiet 'donga' or ravine, in which to settle down . . ."*
—MARTIN JOHNSON

ONE NIGHT, MARTIN having decided to stay in camp and rest
to get some early morning movies of the game, I determined to
go after lion flashlight pictures alone. There were enough lions
about and I was sure of success. Martin protested, but finally gave
in to me. So I had the boys build me a blind of thorn trees and
leaves and grass, and set up a camp cot in it, with a zebra kill
and flashlight apparatus in position. Martin kissed me goodbye
and gave me a great many parting instructions, especially to be
sure to whistle just as I set off the flash so that the lion would lift
his head and make a good picture.

Along about ten o'clock, I began to hear the various night sounds
of Africa—hornbills sounding like anvils, crickets and tree frogs
making a wild din, hyrax screeching and sending shivers down my
spine. Zebra, barking, stampeded by. A herd of wildebeest galloped past, probably startled by prowlers, for they were honking
noisily. Then a dozen giraffe came near, caught my scent, stood
frozen in the moonlight for a time, and moved on with their familiar leisure and dignity. They seemed to grow taller as they moved
away, and their shadows lengthened, magnifying their ungainliness
into grotesque shapes.

326

I could hear hyenas laughing in the distance, and then nearer and nearer as they obviously began to sniff the kill. A jackal called not far off and that, I knew, meant lion, for the jackal is the lion's scout and pilot, and it is usually he who finds the kill, warns the lion, and is then rewarded by being permitted to share the feast.

So I bestirred myself and drew my rifle and sawed-off shotgun beside me and waited. Not far off I heard a succession of growls. Then a hyena moaning, and I knew that a lion was near and had hurt the hyena, for the lion has very little use for this scavenger. I waited, hardly daring to breathe, for a very long time, but nothing happened and I finally grew cramped and weary and decided to crawl into the blankets for a rest. Soon I was fast asleep.

I was awakened by a terrific growl. I looked up at the moon and stars and hardly stirred. I had been dreaming of Kansas and slowly realized where I was. Something seemed to have my big toe in a grip. This seemed curious and I tried to make out what was happening, without moving, and with my heart beating like a sledgehammer. I recognized my blind, peered at my feet and saw nothing there, and gathered that my foot was twisted in the blanket. Then I detected the unmistakable scent of cat, and knew that my lion was outside. I froze with the thought. I reached for my gun, very cautiously.

Then I heard the big cat sniffing. He came right up to the outside of the blind and was not more than a matter of inches away from me. I suddenly remembered how flimsy the blind was, and thought like a flash how easy it would be for him to push it down and leap in on top of me. He sniffed all about the shelter, uttering low throaty sounds that brought out goose bumps all over me. The roots of my hair felt like needles of ice!

Do you remember when you were a child, how you always felt like doing what you shouldn't do, and would surely cough in a prayer-meeting when your mother had told you to be very quiet?

Now I wanted to cough, probably to lighten the tension. I struggled to control it. My mouth filled with saliva. I went rigid with the effort to control myself, but the cough would out, so I buried my face in the blankets and muffled it. I felt better right away. I inched the blankets up to my hand and freed my foot. The cot squeaked. I froze again for the cat was sniffing back to where I lay. I managed to sit up and grasp my gun, but I was trembling like an amateur. I was thoroughly off-guard and very scared.

It seemed to me like hours that he prowled back and forth around the blind. Swallowing had never before seemed to me to be so important nor difficult. I was sure that he could hear me and was sure that my heartbeats must be audible as they swelled through me and struck against my temples. Why wouldn't he go to that kill? Was he afraid or did he regard me as a choicer morsel? But then he did go to the kill. He growled and tore at its hide and smacked his chops.

I felt easier, but began to wish for Martin. No wonder he was so concerned in letting me go on this venture—it was an idiotic thing to do. A lion in broad daylight is one thing, but out here in the night, cramped into a tiny blind, and with this cat in such a rowdy mood . . . I felt almost helpless.

The minutes dragged. My feet and hands were now really cold, and altogether I have never felt more miserable. I peeped out of the blind and in the moonlight could see the huge fellow gorging himself. He crunched into a bone, and I thought: "If he can crush a zebra bone like that, what would he do if he got hold of me?"

Then shame rushed over me. I said to myself, "You little fool! You asked for this. You are here to make pictures, and pictures you are going to make, even if they are your last!"

I found my flashlight and tested it on the ground. Then I remembered that Martin had told me to be sure to get a good pic-ture and not to forget to whistle as I touched off the flashes. I took the light in one hand and the flash-buzzer in the other. (The buzzer was connected by a wire to the cameras and flash synchronizer.)

I screwed up my courage and threw the flashlight beam on the lion. He was such a beauty that I almost exclaimed aloud. He looked up at the light, his eyes like green headlamps. The lion must have thought my flashlight the moon, for he turned back to his food with a grunt. I held the light on him and tried to pucker my lips for that whistle. I simply couldn't manage them, and when I did get my lips set, couldn't get out a single sound. So I just pressed the buzzer and the flash went off like a cannon. The poor lion must have thought himself shot. I heard him growling about the place, and then he came over near me, growling and sniffing all over again. This time I was sure he would make for me, so I drew up my sawed-off shotgun and made up my mind that if he came in, I was going to give it to him in the face.

He finally went back to his kill. I began to feel more like myself now, and wished I could set another flash. I believed that I could whistle the Star-Spangled Banner for him, if need be.

Then I sneezed, one of those loud kerchoo sneezes, and could have kicked myself. The lion ran away, but, still hungry, he soon came back to the kill. He gorged and gorged, stopping occasionally to growl at what was probably a slinking hyena, and finally became quiet. But he wasn't going to leave that kill for anyone—man or beast—and there he lay. The hours dragged on, and I became very restless. I was too cold to sleep and too excited to doze.

For some unaccountable reason, or lack of reason, I decided to bolt the blind. I could stand my cramped quarters no longer. Had I thought twice, I should have known better, but I acted on impulse.

I took my rifle, left everything else, and slipped out the back of the blind. At the sound, the lion let out a growl and I began to run. I heard him growling behind me, and I ran as I have never run before—or since.

I felt him bounding behind me. I was chilled by the thought that at any moment he would pounce upon me and bear me down. I could almost feel his breath. I stopped and whirled, ready to shoot. There was no lion in sight!

I began to run again and every step took on an exaggerated sound. Ahead of me was a large heap of rocks and bush. The moon threw long shadows toward me. Something seemed to be moving there. The something jumped and stood on a rock against the sky, so near that I could almost see its whiskers. I froze and held my gun ready for another lion. Perhaps the big male's mate, I thought. Then something started to laugh. How thankful I was to hear that sound! The hyena was probably laughing at me for doing the crazy thing I was doing or for standing there in such a silly posture. Off he went into the shadows.

It suddenly came over me that I had no bearings. The horizon in every direction looked the same. Where was camp and where was I going? I was hopelessly lost. A little reed-buck leaped up from some rocks and ran off. I reflected that the same rock kopje was probably full of puff adders and cobras and that they are always active at night. I stumbled along, stopping every few feet to strain my eyes for a sign that would guide me.

I crossed a little swamp to reach a small rise of ground. A cat jumped up and crashed off, scattering small stones, probably a leopard that had been lying there watching for game. I could discern nothing familiar and went on over the rise to level ground. Panic overtook me again and I began to run. I wished I were back in the blind, but perhaps I was as well off out here as in that flimsy shelter, and if I could last until dawn, Martin or the boys would scour the place and surely find me.

I detoured around some bush and right there in front of me, gleaming white in the moonlight, were our tents. I was never so happy in all my life. I wanted to yell and rush in and tell Martin that I was back. But I remembered that he didn't know I had been lost and it would be a shame to disturb him. So I crept up quietly and heard a peculiar animal sound. I listened. It was Martin snoring!

As I crept into our tent, he started up and cried, "Thank good-ness you're back. I haven't been able to sleep a wink, worrying about you!"

I told him what had occurred, and he was at first very con-cerned. Then he laughed and laughed. That made me furious.

"You make me feel like a fool," I complained. "Here I almost lose my life and all, just to get a few of your old pictures, and you make fun of me as though it were a big joke. I think you're perfectly terrible!" And I began to sob, more from nervous ex-haustion than from anything else.

"No, no!" he soothed. "Don't get confused about this, honey. I think you're a wonder! This thing is more concern and worry to me than it will ever be to you, for you don't seem to feel fear the way most women do, or else you don't show it. I'm proud of you. I let you go and do these fool things only because I want you to be more and more able to take care of yourself whatever hap-pens. We're going to spend a lot of our lives out here, you know. That is, if you can stand it."

Martin was putting on his clothes over his pajamas.

"Come along, darling," he said. "I'll bet you've made the best lion pictures to date. We'll go right out there and get them before something happens to them. Boculy! Bukhari!"

And we were off to the blind. The lion was still there, snoozing over his dinner, but too stubborn and greedy to leave it. We crept to a good position and I fired my rifle over the animal's head, and off he went in a hurry. The cameras were untouched and we gathered them up and carried them back to camp where Martin, with his usual elation and curiosity, insisted on developing my negatives at once. I watched eagerly while the negatives came out of the bath. There was a beautiful shot of a lion, and Martin was happy.

"But, darling," he said sorrowfully, "his head is down. You forgot what I told you. You must *whistle*, just as the flash goes off!"

27

". . . Only Osa and I and the ele-
phants will know where Paradise is
and Osa and I won't tell."

—MARTIN JOHNSON

"OSA, DO YOU know we have been here almost four years?"

I knew what was coming. I had thought of it too, but I hadn't said anything.

"We will have to be leaving soon." Martin put the thought into words. "I hate to think of the money this trip has cost, but if the Museum and the public appreciate the pictures, that's all I ask."

"Well," I reminded him, "we've had good reports from the laboratory, and Eastman Kodak ought to know what they're talking about."

"Isn't it funny," Martin continued, "we've been here for four years and our work has hardly begun. I guess we could spend our lives out here and still not finish the job."

It would take weeks to close Lake Paradise, not only because of the household details but because there were so many unfinished odds and ends of picture-taking that must be completed to round out the record.

"Osa, let's do the rounds of all the waterholes here at the Lake just once more."

I was hoping Martin would say that. For I loved each and every spot as much as he did, and although each one would be fixed forever in my mind for its beauty and the adventures it had given us, nevertheless I wanted to have just one more glimpse.

One by one we tramped off to the Lily Pool, Margi M'kubwa, Sunga, the Martin Johnson, the Old Lady, Wistonia and the others. Never had there seemed more butterflies, never had the birds sung so melodiously, never had the moss and the rocks and the tumbling streams seemed more beautiful.

"Anyway, the elephants will have plenty of salad," I remarked, eyeing my watercress that had grown a foot high in nearly every pool.

At the Old Lady waterhole, where we went to see our old grandmother elephant for the last time, we found only baboons, hundreds of them, more impudent than ever. They were screeching and rowing and fighting, pushing each other out of branches, snatching each other's food; babies were being mauled and cuffed by their elders. A big grandfather spied me and came running at me as if to tear me to bits. He stopped and stood there, barking and calling me names and showing his ugly fangs.

"Martin, I even like the baboons today," I said with a funny feeling in my throat.

"And I bet you'll tell me you like rhinos by the time we get back to New York."

While Martin was packing his laboratory supplies, I decided to go off and see if the heather was still blooming, if the tiger lilies were still there, for this might be my last chance to see them. On the more practical side, I hoped also to get some guinea fowl and partridge for dinner. But I would have to make a long trip for them, so I took Lazy Bones and started off with Boculy and Bukhari.

Though the lilies were gone, the heather was still there, covering the familiar slopes at the entrance to Paradise and beyond. I turned Lazy Bones loose to graze and climbed a high cliff to have a good look at the Kaisoot. The day was clear and I could see every ridge and valley, and even the N'Groon Mountains, beyond which we had had so many pleasant and successful safaris.

It would be hard to leave this beautiful wilderness, and I said a little prayer that this spot might be kept as it was, to remain a sanctuary for the animals who loved it.

With our dinner bagged and tied to Lazy Bones' saddle, we started back to camp. On the way I saw cannas that I had planted there, but baboons had broken most of the stalks. I passed great banks of white and pink everlasting flowers in the forest.

Suddenly, right through a cluster of flowers, came trotting a rhino and her baby. I leaped off Lazy Bones and made ready with my gun. They stopped and snorted and made a false charge, but with our screams and yells the ugly lady lost her nerve and crashed off into the brush with her youngster.

About two miles farther on, Boculy held up his hand and we halted. Right ahead of us and across the trail came ten elephants, slowly feeding. The wind was right and they had not yet seen us, so we slipped into the woods on a detour. On such occasions Lazy Bones was extremely intelligent and well-behaved. I took his halter and he picked his way along behind me as silently as an elephant.

We arrived safely at camp and found Martin still packing and very provoked with the boys because he couldn't make them understand how carefully his delicate lenses and precious equipment had to be put away for the long journey. But when he saw the fowl his eyes lighted up.

"By George! I can eat six of those myself, Osa. And please make pan muffins. I'm starved!"

As we were having dinner, our Boran herder burst into the room, stark naked and very scared. He was scratched from head to foot; he was bleeding, and mumbling and crying.

"What in heaven's name has happened to him?" Martin asked Suku. "I can't understand a word he says."

"He says elephants chased him," explained Suku. "He ran through the brush and climbed a thorn tree and lost his blanket."

"Take him to Bukhari," Martin ordered, "and after dinner

M'sahib will give him a new blanket." Then he turned to me:
"Those must have been the nice elephants you saw. That will be
one advantage in going home: I won't have to worry about you
roaming around out there among elephants and rhino."

We spent many of these last days at the Lake, lying on a
rock to watch the animals and birds, or walking around its rim
as a relief from the work of packing and writing letters and
reports.

There in the water one afternoon, we saw a great elephant
giving himself a bath. He was having a wonderful time all by
himself, throwing great streams of water over his body and into
the air. As the spray fell it caught the sun and draped a broad
rainbow over his bronze back.

I began to cry; it was too beautiful to leave.

"Never mind, dear," Martin said soothingly. "We're going to
come back here. If everything goes well, we'll be back in a year.
These houses are good and strong; they'll wait for us. Why, our
work at Lake Paradise will never be finished. We could spend
twenty years here and every day we would have something new."

"I wonder if my nasturtiums will live by themselves," I mur-
mured. "I suppose the birds will carry seeds from the garden
and there will be cucumbers and watermelons all over the place."

"Life is just too short," Martin went on. "It's a pity we can't
live five hundred years with so much beauty to enjoy and so much
work to accomplish."

As we climbed back up toward camp, his voice trailed on:

"The baboons will live in our houses. They will stuff themselves
with tomatoes and the elephants will have a good time in the sweet
potatoes. The birds will feast on your flower seeds and on the
melons. But only you and I and the animals, Osa, will know
where Lake Paradise is. And you and I won't tell."

Early the next morning, with every porter loaded to capacity
and the motor cars piled high, we started away.

Driving over the rim of the crater, we stopped for a final look. "It's a Garden of Eden, Martin. I hope it never changes."

"I hope it never will," he said. "I hope that Lake Paradise will always remain just as God created it."

*   *   *   *

Lt. L. C. Sleigh, No. 125013
No. 2 Mobile General Workshop
c/o Army Post Office
Durban, South Africa
January 16, 1941

Mrs. Martin Johnson
New York City, U. S. A.

Dear Mrs. Johnson:

I hope you will forgive me, writing to you, but thought that the enclosed might interest you, knowing this part of the world so well.

Our last Camp was right next to your old house, by the Lake; what a Paradise of a place! Did you ever lose a water pump, down a deep hole? We rescued it, and after a clean-up, it's doing good work for the troops, drawing water.

The famous butterflies are still in the district by the million, not to mention, of course, the rhino, hyena, elephants, leopards, baboons, and the rest.

We are now on the move again, right out in the desert. The Arabs are still herding their goats and the camel girls still smell. It's 116 degrees in the shade this morning, the trouble is to find the shade; what I wouldn't give for a real iced beer.

Do drop me a line, if you feel that way inclined.

All the very best for 1941,

Yours sincerely,
L. C. Sleigh

GLOSSARY

ABERDARE MOUNTAINS . . . . a wooded range in Kenya
ASKARI . . . . native black soldier

BAKSHISHI . . . . gift or "tip"
BILTONG . . . . strips of dried meat which porters carry on safari
BOCULY . . . . the Johnsons' elephant guide at Lake Paradise
BOMA . . . . a stockade surrounding a camp or village
BORAN . . . . a tribe of nomadic herdsmen on the Northern Frontier
BUKHARI . . . . Osa Johnson's headman on Lake Paradise expedition
BUSTARD . . . . African wild turkey
BWANA . . . . Swahili for "master" or "mister"

CHAI . . . . Swahili for "tea"
CHANIA FALLS . . . . a beautiful waterfall discovered by the Johnsons on
   the Northern Frontier
COLOBUS . . . . a monkey with long lustrous black and white fur inhabit-
   ing Mount Kenya and other forests at high altitudes in East Africa

DHOW . . . . an Arab boat with triangular sail
DIK-DIK . . . . the smallest antelope in East Africa
DONGA . . . . ravine
DUKA . . . . a Hindu or native tradesman; the "duka" shop is equivalent
   to the old American country store

EAUSO NYIRO . . . . river of the Northern Frontier
ELAND . . . . the largest antelope of East Africa

FARU . . . . contraction of "Kifaru," the Swahili word for "rhino"

GENET . . . . a small African wildcat
GERENUK . . . . a nimble East African antelope which makes jumps of
   from 20 to 30 feet

339

GHEE . . . . a rancid butter made by the African herdsmen from the milk of camels, goats, sheep and cows

GURA . . . . a river of the Northern Frontier

HABASH . . . . Abyssinian chief

HALLALLA . . . . a Mohammedan practice of cutting the throat of an animal so that the flesh will be "purified" for eating

HAPANA . . . . Swahili word meaning "no"

HYRAX . . . . the small brown "rock rabbit" of East Africa

ISIOLO . . . . a government station on the Northern Frontier

KAISOOT . . . . a famous desert of East Africa which the Johnsons crossed in their trip to Lake Paradise

KAMPIA TEMBO . . . . a small government station on the Northern Frontier

KANZA . . . . a white cotton robe worn by native houseboys and personal servants

KAPANDI . . . . a license issued by the government to native servants in East Africa. Also applied to other licenses

KARO . . . . a waterhole enroute to Lake Paradise

KIBOKO . . . . Swahili for hippopotamus. Also a whip or stick made of hippo or rhino hide

KIDOGO . . . . Swahili word for "small"

KIKUYU . . . . an East African tribe of farmers and gardeners

KILINDINI . . . . the port of Mombasa

KISSIMINI . . . . a waterhole enroute to Lake Paradise

KOPJE . . . . an outcropping of boulders or rocks

LASAMIS . . . . a waterhole enroute to Lake Paradise

LONGAIA . . . . a waterhole enroute to Lake Paradise

LONGANIA . . . . a waterhole enroute to Lake Paradise

LORIAN SWAMP . . . . a large swamp on the Northern Frontier into which the Eauso Nyiro River flows and disappears

LUGGAR . . . . a dry sand wash or river

MAJI . . . . Swahili word for "water"

MAKELELE . . . . Swahili word for "noise"

MANYETTA . . . . this Swahili word means "home" to the natives but may represent a hut, or several huts surrounded by a stockade

MARDUFF . . . . cheap muslin

MARSABIT . . . . a government station on the Northern Frontier

MASAI . . . . a tribe of nomadic East African natives

M'BOGO . . . . Swahili word for "buffalo"

MEMSAHIB . . . . Swahili word for "mistress" or "missus"

MERILLE . . . . a waterhole enroute to Lake Paradise

MERU . . . . a trading center and government post on the Northern Frontier

M'KUBWA . . . . Swahili word for "large"

MOMBASA . . . . famous seaport of East Africa rented by the British from the Sultan of Zanzibar

M'PIGA . . . . Swahili word for "to shoot"

M'PISHI . . . . first cook for the Johnsons at Lake Paradise

MUMBORA . . . . second cook for the Johnsons at Lake Paradise

MUNGU . . . . Swahili word for "God"

NAIROBI . . . . principal city of British East Africa and capital of Kenya colony

NANYUKI . . . . a white settlement north of Nairobi

N'DIYO . . . . Swahili word for "yes"

N'DOTO MOUNTAINS . . . . a range near Lake Paradise

N'GOMA . . . . Swahili word for "dance" or "celebration"

N'GROON MOUNTAINS . . . . a range near Lake Paradise

NYERI . . . . a white settlement north of Nairobi

OURANGA . . . . the Johnsons' chief camera boy and laboratory assistant

PANGA . . . . a long sharp native knife for cutting grass and bushes

POSHO . . . . ground cornmeal—staple food of the African native

RENDILLE . . . . a tribe of East African herdsmen and nomads

RET . . . . a waterhole at the end of the Kaisoot Desert enroute to Lake Paradise

RUSHA . . . . Swahili word for "splash"

SAFARI . . . . expedition, caravan or trip

SAMBURU . . . . a tribe of Northern Frontier nomadic herdsmen

SHENZI . . . . Swahili word for rude savage, especially in derogatory sense

SHILLING . . . . a silver East African coin worth approximately 25¢ in American money, and the principal coin used in trade

SIMBA . . . . Swahili word for "lion"

SOMALI . . . . a tribe of Northern Frontier nomadic herdsmen, partly Arab in their origin

SPIRRILUM TICK . . . . a large infection-carrying tick, fever contracted from which is regarded as one of the most dangerous maladies in East Africa

SQUEAKERS . . . . slang for baby game fowl

SUKU . . . . chief houseboy of the Johnsons at Lake Paradise

SUNGA . . . . a waterhole on the Northern Frontier

SWAHILI . . . . an "Esperanto" introduced by the Arab slave traders, now used and understood by approximately 100 tribes in East Africa

SYCE . . . . a camel boy

TEMBO . . . . Swahili word for "elephant"

THIKA . . . . a white settlement north of Nairobi

THORN-TREE . . . . a popular designation of acacia and other trees found on the plains and desert with sparse foliage but long sharp thorns, often growing to considerable size

THORNBUSH . . . . the small, scrubby bushes of the East African plains and desert, bearing long thorns

TINGA-TINGA . . . . Swahili word for swamp

TOTO . . . . baby or small child, in Swahili, also used by East Africans to describe a son or daughter of any age

TURKANA . . . . a savage tribe of the Northern Frontier living in the Lake Rudolph section

TWIGA . . . . Swahili word for "giraffe"

UZEE . . . . Swahili word for "old person"

VULTURINE GUINEA FOWL . . . . East African guinea fowl with vulture-like head and beak and lustrous striped turquoise blue and purple plumage about the throat, and purple back

WANDEROBO . . . . a savage tribe of small-bodied East African natives who roam the forests, have no permanent dwellings and live on game, fruits and nuts

WILDEBEEST . . . . an East African antelope, smaller but somewhat resembling the American bison

WISTONIA . . . . the Johnsons' favorite waterhole and waterfall at Lake Paradise

INDEX

343